D1716901

Machine Organization:
An Introduction to
the Structure and Programming
of Computing Systems

Machine Organization

An Introduction to the Structure and Programming of Computing Systems

Charles P. Pfleeger
The University of Tennessee

JOHN WILEY & SONS
New York   Chichester   Brisbane   Toronto

Library of Congress Cataloging in Publication Data:

Pfleeger, Charles P., 1948–
Machine organization.

Includes index.
1. Computer architecture. 2. Electronic digital computers—Programming. I. Title.

QA76.9.A73P47	621.3819′52	81–11380
ISBN 0-471-07970-7		AACR2

Printed in the United States of America

10 9 8 7 6 5 4 3 2 1

Preface

This textbook is for those who want to know more about the relationship between programs and computers. Introductory programming courses tend (justifiably) to gloss over the internal construction of computers and concentrate instead on programming and algorithm development. Until people have written a few programs, they cannot really appreciate the components of any computing system.

However, programmers eventually need to know something about the internal construction of a computer. As programmers mature, they are likely to ask questions such as the following. "Why do I get 2.99999 instead of 3.0?" "Why does it take so long for my output to be printed?" "Why must I differentiate between character mode and arithmetic mode variables, even if the character variables contain strings of digits?" "Why does my program have to be recompiled each time I remove or insert one instruction?" This book deals with these questions and helps programmers become more sophisticated, more qualified computer users.

Chapter 0 introduces a building block model of a computer—CPU, memory, and I/O devices; it also introduces the machine language.

Chapter 1 describes the typical circuit design of digital computers as a central processing unit with registers, an arithmetic logic unit, and a memory. Circuit design, to the point of designing a half adder, is introduced. Although the goal of this book is not to train people to design new circuits, it does begin with a low-level element of computing devices. This chapter also presents the organization of memory, again starting at the atomic level. The chapter concludes with functional descriptions of the three computers that will be used throughout the book: the Intel 8080, the PDP-11, and the IBM 360-370 computers.

Chapter 2 presents representations of data: integers, characters, and floating point numbers. It also covers the binary numbering system and octal and hexadecimal notation.

Chapters 3 and 4 concentrate on machine and assembler languages as a way of driving the computing machinery already studied. Instruction formats and addressing modes are described at the machine level. The section on assembler languages discusses typical features of assembler languages and indicates the more common machine instruction types. Chapter 4 concludes with a description of the kinds of errors that can occur during assembly or execution.

Chapter 5 traces the flow of control during the execution of a program. Simple instruction flow, procedure calls, and interrupts are explained.

Chapter 6 covers I/O devices, another important part of the study of the hardware components of a computer. This chapter does not try to be exhaustive; instead, it shows representative characteristics of different device types. This chapter also concludes the first part of the book, computer hardware.

It is foolish to discuss assembly language without talking about assemblers. It is pointless to describe subprocedure calls and relative addressing without telling about loaders. And it is unusual to describe hardware resources without mentioning monitors and executive systems. The second part of this book concerns software support for execution. Chapter 7 overviews the chapters to come. Chapters 8 and 9 investigate translators for assembler and higher-level languages. The emphasis is on understanding what these programs do and how they operate. The discussion frequently relates to a section in the first half of the book on hardware for motivation or for clarification.

Chapter 10 considers linking and loading, giving brief descriptions of relocation schemes such as base registers and paging. Chapter 11 considers operating systems as resource managers and shows how operating systems use and distribute the hardware units at their disposal.

This book is intended for a one-semester course in machine organization for first- or second-year computer science students. The only prerequisite assumed is knowledge of some higher-level language such as PASCAL, PL/I, or FORTRAN. It would be ideal if students could also have access to one or more actual computing systems for assembler language programming to complement the text. The book has intentionally avoided specific or thorough description of any one machine, assembler language, or operating system, although examples of several are present. Hopefully, students will study supplementary materials on the systems available.

I have developed this book for a class of students in Computer Science 2710 at The University of Tennessee, and it is to those students that I owe my appreciation. They tolerated rough manuscripts, missing pages and sections, and countless typographical errors. I received and used many good suggestions for improvement from them. I thank my colleagues, especially Robert Heller, Charles Hughes, J. Michael Moshell, and David Straight, for sharing with me their insights on teaching this material and their candid constructive suggestions for improving this manuscript. Finally, my wife, Shari Lawrence Pfleeger, gave me the moral support and encouragement to complete this work. She tolerated my moods and time constraints with a great deal of understanding.

Charles P. Pfleeger

Contents

part 1
Computer Hardware

chapter 0

Introduction to Machine Organization

When some people see a new device, such as a car, a camera, or a jet airplane, they are curious about what makes it work. Seldom are they interested in building one or taking one apart and putting it back together again; they are more often intrigued by what it can do and how it operates. Of course, some things are so complex that most people want only an introduction to the internal structure of the item. Computers are complex devices about which a large mythology has developed; there are many common misconceptions about what a computer can and cannot do. One reason for studying the internal structure of computers is to be able to appreciate how a computer works and to dispel some of these misconceptions.

Every computer specialist should know something about the internal structure—called the "machine organization"—of computers. Knowing the structure of computers can help you program more efficiently; it can help you understand some of the features and restrictions of compilers and programming languages. Furthermore, understanding some basic machine organization principles is important to learning more advanced material in computing, material such as systems programming (support programming that makes the resources of a computer readily accessible to a number of users), information retrieval (programming that makes a collection of data available to users who may request all or some part of the collection), and teleprocessing (hardware devices plus programs that permit users to obtain access to a computer miles, or even thousands of miles, away). These are all important areas of computing, and a knowledge of machine organization is essential to their understanding. In this book you will learn about the internal components of a computer.

To understand internal combustion engines, you do not have to understand what every valve, hose, and bolt does in a particular model of automobile. Similarly, to understand computers, you do not have to understand every wire, or even every circuit, in a particular model of computer. Throughout this book you will see a simplification of the internal structure of computers. These explanations will be fairly high level, presenting only major building blocks of a computing system. The book will not teach you specifically what electronic circuitry exists in computers, but it will show you the high-level components from which computers are constructed.

Although a variety of internal structures are explained in this book, no one computer currently has all of the characteristics detailed here. Instead, representative features of many popular computers will be presented. Three representative models of computers used will be the IBM 360-370 series machines (large, general-purpose machines), the PDP-11 family (medium-sized machines, often dedicated to one task or for a small group of users), and the Intel 8080 microcomputer (a small but powerful computer often used by one person).

The rest of this chapter is a brief discussion of the components of a typical computer system. The next chapter will examine these components in more detail. After you understand the components of a computing system, you will learn about the internal forms of instructions for computers and how these instructions are executed. Assembler language is a means of programming at the machine language level. After learning some of the features of assembler language, you will begin to study systems software, including assemblers and compilers, loaders, and operating systems. Finally, this book will end with some information on programs that support I/O activities and other operating systems functions.

0.1 A COMPUTER MODEL

You have probably already programmed a computer, so you may have some idea of what it is. Medium to large computer installations are often called *computer systems* to indicate that the system is a complex but unified group of components. There is no harm in using the term computer system to describe a minicomputer or a microcomputer and its attached devices.

It is common to divide computer components into hardware and software. The visible, tangible devices of a computing system are its *hardware.* Typical hardware components are a printer, a video display terminal, and a data storage unit. The term *software* denotes computer programs. In addition to programs a user writes, other common pieces of computer software are compilers (to translate other programs into a form so that they can be executed on a computer) and text editors (to assist users in typing programs).

Although the division between hardware and software seems obvious, this is not necessarily so. Another term you may hear is *firmware,* which describes tangible pieces of hardware that contain a sequence of instructions that may be executed, just like a program. More information on firmware will appear later.

Just as it is hard to use a computer program without having a computer on which to execute it, it is difficult to use a computer without a program to guide its use. Although this book is more oriented to hardware, there will be a number of references to the software needed to utilize that hardware.

Figure 0.1 shows the major hardware components of a computer system.

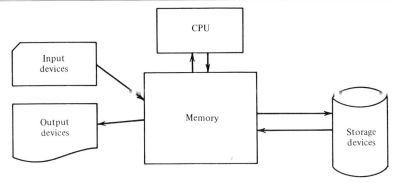

Figure 0.1   Components of a computer system.

These components are a *CPU* or central processing unit, some amount of *memory,* and a combination of *input, output,* and *storage* devices. This chapter contains a quick overview of all the parts of a computer. Later chapters offer more detailed explanations of the form (construction) and function of each component.

The CPU does the actual computation of a computer. It executes the program instructions one at a time. The activities of the CPU are divided into categories in the next chapter. Furthermore, the CPU consists of several distinct functional modules; these will also be explained in the next chapter.

On most computers both a program and its data are held in the memory unit. The program is coded in a numeric form. Memory devices are *bistable devices.* A bistable device has two possible settings, like a light switch, which is either on or off. The binary numbering system is convenient for use with bistable devices, since binary numbers are composed of the digits 0 and 1; these digits can represent the two states of a bistable device. Both a program and its data are stored in memory in binary number notation.

A computer memory is usually divided into many fixed-size independent storage locations called *bytes* and *words.* A byte is the smallest unit of computer memory that may be referenced directly. Each binary digit in a number is called a *bit.* A byte consists of a certain fixed number of binary digits. Usually, but not always, a byte consists of 8 bits.

A *word* is a series of consecutive bytes. A word may consist of 1, 2, 4, or more bytes. The number of bits in a word is called the *word size* of the computer. Typical word sizes are 8, 16, 32, 36, 48, or 64 bits.

Input, output, and storage devices are often called *I/O devices;* I/O represents *input/output.* I/O devices are used for transmitting data to the computer and retrieving data from a computer, respectively. We normally think of input devices as those by which humans can provide data to a computer. Examples of such devices are typewriterlike keyboards and readers for punched cards. Similarly, humans can acquire data from a computer through output devices, which include video display screens (also called CRTs, for cathode ray tubes) and different types of printers, from typewriters to printers that produce an entire line at a time (called *line printers*) to those that work by a xerographic process to produce an entire page at a time.

Storage devices are used for short- or long-term storage of data. This data is usually not immediately destined for human use and is kept in a form that is not readily visible to humans but that is easily accessed by computers. Storage devices are normally both input and output devices, because data is written (used for output) and read (used for input) by the computer. Storage devices range from cassette recorders (identical to those used for home audio recording) to other devices using disks, strips, or drums of magnetic oxide material as well as other more advanced pieces of technology. The relationship among input devices, output devices, and storage devices is shown in Figure 0.2.

A program may be entered into a computer through an input device. Execution of this program may cause additional data to be read from the input devices; this data is used in computation, and results may be written on the output devices. If the program is especially important or if the input or output data is valuable, the program or the data (or both) can be retained on a storage device. Subsequent programs can retrieve data from a storage device and perform other computations with it. The same program can be executed numerous times from one copy retained on a storage device.

Different computer systems will have different complements of I/O devices, depending on the tasks they must perform. It is possible to have several types of memory attached to one computer system or various CPUs that operate at different speeds. In fact, it is difficult to balance all components of a computer system so as to maximize computing power for the money spent. Frequent new technological developments make it especially difficult to keep a system at maximum efficiency.

0.2 MACHINE LANGUAGE PROGRAMS

Your programming experience may have familiarized you with hardware components. As we get further into the internal construction of computers, you will also learn more about the actual machine language programs that are executed on a computer. This section contains an introduction to machine language programs.

First, no computer directly "understands" or executes FORTRAN or PL/I or

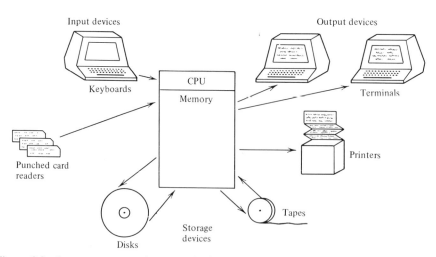

Figure 0.2 Input, output, and storage devices.

PASCAL. In programs you have written the translation of your program very likely was not apparent. In some cases you were simply told to prepare a few standard control cards or to type a few stock commands to force your program to be run. In fact, in some systems that support BASIC and similar languages, executing the program seemed to be a natural extension of typing the program. Actually, however, your programs were translated to machine language by a program called a *compiler.* Some of the compilers you used may have keyed errors detected during execution to variable names, line numbers, or conditions in the higher-level language source program.

Languages such as FORTRAN, PL/I, PASCAL, BASIC, ALGOL, and COBOL are called *higher-level languages.* This means that a single statement in one of these languages is more powerful than a single machine instruction, since many machine instructions may be needed to produce the effect of one higher-level language instruction. However, a CPU can execute only its machine language commands. Thus any higher-level language program must be translated to an equivalent machine language program. A software component that translates higher-level language to machine language is called a *compiler.* You will learn more about compilers in Chap. 9. Fig. 0.3 shows the relationship among a compiler, a source language program, and an executable machine language program.

Machine language is a programming system where each operation to be performed consists of a numeric code to identify the operation and one or more numeric codes to identify the sources of the data for the operation and the destination of the result. As an analogy, consider the case of a person handling a lot of routine correspondence. Suppose that people regularly write letters, asking many of the same questions. It would be efficient to draft a response to each common question and number the responses. The person handling the correspondence could then tell a secretary to type a letter with responses 1, 3, and 7. This numeric shorthand becomes a simple means of specifying a letter to be produced. Furthermore, if both the correspondent and the secretary understand the coding scheme, there is no uncertainty about which letter will be produced. Think of the numbers as commands to the secretary to type certain paragraphs. Not every sequence of numbers represents a meaningful letter; for example 1, 1, 1 is a valid coding for a letter, but it is dubious if the same answer three times in succession will be useful.

One additional feature that could be added to this system would be some form of variable in a response. For example, one question that might be asked is

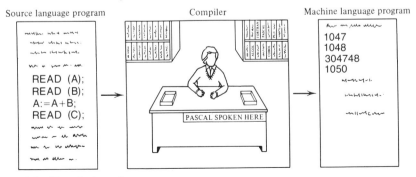

Figure 0.3   Translation of a program.

"Which room will I be assigned in the dorm?", to which the response might be "You will be occupying room X in Lincoln Hall," where X is some room number. If this is response number 8, a possible letter coding would be 3, 5, 8(337). The 337 is the value to be substituted for X in the stock response.

In a machine language each machine operation has been assigned a numeric code, called its *operation (op) code.* To have an operation performed, you specify its number. Some operations have modifiers, also called *operands,* that specify with which data the computation is to be done and where the result is to be placed. The operands act like the variable items in the preceding example.

Commands (Op Codes)	Variable Items (Operands)
3	
5	
8	337

A possible machine language (for a very simple machine) is shown next.

Op Code	Operation	Operands
10	Input a value; place it at memory location X	Address of X
20	Output the value currently in memory location X	Address of X
30	Add contents of memory location X to location Y, placing result in location Y	Addresses of X, Y

Now suppose the machine for which this is the machine language has 100 words of memory. Memory addresses are numbered, usually going up from 0. Thus the memory addresses of this machine would be 00 to 99.

A typical instruction for this machine would be

Input a value, placing it in memory location 47

which would be coded in machine language as

10 47

A program consists of a series of these instructions, such as the following example.

English Instruction	Machine Language
Input a value, placing it at location 47	10 47
Input a value, placing it at location 48	10 48
Add the values at locations 47 and 48, placing the sum in location 48	30 47 48
Output the value at location 48	20 48

This example corresponds to the following higher-level language program.

```
READ (A);
READ (B);
B := A + B;
WRITE (B);
```

Not all machine language instructions are the same length. The I/O instructions (1 0 and 2 0) are 4 decimal digits long—2 to specify the operation and 2 more to specify the address of the operand. Since an add instruction (3 0) has two operands, it needs 6 decimal digits—2 for the operation and 2 for each operand. If we assume that 2 decimal digits could be contained in 1 byte of memory, the I/O instructions would be 2-byte instructions while the add instruction would be a 3-byte instruction.

This series of instructions can also be written as follows.

10 47   10 48   30 47 48   20 48

Here spaces have been inserted to show the separation between instructions and between the operation and the operands. All input (1 0) instructions are 4 digits long, and all add (3 0) instructions are 3 bytes long. Assuming we start with an instruction, it is possible to tell the length of that instruction (and hence the point where the next instruction starts) by examining the op code portion of the first instruction. Thus spaces are unnecessary between instructions or between an op code and its operands. The previous sequence could be written as follows.

104710483047482048

It is difficult but not impossible for humans to break that string down into its component instructions. However, the computer analyzes one instruction at a time, so there is no difficulty about separating the program into individual commands.

This is the essence of a computer machine language program. A machine language program is simply a series of numbers, which are op codes and operand addresses. There may also be flags and data values that affect the execution of the operations.

Most digital computers operate under the *stored program* concept. This means that the program is stored in the same memory that contains the data values. For example, the preceding program might be placed in memory beginning at byte 20. Since the program is 9 bytes long, it would occupy memory locations 20 to 28.

Using one block of memory for a program and its data can be convenient, except that care must be taken in the placement of the program. For example, the program could not be placed beginning at location 40, since it would then occupy addresses 40 to 48, but locations 47 and 48 are used as data addresses in the program. A memory location can contain a piece of data or a program instruction part, but not both. A problem would arise when the computer tried to execute the instruction at location 47. Instead of containing the 2 0 4 8 instruction, as in the program, that location would contain the sum of A + B (placed there after A + B was computed), which would probably not be interpreted as a valid instruction.

This would cause different results on different computers, but most would generate some sort of error.

This concludes the introduction to the internal structure of computers. In later chapters you will learn more about varied computer devices and their uses in modern computer systems. Descriptions of the internal structures of certain typical computers will be given, but you should plan to seek out specific information on the computer model to which you have access.

Each chapter will conclude with a list of terms that have been introduced in the chapter. Before leaving the chapter, you should be familiar with all these terms. If you need help, the index can tell you where the word was first used. The chapters also conclude with questions that you should answer before moving on.

0.3   TERMS USED

The following terms have been introduced in this chapter. Those marked with an asterisk (*) have only been introduced; they will be defined in later chapters.

Machine organization
Systems programming*
Information retrieval*
Teleprocessing*
Compiler*
Computer system
Hardware
Software
Text editor*
Firmware*
Central processing unit (CPU)
Memory
Input device
Output device
Storage device
Binary (base 2) numbers
Bistable device
Memory storage location
Byte
Bit
Word
Word size
I/O device
Machine language program
Higher-level language
Operation code (op code)
Operand
Stored program computer

0.4 QUESTIONS

The following questions are designed to review your study of this chapter and to motivate you to locate more related material. Answer these questions before you progress to the next chapter.

1. What model computers are available to you? What is the word size of each? How much memory does each have?
2. What are the principal components of a computer? What function does each serve?
3. If a machine language program, such as

    1025102910343025403029403034402040

    is in memory, how is it possible to locate the separate instructions of this program? Of how many instructions does this program consist? What are they?
4. Using the programming language presented here, write a program to read three numbers and add them.
5. The example program in this chapter uses two separate storage locations in order to read two numbers and compute their sum. Write a similar program to do that task, but use only one storage location.
6. If a computer has, for example, 100 memory locations, what is the advantage of numbering these locations from 0 to 99 instead of 1 to 100?

chapter 1

Hardware Components of Computer Systems

This chapter contains more detailed information on the CPU and on memory. The first topic explored is the variety of components and operations normally associated with the term CPU. After you understand a CPU better, you will see how some of the basic circuits of the CPU are constructed. Although this book does not develop the design of all computer circuitry, it is illustrative to know some of the pieces that go into a computer. The memory unit is also examined in detail. Various technologies are presented in order to help you understand some of the popular jargon of memory devices. The chapter ends with a brief discussion of microprogramming.

1.1 THE CENTRAL PROCESSING UNIT

As you learned in the last chapter, the CPU actually does the computing (arithmetic and decision making). This computing involves at least three major aspects:

1. Performing arithmetic, logical, and other transformations on data.
2. Decoding, sequencing through, and performing the instructions of the program.
3. Analyzing and responding to conditions pertaining to the status of the computer system.

These activities are shown in Figure 1.1.

A CPU consists of a number of *registers* and some *arithmetic* and *logical functional units.* Registers may be thought of as fast-access storage locations used to hold data values during computation. Some are called *scratchpad registers,* which indicates that one of their primary uses is as temporary storage areas for intermediate results in computations. Others are used internally to the CPU.

13

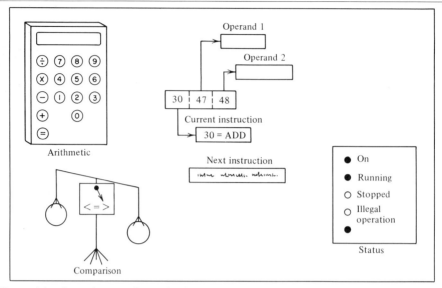

Figure 1.1   Central processing unit (CPU).

The *arithmetic logic units* (ALUs) perform arithmetic and logical operations such as adding, comparing, and testing for a carry as the result of an arithmetic operation. Furthermore, the arithmetic and logical units monitor the status of the machine and cause action in the event of an exceptional condition, such as a hardware failure or a program error. The various components of the CPU are shown in Figure 1.2.

1.1.1   Registers

A register is a storage device used to contain data that will likely be referenced soon. Some registers are for the programmer, while others internal to the machine are beyond the programmer's access. A user may place data in a register to improve the speed of computation. Although timings will vary from computer to computer, access to a data value in a register is often twice as fast as access to the same value in regular memory. For example, on a typical IBM 360-370 machine it

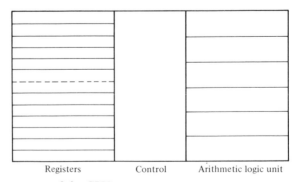

Figure 1.2   Components of the CPU.

takes 0.65 microseconds to add the values in two registers; it takes 1.3 microseconds to add a value in main memory to a value in a register. (A microsecond is 10^{-6} second $= 1/1,000,000$ seconds.) On the PDP-11 family of computers it can take almost 2 microseconds longer to perform an instruction if the destination is a memory address instead of a register.

A CPU may contain zero or more user registers. These may be called *general-purpose registers, scratchpad registers,* or simply *registers.* If there is just one register, it is often called an *accumulator.* Registers are either numbered, from zero to the number of registers, or they are known by names such as the HL register or the A register. Some machines have a number of different types of registers. For example, the IBM 360-370 family has a group of general-purpose registers that may be used for general computation and another set of registers used exclusively for floating point (real number) computation. The Intel 8080 microcomputer has several 8-bit registers (called B, C, D, E, H, and L) and a 16-bit register (called SP); however, the 8-bit registers can also be used in pairs (B-C, D-E, H-L) for 16-bit computation. These registers are shown in Figure 1.3.

Registers are sometimes used to hold intermediate values in a computation. Suppose you need to compute $(A+B)*(C+D)$. One way to do this is to compute the result $(A+B)$ and place this result in a general-purpose register. Then compute $(C+D)$ and put it in a different register. Finally, multiply the contents of these two registers. Although the intermediate result $(A+B)$ could be stored in memory, the computation will be faster if the final multiplication has registers instead of memory locations as its operands.

On a machine with registers the machine language instructions will have a means of designating a register as the destination for a computed result. For example, an English representation of a machine language program to compute $(A+B)*(C+D)$ would be as follows.

Add A to B, placing the result in register 4.

Add C to D, placing the result in register 1.

Multiply register 4 by register 1.

(The actual machine code would be a numeric encoding of these instructions.)

A register can hold only one value at a time. Each time a new value is placed

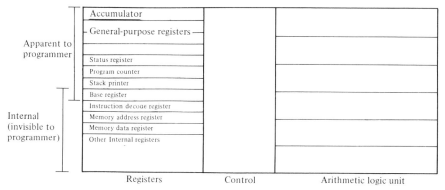

Figure 1.3 Kinds of registers.

in a register, the previous contents of the register are lost. However, a value can be retrieved from a register any number of times without affecting the value. In the preceding case, for example, once (A + B) has been assigned to register 4, the contents of register 4 could be used in computing (A + B) * 2 , (A + B) * (A − B) , and so forth, and the value will be (A + B) until a new value is placed in register 4.

As a programmer, you can place values in and retrieve them from general-purpose registers. In contrast, the *program counter register* is a register whose value is changed only by the CPU. The program counter (sometimes abbreviated PC) keeps track of which machine language instruction is to be executed next. Recall that in a stored program computer the program resides in main memory along with the data. The program counter contains the address of (i.e., the number of) the memory location that contains the next operation in the machine language program being executed. If the next instruction is 2 (or more) bytes long, the address in the program counter is the first byte of the next instruction.

The sample program in the previous chapter was 9 bytes long, consisting of four instructions. The program is repeated here for reference.

    1047   1048   304748   2048

Suppose it were placed in memory beginning at location 20. This situation is shown next.

Address	20	21	22	23	24	25	26	27	28
Contents	10	47	10	48	30	47	48	20	48

Just before the program begins execution, the program counter will have the value 20, showing that byte 20 contains the start of the next instruction. After the CPU begins executing the first instruction (1047) , the program counter is set to 22 to show that the next instruction begins at byte 22. Similarly, when that instruction (1048) begins, the program counter is updated to 24. In Chapter 4 you will learn more about the method by which the CPU updates the program counter during execution; at this time it will suffice to know that the program counter points to the next instruction to be executed.

Another register maintained by the CPU is the *status register*. This register reports on the status of the program's execution. Examples of status information maintained include whether the result of the last instruction was negative, whether the last two numbers compared were equal, and whether the last result computed exceeded the limit of the machine.

The answer to the first of these questions is maintained because you sometimes need to know the sign of an arithmetic computation in progress; for example, before taking the square root of a sum it is important to know if the sum is positive or negative.

The second question is related to the machine instructions available for decision-making. Usually the decision-making process in machine language is split into two parts: checking a condition and taking appropriate action. In higher-level languages conditional statements usually consist of two (or three) parts:

```
IF   (some condition is true)
THEN   perform some action
<ELSE   perform some other action>
```

where the ELSE part of this construction is optional. While this conditional statement is one single statement, it is represented in machine language by at least two separate instructions: one to test if the condition is true and another to execute either the THEN or the ELSE part of the statement.

One means by which information is communicated between two machine language instructions is by way of the status register. The status register contains flags that tell, for example, whether the last two numbers compared were equal or whether the first was less than or greater than the second. Other comparisons are possible. There are machine instructions that will execute or skip a particular group of instructions, depending on the settings of flags in the status register.

The third question is normally an error condition. As mentioned in the previous chapter, each word in computer memory consists of a fixed number of bits. This implies a limit on the size of a value that a computer word may contain. As an analogy, imagine that each word in a computer could hold, at most, 5 decimal digits. Then numbers such as 12,345, 1, 99,999, and 347 could each be contained in a word. However, the result of adding two of these numbers would not necessarily fit in a computer word; 12,345 + 54,321 = 66,666, which is only 5 digits long, but 99,999 + 1 = 100,000, which is 6 digits long. Generating a result that will not fit in a computer word is called *overflow*.

The action taken on detecting an overflow will vary from computer to computer. Some retain the rightmost n digits of the answer (where the word is n digits long), while others leave the original value unchanged. In any event, since the true result cannot be placed in a computer word, it will not be retained, so the apparent result from the operation will be incorrect. If the most recent result obtained exceeds or overflows the size of a word (meaning the result stored will be incorrect), computers set an overflow flag (a bit in the status register). The program can test this flag after an arithmetic operation and take remedial action.

There are other registers in computers; these will be noted briefly here and described in depth later. The *stack pointer register* is used primarily for passing arguments between procedures or subprograms and for maintaining return addresses. The stack pointer will be described fully in the section on subprograms in Chapter 5. The *base register* is used to show the address at which a program begins in memory. Some computers—particularly small ones—do not have a base register. The use of a base register will be explained in more detail in Chapter 10. The *instruction decode register* contains the machine language instruction that is currently being performed. As shown in the preceding example, machine language instructions have different parts, such as an op code and operands; these parts must be processed separately. The instruction decode register is a place where the current instruction can be held and the various fields of the instruction can be separated. The instruction decode register will be explained in Chapter 3. The instruction decode register is invisible to the programmer in that machine language programs do not manipulate this register explicitly. Two other registers that the programmer does not manipulate directly are the *memory address register* (MAR) and the *memory data register* (MDR). These are used during references to memory to hold the address and contents of the memory word being referenced. The use of the MAR and the MDR will be explained in the next section. Typical CPU registers are shown in Figure 1.4.

The essential characteristics of registers that you should now know are these.

1. Registers are a small set of storage locations separate from main memory. They are of fixed sizes. Access to a register is faster than access to main memory.

2. Most machines have an accumulator or a set of general-purpose registers for the programmer's use. These may hold intermediate data during a computation.

3. Other system-maintained registers include the program counter and the status register. These registers provide information to the programmer and to the computer regarding the execution of the current program.

4. The register complement of different computer models differs. Some computers have additional registers, such as a stack pointer and a base register. There will also be a variety of internal registers that the programmer does not access directly, such as the instruction decode register and the MAR and MDR.

1.1.2 Arithmetic Logic Unit

Registers are only holding places for data; some additional circuitry is needed to combine the values to produce new results. This section contains information on the *arithmetic logic unit* (ALU) of a computer; this is the unit that performs computations. Examples show the types of computations possible on modern

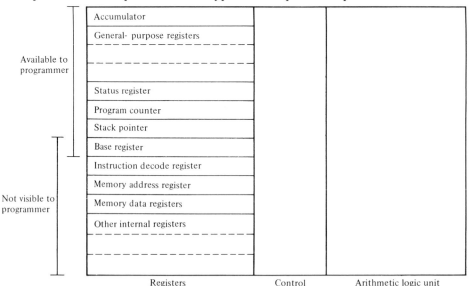

Figure 1.4 Typical registers of the CPU.

computers; in a few instances, the exact circuitry is shown to give you a better feeling for the method by which a computer is constructed. Before describing the types of computations, it is necessary to present some idea of the internal form of information.

Consider the decimal number system with which you are familiar. This common numbering system uses *positional number representation,* which means that the value of each digit depends on the position it occupies in a number. For example, the 5 in 295 means 5 1s or 5*1 or 5; however, the 5 in 5784 means 5 1000s or 5*1000 or 5000; thus the value of a digit in a number depends on what position it is in.

The positions of decimal numbers represent powers of 10: from the right end of a number, the positions have value 1 (10^0), 10 (10^1), 100 (10^2), 1000 (10^3), and so forth. To determine the value of a decimal number, take the digits of the number, multiply them by the values of the positions in which the digits appear, and add the products. For example, the number 3562 is interpreted as follows.

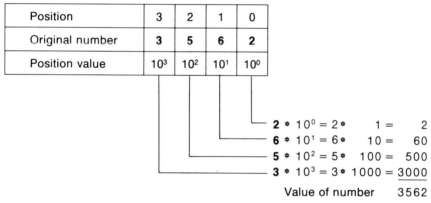

Position	3	2	1	0
Original number	3	5	6	2
Position value	10^3	10^2	10^1	10^0

$2 * 10^0 = 2 *\quad 1 = \quad 2$
$6 * 10^1 = 6 *\quad 10 = \quad 60$
$5 * 10^2 = 5 *\quad 100 = \quad 500$
$3 * 10^3 = 3 * 1000 = \underline{3000}$

Value of number   3562

Computers operate using the binary (base 2) numbering system. This system has only 2 digits—0 and 1. It is a positional representation system, much like the decimal system, except that the position values are powers of 2 instead of powers of 10. Numbers in binary are decoded in exactly the same manner as decimal numbers; in the decoding process you can also determine the decimal equivalent of a binary number by multiplying the digits by their values in decimal. The following example shows the decoding of a binary number.

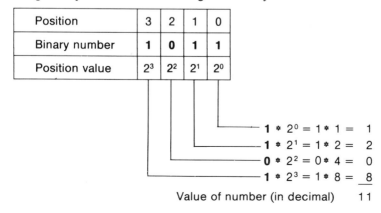

Position	3	2	1	0
Binary number	1	0	1	1
Position value	2^3	2^2	2^1	2^0

$1 * 2^0 = 1 * 1 = \quad 1$
$1 * 2^1 = 1 * 2 = \quad 2$
$0 * 2^2 = 0 * 4 = \quad 0$
$1 * 2^3 = 1 * 8 = \quad \underline{8}$

Value of number (in decimal)   11

The process for interpreting binary numbers is the same as that for interpreting decimal numbers (or numbers in any other base, for that matter).

For reference, here is a table of the first few binary numbers.

Decimal	Binary
0	0
1	1
2	10
3	11
4	100
5	101
6	110
7	111
8	1000
9	1001
10	1010
11	1011
12	1100
13	1101
14	1110
15	1111

The binary numbering system and representation of numbers will be explained more fully in Chapter 2.

With this basic understanding of the internal storage of values, you will be able to learn about the internal operation of the ALU. The first operations to be described will be the logical operations, AND, OR, exclusive OR, and NOT.

One useful feature of binary numbers is that the digits of the binary numbers can be used as separate flags to indicate the presence or absence of a particular condition. Suppose that you are setting up a dating bureau and arranging matches between people. You may have a number of characteristics on which you wish to pair people. For example, all applicants may be required to answer the following questions.

1. Do you enjoy going to athletic events?
2. Do you enjoy going to plays?
3. Do you enjoy going to rock concerts?
4. Do you enjoy going to classical music concerts?
5. Do you enjoy outdoor activities such as hiking and camping?
6. Do you enjoy individual sports such as jogging and bicycling?
7. Do you enjoy group activities such as clubs and team sports?
8. Do you enjoy individual activities such as reading, cooking, and woodworking?

Each person's responses could be coded in 8 bits of memory by using a convention that 1 would represent *yes* and 0 would represent *no*. Then a person's responses, such as

(1) Y (2) Y (3) N (4) Y (5) Y (6) N (7) N (8) N

could be encoded as

1   1   0   1   1   0   0   0

which is the 8-digit binary number 11011000.

The AND function has 2 binary digits as input and 1 binary digit as output. The AND of 2 digits is 1, just in case both of the input digits were 1s. The value of the AND function is shown in the following table.

Inputs	Output
A B	A AND B
0 0	0
0 1	0
1 0	0
1 1	1

Assume that 1 represents *true* and 0 represents *false*. The AND function performs the same as the English connective *and*. For example, the English statement "You will receive an A only if your test scores are better than 86 and your homework average is 90 or above" has the following interpretation. A student with test scores better than 86 (1) and homework average 90 or above (1) will get an A (1 AND 1 = 1). A student with test scores better than 86 (1) but homework average less than 90 (0) will not get an A (1 AND 0 = 0), nor will a student with test scores below 86 (0) but homework above 90 (1), since (0 AND 1 = 0). And a student who meets neither condition should not expect an A (0 AND 0 = 0).

We can apply the AND function to binary numbers of more than 1 digit by computing the AND digit by digit. For example, 101 AND 110 = 100, as shown here.

101	1 AND 1 = 1	101	0 AND 1 = 0	101	1 AND 0 = 0	101
AND 110		AND 110		AND 110		AND 110
???		1??		10?		100

Since there are no carries in an AND operation, we can compute the AND of 2 binary values from left to right or from right to left. Also, the order in which we compute the AND of two numbers does not affect the result; that is, if A and B are any two numbers, (A AND B) = (B AND A). We say that AND is commutative, since it has this last property. Furthermore, AND is associative, meaning that for any three numbers A AND (B AND C) = (A AND B) AND C = A AND B AND C.

In the dating bureau example it may be desirable to determine the applicants who have an overlap of interests. Two applicants who respond 01101100 and 10010011 have no affirmative overlap. This is readily computed by taking the AND of their two responses; 01101100 AND 10010011 = 00000000, which implies there is no question to which both people answered *yes* (i.e., there is no question to which the first person answered *yes* and the second person answered *yes*). Two people responding 01011100 and 10111000 have an overlap of 00011000, which shows they both answered *yes* to questions 4 and 5. Two respondents who both answered 01010010 would have an AND of 01010010, showing that they both answered *yes* to questions 2, 4, and 7. (Notice that the AND function is sufficient to determine cases where the respondents both answered *yes,* but it does not detect situations where both answered *no.* It is possible to compute this last situation by some other logical functions that will be described shortly.)

The AND function is useful in computing these and similar things as well as extended conditions in conditional (I F) statements in higher-level languages. It is also necessary in computing arithmetic results, as will be shown later. The AND function is one of the principal building blocks in an electronic circuit. The symbol for AND is shown in Figure 1.5. Because AND is also the arithmetic product of its inputs, the AND of two values may also be denoted A*B or AB.

Figure 1.5   Symbol for the AND function.

Another useful logic function is the OR function. This is a function that takes two inputs and produces a 1 output just in case either or both of the inputs was a 1. The function table for OR follows.

Inputs		Output
A	B	A OR B
0	0	0
0	1	1
1	0	1
1	1	1

The OR function just described is also called the *inclusive* OR, implying that it includes the case where both A and B are 1: A OR B is 1 just in case A or B *or both* were 1.

Another function, the *exclusive* OR is similar to inclusive OR, except it excludes the case where both A and B are 1: its result is 0 if both inputs were 1. That is, exclusive OR has a table that resembles the table for inclusive OR, except for the last line.

Inputs		Output	
A	B	A XOR B	(XOR means exclusive OR)
0	0	0	
0	1	1	
1	0	1	
1	1	0	

The term OR alone means inclusive OR; any time exclusive OR is intended, it will be called exclusive OR. The rest of the discussion in this chapter refers to inclusive OR.

The OR function also corresponds to the common English usage of the word *or*. For example, the statement "If you are under 18 or over 65 years old, you pay half fare" has the following interpretation. A person who is 15 pays half fare (under 18 = 1, over 65 = 0, 1 OR 0 = 1), as does a person who is 72 (0 OR 1 = 1). A person aged 31 pays full fare (under 18 = 0, over 65 = 0, 0 OR 0 = 0).

In the dating bureau, suppose it is desired to have a *well-rounded* pair—that is, a couple who covers as many *yes* answers as possible. Two people having responses of 00101100 and 00010100 have, between them, a *yes* answer for questions 3, 4, 5, and 6, since the OR of the two responses is 00111100. (The OR function is applied to multiple-digit inputs digit by digit, as was the AND function.) People with responses of 10101010 and 01010101 cover all questions with an OR of 11111111, although they agree on none. (Some say that opposites attract.)

As with the AND function, the OR can be used to compute compound conditions for IF statements. It is also used in computer arithmetic. The OR function is often represented by a plus sign, as in A + B, although it is not strictly the arithmetic sum of its inputs (1 + 1 ≠ 1). The OR function is also a basic component of electronic circuitry. The symbol for OR is shown in Figure 1.6.

Figure 1.6   Symbol for the OR function.

The final function that will be described here is the NOT, or negation or complement function. This is a function of only one input, and it produces an output that is the opposite of its input. The table of values for the NOT function follows.

Input	Output
A	NOT A
0	1
1	0

The NOT function may be represented by a minus sign ($-A$), a bar over a variable ($\bar{A}$), or by the ¬ symbol (¬A). Two different circuit symbols for NOT are shown in Figure 1.7.

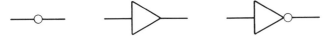

Figure 1.7   Symbols for the NOT function.

The NOT function parallels its usage in English. The statement "If you have not registered for more than 12 hours, your tuition is figured on a per-hour basis" is interpreted as follows. Someone who has registered for 13 hours (more than 12 = 1) does not have tuition figured on a per-hour basis (NOT 1 = 0), but a person who registers for only 6 hours (more than 12 = 0) does have tuition figured on a per-hour basis (NOT 0 = 1).

The complement of a multiple-digit value is computed digit by digit. In the dating bureau you may decide to match exact opposites. To do this, each pair of people must be compared to see if one is exactly the complement of the other. For example, 11101110 and 10010001 are not complements, since the NOT of the first, (NOT 11101110) = 00010001, does not equal the second, 10010001. Notice that if (NOT A) = B, then A = (NOT B); that is, it does not matter which we complement if we are testing for one value to be the complement of the other.

More realistic and useful than checking for one person to be the opposite of the other is to combine NOT with OR and AND. For example, we might desire to know the degree of agreement between two people. We have previously seen that A AND B computes a result that has a 1 in each place that both respondents answered *yes* and a 0 elsewhere, as in the following example.

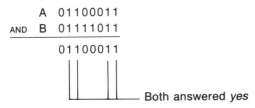

Similarly, (NOT A) will give a word that has a 1 in each place that A answered *no* and 0 otherwise; (NOT B) is similar for B. Then (NOT A) AND (NOT B) will have a 1 in each place that both (NOT A) and (NOT B) have a 1, but this is so just in case both A and B had a 0 in that position, as shown here.

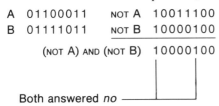

Therefore (A AND B) shows all places A and B agree with a *yes,* and (NOT A) AND (NOT B) shows all places A and B agree with a *no.* Conveniently, both functions leave 0s in all other places. The expression

(A AND B) OR ((NOT A) AND (NOT B))

has a 1 wherever both A and B had a 1, a 1 wherever A and B both had a 0, and a 0 everywhere else. In other words, the function shows the places where A and B agreed, either with a *yes* or a *no.* This result is shown in the following example.

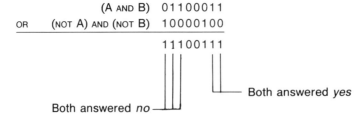

The logical functions AND, OR, and NOT are the basic components of digital computer logic. In the examples in this section we used these functions to produce pieces of results that we wanted, and we then combined the pieces. Another method to select logical elements is to determine the answer desired from each set of inputs and derive a logical function that computes those results. This method is shown next in the construction of a circuit to perform addition.

The basic circuit that can perform arithmetic is an *adder*. The elements from which to design an adder are AND and OR gates and NOT circuits (a NOT circuit is called an *inverter*).

A way to begin this process is to study how the adder is to perform; that is, write down each possible pair of bits coming into the adder and show what output is wanted. This is shown in the following table.

Case	Inputs		Output
	A	B	A + B
1.	0	0	0
2.	0	1	1
3.	1	0	1
4.	1	1	10

The first three should look reasonable. For case 4 remember that $1 + 1 = 2$, but that 2 in binary is 10. Although 10 is the correct answer, this really means that a 1 is to be carried to the next digit to the left in the sum. There are two outputs: a *result* digit and a *carry* digit.

For cases 1, 2, and 3 the carry digit is 0; for case 4 it is 1. The carry should be 1 just in case both A and B were 1. Thus the AND function can be used to compute the carry.

The result digit is 1 just in case A was 1 and B was 0 or A was 0 and B was 1. This is A XOR B (where XOR indicates the exclusive OR function). Another function that is equivalent is

(A AND (NOT B)) OR ((NOT A) AND B)

This function can be computed just from AND, OR, and NOT circuits. (Verify that this function does produce the values shown in the preceding table.)

In summary, an adder is a function that takes two inputs, A and B, and produces two outputs, D (digit) and C (carry). The functions to compute D and C are repeated here.

D = (A AND (NOT B)) OR ((NOT A) AND B)
C = A AND B

A circuit that computes these functions is called a *half adder*. The circuit diagram for these functions is shown in Figure 1.8.

The half adder in Figure 1.8 computes both a result digit and a carry digit. The carry digit should be added to the pair of digits immediately to the left.

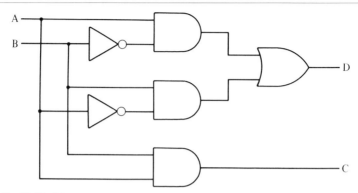

Figure 1.8 Half adder.

However, the half adder accepts only two inputs, A and B; it has no provision for a carry digit as input. Thus the half adder is usable only for the least significant digit of an addition (because there is no carry into the least significant digit). A *full adder* needs three inputs, A, B, and C (carry), and it produces two outputs, C′ (new carry) and D (digit). The values to be produced are shown in the following table.

Case	Inputs			Outputs	
	A	B	C	C′	D
1.	0	0	0	0	0
2.	0	0	1	0	1
3.	0	1	0	0	1
4.	0	1	1	1	0
5.	1	0	0	0	1
6.	1	0	1	1	0
7.	1	1	0	1	0
8.	1	1	1	1	1

The functions that compute these results are shown next. Cases 2, 3, 5, and 8 produce a 1 for the digit (D). These cases have the following values.

2. ((NOT A) AND (NOT B) AND C)
3. ((NOT A) AND B AND (NOT C))
5. (A AND (NOT B) AND (NOT C))
8. (A AND B AND C)

The cases that produce a carry are 4, 6, 7, and 8, which have values as follows.

4. ((NOT A) AND B AND C)
6. (A AND (NOT B) AND C)
7. (A AND B AND (NOT C))
8. (A AND B AND C)

Another way of looking at this is that cases 4 and 8 are identical with the exception of A; in other words, any time B and C are 1, then C′ (the carry output) should be 1, whether A is 0 or 1. Cases 6 and 8 are identical with the exception of B, so any time A and C are 1, then C′ should be 1, whether B is 0 or 1. Cases 7 and 8 are identical with the exception of C, so any time A and B are 1, then C′ should be 1, whether C is 0 or 1. These last three terms have covered cases 4 and 8, 6 and 8, and 7 and 8, so this combination covers cases 4, 6, 7, and 8, all of the cases in which C′ must be 1. Functions for D and C′ are shown here.

$$D = ((\text{NOT A}) \text{ AND } (\text{NOT B}) \text{ AND C}) \text{ OR}$$
$$((\text{NOT A}) \text{ AND B AND } (\text{NOT C})) \text{ OR}$$
$$(\text{A AND } (\text{NOT B}) \text{ AND } (\text{NOT C})) \text{ OR}$$
$$(\text{A AND B AND C})$$

$$C' = (\text{A AND C}) \text{ OR}$$
$$(\text{A AND B}) \text{ OR}$$
$$(\text{B AND C})$$

These functions can be used to construct a full adder. However, as just stated, the functions would require 11 ANDs and 4 ORs. A simpler circuit involves joining two half adders: one to add A and B, and the other to add the result from (A + B) to C. A carry output C′ is generated any time either adder generates a carry. Figure 1.9 shows the circuit diagram for this form of a full adder. (There are other circuits that will work as a full adder.)

The circuitry designed so far will compute a single-bit result, including carry in and carry out. The result of adding two multiple-digit numbers can be determined by either of two methods. One approach is to perform the addition in serial, digit by digit, using one adder. That is, the C′ output feeds back into the same adder as the C input along with the next 2 digits to the left. This simulates the way humans work, adding each pair of digits, working from right to left. Humans require some time to record a result digit, move to the next pair of input digits, and begin the next addition. Computers have a similar lag time in reusing the same circuit to perform addition of each pair of digits.

Another more common circuit for multiple-digit addition is a *parallel adder.* An n-bit parallel adder is n full adders ganged together to compute an n-bit sum. The carry from each adder is passed to the adder immediately to its left. This form of circuit is more complex than a serial adder, but it is faster. A 4-bit parallel adder is shown in Figure 1.10.

It turns out that subtraction can be done with the same circuitry as addition simply by selecting the right representation of negative numbers. In Chapter 2 you will learn about different forms of number representation, and you will understand how subtraction can be accomplished using an adder.

Multiplication can be performed in several ways. One way to multiply X by n is to add X n times. For small values this is feasible but, in general, the time required for these additions is intolerable.

In decimal arithmetic it is easy to multiply by 10; you simply append a 0 to the end of the number being multiplied (e.g., 3576 * 10 = 35760). The same is true for multiplying by 100, 1000, 10,000, and so forth. This feature is a result of the positional representation. When you multiply by 10, you are simply increasing the

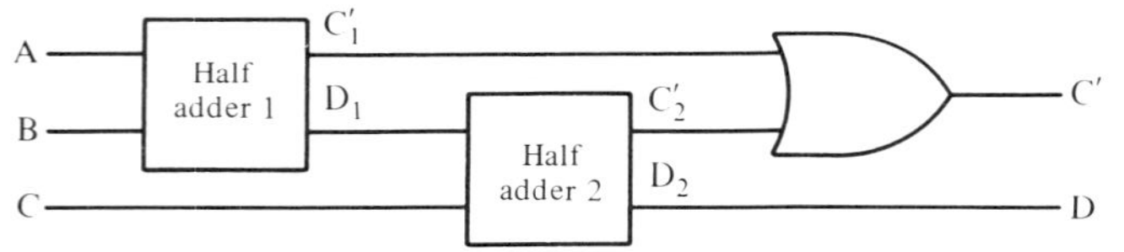

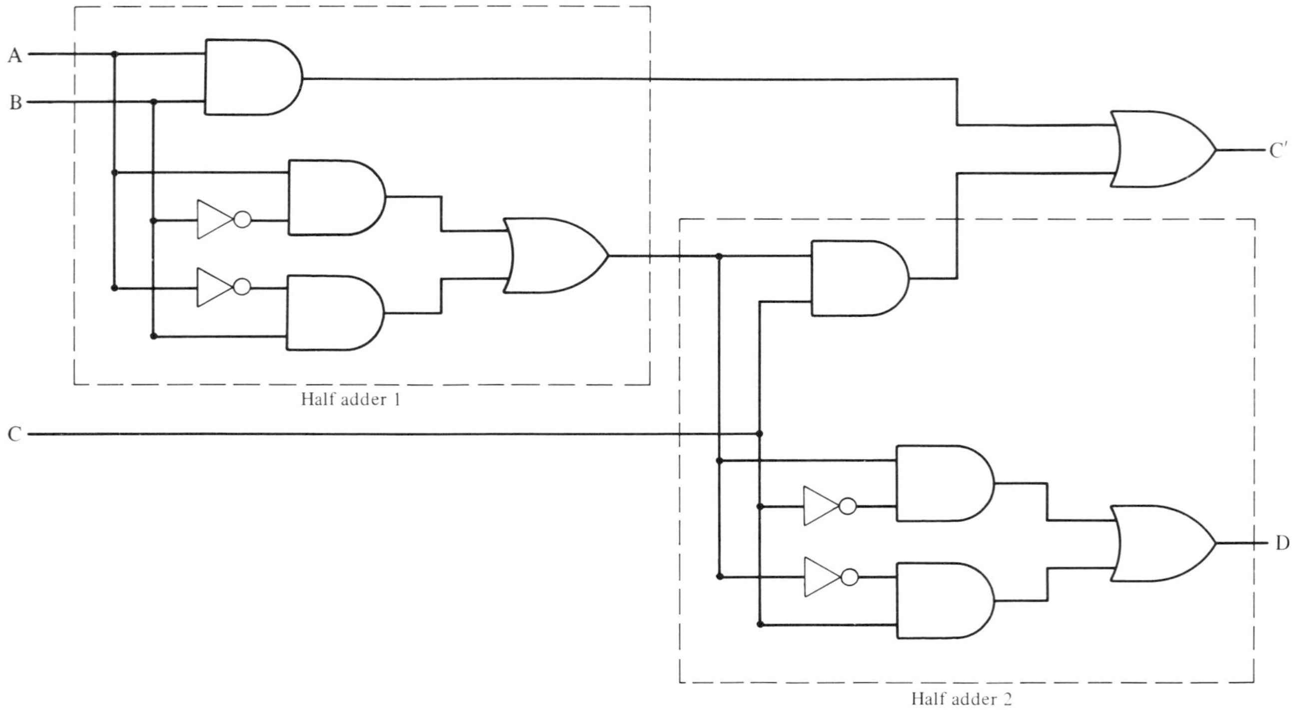

Figure 1.9 Full adder constructed from two half adders

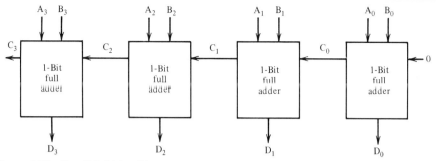

Figure 1.10 Parallel 4-bit adder.

value of each digit by a factor of 10. This is done by shifting each digit into the next position and moving a 0 into the rightmost position. For example, 3576 * 10 is computed as follows.

Position	3	2	1	0		4	3	2	1	0
Number	3	5	7	6	* 10 =	3	5	7	6	0
Power	10^3	10^2	10^1	10^0		10^4	10^3	10^2	10^1	10^0

Moving all digits of a number to the left (or the right) is called *shifting* the number. To multiply a number by a power of 10, say 10^n, you shift the number n positions to the left.

Because the binary number system is a positional system, a similar technique is true for binary numbers. However, since the binary number system is based around powers of 2, multiplication by powers of 2 (not 10) is performed by shifting to the left. An example using binary numbers instead of decimal ones should convince you this is true.

$$(5)\,(4)\,(3)\,(2)\,(1)\,(0)$$
$$1\ 0\ 1\ 1\ 0\ 1\ *\ 2^2 = 10110100$$
$$= 45 \qquad *\ 4\ = 180$$

Shifting circuitry is an important part of the ALU of a computer. Most computers provide instructions for shifting numbers both to the left and to the right.

Shifting can take care of multiplication by powers of 2, but it does not solve the general problem of multiplying. A multiplication algorithm will now be shown; this algorithm is the direct counterpart of the technique most people learn in school. Consider the following binary example.

```
        110100
   ×     10011
      ─────────
        110100
        110100
        000000
        000000
       110100
      ─────────
      1111011100
```

In each step of this computation the multiplicand (the top number) was multiplied by a digit from the multiplier, which produced one row of partial product. In fact, the multiplication was extremely easy, since the multiplicand was multiplied only by 0 and 1; when it was multiplied by 1, it was copied exactly, and when it was multiplied by 0, a row of 0s was supplied. In school students are usually taught to compute all partial products and add them at the end. However, because adders are built for two inputs instead of five (in this example) or n (for an n-digit multiplier), it is easier to compute a running sum during the multiplication. It is not really necessary to multiply at all: the digit 1 in the multiplier specifies adding the multiplicand, and the digit 0 specifies not adding it. The full algorithm is shown in the following example. To multiply 110100 * 10011:

1. Initialize: Product = 0.
2. Inspect the rightmost digit of the multiplier: If it is 0, go to step 4; otherwise, go to step 3.
3. (The multiplier digit was 1.) Add the multiplicand to the product.
4. (Adjust the multiplicand and multiplier.) Shift the multiplicand 1 digit to the left; discard the rightmost digit of the multiplier.
5. If the multiplier is 0, halt; otherwise, return to step 2.

Step	Multiplicand	Multiplier	Product
1	110100	10011	0
2			
3	110100	10011	110100
4	1101000	1001	110100
5			
2			
3	1101000	1001	10011100
4	11010000	100	10011100
5			
2			
4	110100000	10	10011100
5			
2			
4			
4	1101000000	1	10011100
5			
2			
3	1101000000	1	1111011100
4	11010000000	0	1111011100
5	Halt		

This shift-and-add algorithm is a simple means of performing multiplication, but it does take time; on most machines multiplication is substantially slower than addition, often by a factor of 5 or 10. Some machines—some mini- and microcomputers—do not have multiplication circuitry because it is so time consuming and because many users of these machines do not need to multiply often.

Notice that multiplication can be built from circuitry that can add, shift right and left, test for a single bit to be 0, and test for a number to be 0. The adder and shifter have already been described as being important parts of an ALU. Circuitry to inspect a single bit and to test a full word for the value 0 are both found in all arithmetic units as well.

Figure 1.11 summarizes the elements of an ALU.

In this section you have seen the components found in most ALUs. Different machines are built for different purposes. Some users may require the ability to perform floating point (real number) arithmetic, while others may require an extensive character-manipulating repertoire, and still others may desire the ability to perform arithmetic on decimal values coded in binary, decimal digit by decimal digit. Later chapters have examples of special-purpose instructions that imply extra circuitry in the ALU. What you have seen here is a part of the basic circuitry of an ALU so that you can appreciate the types of basic operations with which each machine operates. A summary of the information on the ALU follows.

1. The three basic logical functions are AND, OR, and NOT; the exclusive OR function is also sometimes provided. The AND of 2 digits is 1 only if both of the digits are 1; otherwise, it is 0. The OR of 2 digits is 0 only if both of the digits are 0; otherwise, it is 1. The NOT of 0 is 1, and the NOT of 1 is 0.
2. A half adder is a circuit that takes two inputs and produces the sum digit and carry digit from the input digits. A full adder is a circuit that takes two input digits and a carry input; it produces a sum digit and a carry digit as output.
3. A shift unit is one that can move all digits of a binary number left (or right).
4. Multiplier units are available with only some ALUs. One algorithm for multiplication is the shift-and-add method; however, there are other techniques.

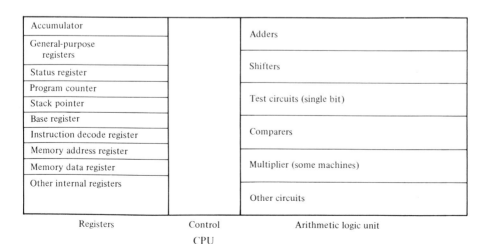

Accumulator		Adders
General-purpose registers		
Status register		Shifters
Program counter		
Stack pointer		Test circuits (single bit)
Base register		
Instruction decode register		Comparers
Memory address register		
Memory data register		Multiplier (some machines)
Other internal registers		
		Other circuits
Registers	Control	Arithmetic logic unit
	CPU	

Figure 1.11   Components of an arithmetic logic unit (ALU).

1.2 MEMORY DEVICES

In this section you will learn about some of the internal memory organization forms. The classic form of memory is *core memory*, which will be used as the standard description. In spite of the fact that there are faster devices to serve as computer memory, core memory remains a popular form. Other forms of memory will be described in terms of their difference from core memory.

1.2.1 Core Memory

A bit of *magnetic core memory* is a doughnut-shaped disk of ferrite or similar material. As you may recall, magnets have two poles, north and south. The north pole of one magnet is attracted to the south pole of another and repelled by the north pole of another. The magnets in a core are aligned in a circle, as shown in Figure 1.12.

Figure 1.12   Magnetic core memory.

If a sufficient current is passed along a wire through the core, the poles of the magnets align themselves in agreement with the direction of the current. Since there are two possible directions to the current, there are two different arrangements of the magnetic poles, as shown in Figure 1.13.

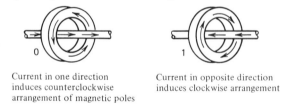

Current in one direction
induces counterclockwise
arrangement of magnetic poles

Current in opposite direction
induces clockwise arrangement

Figure 1.13   Arrangement of magnetic poles in a core memory.

A core thus has two possible configurations, depending on the direction of the current passed through the core. One of these configurations will be arbitrarily called 1, and the other will be called 0. These labels are shown in Figure 1.13. A core retains its magnetic alignment until another strong current is passed along a wire through the core. Cores can thus be used as bistable storage devices: they have two different settings and they will hold their values until changed.

We have to be able to set and test each bit individually. One way this could be done would be to have one wire associated with each bit. A decoding switch would then be needed to select the one wire with which a particular bit was set. Figure 1.14 shows magnetic cores with one wire per bit.

The circuitry to manage one wire per core would be very complex for even a moderately small computer memory. Furthermore, this one circuit would disable the entire memory if it were to fail; it is sensible to make units in a computing system independent, so that if one unit fails the whole system is not disabled.

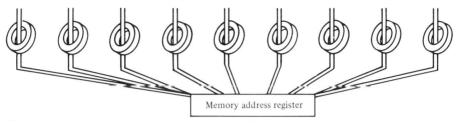

Figure 1.14 Magnetic cores with one wire per bit.

A *threshold* current exists for cores; if a current less than the threshold amount is passed along a wire through a core, no change to the core occurs; if, however, an amount greater than the threshold current is passed through the core, the core will adopt the magnetic alignment that matches the direction of the current. Furthermore, if two or more wires pass through a core, the current sensed by the core is the sum of the currents passed along the wires.

Because of the disadvantages of having an individual wire per core and because of the threshold property, cores are arranged in a square or rectangular pattern. Each core has two wires passing through it. This pattern is shown in Figure 1.15.

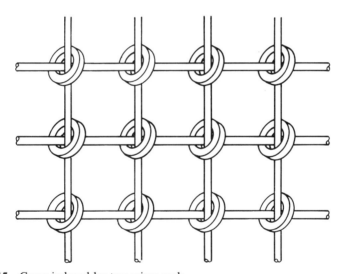

Figure 1.15 Cores indexed by two wires each.

In order to set a particular core an amount of current approximately equal to one-half of the threshold amount is sent along each of the wires passing through the particular core. The one desired core will receive the full threshold amount, and its magnetism will conform to the direction of the current. At cores along the same row or column as the desired core, no change will occur, since the amount of current each of these receives is only one-half its threshold amount. The setting of one core is shown in Figure 1.16. This organization of core is called *coincident current core,* since setting a bit depends on two half currents coinciding at the bit.

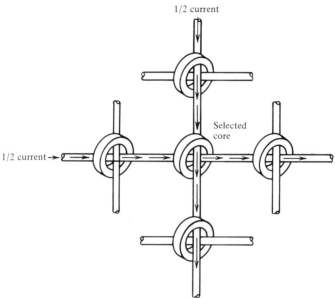

Figure 1.16 Setting one core.

So far the method for setting a bit has been described but, to be useful, core must also be read to determine the setting of a particular core. Through each core passes another wire, called the *sense wire*. When a current flow causes a change in the direction of magnetism, this induces a current along the sense wire. Thus, when a bit changes from 0 to 1 or from 1 to 0, a pulse is generated along the sense wire. However, when a 1 bit receives a 1 current, no change to the bit occurs; the same is true for 0 bits receiving a 0 current. There is a current along the sense wire only when the setting of a bit changes from 0 to 1 or from 1 to 0.

One way to determine the value of a bit is to set it to 1 and to monitor the sense wire. If there is a pulse along the sense wire, the bit was originally a 0, and it changed to a 1. If there is no pulse along the sense wire, the bit was a 1 and remained unchanged. It is possible to determine the value of a bit by setting the bit to one value and observing the sense wire to see if the bit changed in going to that value.

This means of determining the value of a bit requires destroying the value previously stored in the bit. For this reason this type of memory is called *destructive read memory*. After destroying the value in a bit, it is necessary to reset the bit to its original value if it was changed (i.e., if a pulse was generated along the sense wire). Reading the contents of a bit of this memory involves a two-step cycle: fetching the value and rewriting the original value.

Two bits may not be accessed simultaneously in one grid of core. This is because of the coincident current property and the use of just one sense wire for a grid. Two bits have potentially two different pairs of horizontal and vertical coordinates, but two pairs of wires means up to 4 different bits being affected by a 1/2 current threshold passing along two pairs of wires at once. Similarly, it is not possible to determine which of 2 bits changed if one pulse is generated as 2 different bits are being fetched. These problems are pictured in Figure 1.17.

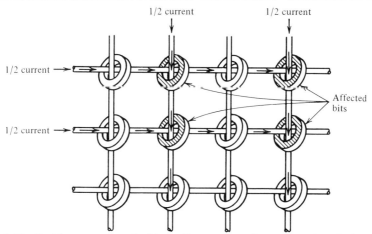

Figure 1.17 Problems associated with sending current along two pairs of wires at once.

During both steps of the fetch-restore cycle, all bits in a plane are inaccessible. To permit simultaneous access to all bits of a byte or a word, the bits of a byte usually appear on different planes of core. If, for example, the grid contains 256 bits (a 16-by-16 square) and a word consists of 8 bits, there would be eight 256-bit planes stacked together. The bottom plane would contain the zeroth bit of all words, the next plane would contain the first bit of all words, and so forth, and the top plane would contain the seventh bit of all words. In this way it is possible to access all 8 bits of a word at once, and the same circuitry that selects a horizontal and a vertical wire to identify a particular bit can be used to select the corresponding horizontal and vertical wires in all planes. This notion is shown in Figure 1.18.

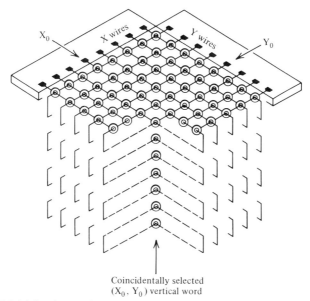

Coincidentally selected
(X_0, Y_0) vertical word

Figure 1.18 Multiple planes of core.

The fact that a plane (or, as just described, a bank of planes) is inaccessible during a restore cycle can slow down the speed of computation. The registers and the ALU circuitry are both normally faster than main memory. While a bank of core is being restored, the ALU may be ready to use another value. In order to reduce the amount of time that the ALU must wait while one bank is being restored, memory is interleaved. *Interleaving* is a technique in which memory is divided into a number of separate banks. If memory is four-way interleaved, for example, four separate banks of memory exist, each containing one-quarter of the words of memory. This is shown in Figure 1.19.

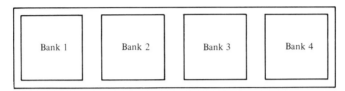

Memory

Figure 1.19 Interleaved memory (four-way interleaved).

Thus, while a fetch or restore is in progress for a word in one bank, a word from a different bank may be fetched. It is common to divide the words in the banks (again, assuming the example of four-way interleaving) so that words 0, 4, 8, 12, 16, and so forth, are in bank 0, words 1, 5, 9, 13, and so on, are in bank 1, words 2, 6, 10, and so forth, are in bank 2, and words 3, 7, 11, and so on, are in bank 3. In this way it is possible to access consecutive words of memory rapidly. This memory arrangement is shown in Figure 1.20.

Word 0	Word 1	Word 2	Word 3
Word 4	Word 5	Word 6	Word 7
Word 8	Word 9	Word 10	Word 11
Word 12	Word 13	Word 14	Word 15
⋮	⋮	⋮	⋮
Word $4 \cdot k$	Word $4 \cdot k + 1$	Word $4 \cdot k + 2$	Word $4 \cdot k + 3$
⋮	⋮	⋮	⋮

Figure 1.20 Arrangement of interleaved words of memory.

Interleaving can have a dramatic effect on the speed of computation. Assume that a new data fetch can be commenced when the previous fetch is half completed. (This assumption is reasonable.) Then, with interleaving, memory can seem to operate twice as fast as its actual speed, as shown in Figure 1.21.

In Section 1.1.1 on registers, *the memory address register* (MAR) and the *memory data register* (MDR) were introduced without much explanation. The MAR holds the memory address of the word that is about to be accessed. From

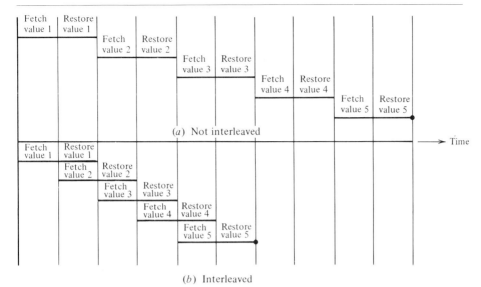

(a) Not interleaved

(b) Interleaved

Figure 1.21 Apparent access speed of interleaved memory.

the preceding discussion on core, you can see that some circuitry is needed to decode a memory address and translate that into a pair of coordinate wires. For example, in a 256-by-256 memory, addresses may range between 0 and 65,535 (= 256*256 − 1). These addresses must be decoded so as to select one pair of the 512 wires. The address desired is placed in the MAR where it can be decoded and the right pair of wires can be selected. Similarly, after a data value has been extracted from a destructive read memory, the value must be restored. The MDR is a register where the value read from memory can be held while pulses are being generated to restore the value in memory. The relationship between these two registers and memory is shown in Figure 1.22.

The operations involved in obtaining a value from memory are listed here.

1. The address of the data is placed in the MAR.
2. The memory module is signaled for a read.
3. This causes the address to be decoded and a pair of coordinate wires to be selected.
4. The sense wire signals (bits of the data value) are directed into the MDR.
5. At this point, the value in the MDR is available for further computation. However, the value there must be restored in memory.

For a store (memory modifying operation), a similar sequence occurs. Steps 1, 2, and 3 are the same. However, instead of directing the values from the sense wires into the MDR, the value from memory is discarded. The value to be stored is then placed in the MDR. The memory unit will then attempt to restore the value destroyed by copying the contents of the MDR back into memory. Since the MDR contains the value that is to be stored, this "tricks" the memory unit into storing that value in memory.

Magnetic core memory is only one common memory technology. Since each core is individually wired, there is a limit to how small a bit of core can be.

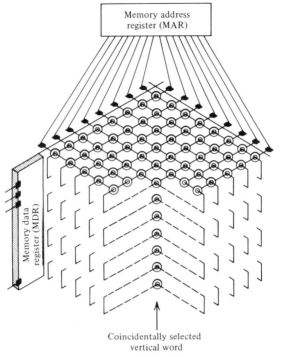

Memory address
register (MAR)

Memory data
register (MDR)

Coincidentally selected
vertical word

Figure 1.22 Memory address and memory data registers.

Typically, the diameter of a core is approximately 0.02 to 0.05 inches, and it will be hard to improve on this size. Magnetic core has the advantage that its memory is not "volatile." This means that even if power is interrupted, the values stored will not be lost. This property is not shared by some other memory technologies. Core memory is fairly fast and inexpensive, although newer forms of memory are faster and cheaper. Nevertheless, because it is rugged, can operate in a wide range of temperature conditions, and is nonvolatile, core memory is not likely to be altogether replaced soon.

1.2.2 Semiconductor Memory

Another variety of memory device is the *flip-flop*. This is a switchlike device that has two inputs. An *SR* flip-flop uses the two inputs to select either of two positions. Call the two positions of the flip-flop the *set* (S) and *reset* (R) positions. If a flip-flop is in the set position and receives a pulse along the reset input line, it moves to the reset position; if it was in the reset position nothing happens. Similarly, if a flip-flop is in the reset position and receives a pulse along the set line, it moves to the set position; if it was in the set position nothing happens. The two input wires act very much like the two directions of current for a magnetic core. The operation of a flip-flop is shown in Figure 1.23.

Originally flip-flops were electromechanical devices. This means that they were relay arms attracted to and held by either of two electromagnets. One electromagnet would be the set side, while the other would be the reset. One electro-

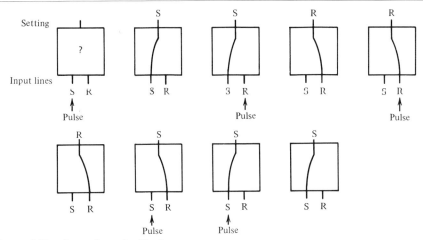

Figure 1.23 Operation of a flip-flop.

magnet at a time would be energized, and it would pull and hold the relay arm. Such relays were used on the first computers such as the ENIAC and the MARK I at Harvard. Flip-flops were also implemented using vacuum tubes.

More recently, however, a flip-flop circuit has been designed using transistors, and now metallic oxide semiconductors (MOS) are used. Single transistors individually wired were used for registers in computers during the 1960s. At that time, their cost made them prohibitive for use as general memory devices. However, with the advent of integrated circuits (multiple transistors fabricated on a single silicon chip) and large-scale integrated circuits (large numbers of semiconductors fabricated on a single chip), flip-flops have become very attractive memory devices. They can be manufactured at reasonable cost, and they have a response time generally better than core memory. The usual range on core memory access is from 0.3 to 2.0 microseconds, while the time for semiconductor memory ranges from 0.02 to 0.4 microseconds. (A microsecond is one millionth of a second, 10^{-6} second.) Furthermore, the size of these devices is substantially smaller than core. A semiconductor memory is commonly one-quarter or less than the size of a core memory of the same number of bits. More than 4000 bits of memory may be placed on a chip approximately 1 square inch in surface size. Furthermore, semiconductor flip-flops can be read without destroying their contents.

Semiconductors are not without their disadvantages. First, although they are highly reliable, their reliability does not equal that of core memory. Second, semiconductor memory does not have to be restored after reading; however, it must be recharged periodically, about once per millisecond (one-thousandth of a second, 10^{-3} second). Finally, because they need to be refreshed periodically, they are sensitive to power loss. In spite of these disadvantages, semiconductor memory devices are becoming more popular, largely because of their better response time and their lower cost than core memory.

1.2.3 ROM and PROM

The type of memory just described is called *random access memory* (RAM). This is the standard computer memory used for storing programs and data. Random access means that any location of memory can be accessed as rapidly as any other. (This contrasts with some kinds of auxiliary I/O storage devices, where it may take considerably longer to access some pieces of information than others, depending on where the information is located and on where information was taken from last.)

Associated with microcomputers is another variety of memory called *read-only memory* (ROM). This memory also has the random access property in that all locations take an equal amount of time to access. However, it is not possible for the programmer to write in this memory, either to store data or instructions there.

ROM is frequently used in conjunction with the CPU to facilitate instruction execution. A section of ROM might contain information on what the "meaning" of certain machine instructions is; that is, information contained there might indicate what action the computer performs to execute each of its instructions. For example, there may be many instructions that cause addition: 8-bit and 16-bit add instructions, 8-bit and 16-bit subtract instructions (in the next chapter we will see how subtraction can be performed as a variation on addition), and other instructions that may use addition, such as a shift-and-add multiplication algorithm or an instruction designed to facilitate iterative looping.

There are several approaches to constructing a machine to perform these instructions. First, there could be a separate hardware adder for each instruction. This duplication in circuitry is unnecessary and costly. A second approach is to have one adder, but to wire it so that it is activated each time one of these instructions is executed. This wiring can be complex, especially with a machine that has a large and comprehensive instruction set. The design of such machines is complicated and, once designed, the machines are virtually impossible to change. (One might want to change such a machine if a newer, faster, more efficient algorithm were found to perform some operation, such as multiplication.)

A final approach uses a technique called *microprogramming,* in which effectively the interpretation of each instruction is done by programming. When a computer instruction is being executed, the CPU actually executes a number of microinstructions in a ROM; these microinstructions direct data movement to and from memory and the computational units, such as adders. A simple 8-bit add instruction might be performed by fetching the two values to be added and forcing them through an 8-bit adder. A 16-bit add instruction might be performed by fetching the two values, forcing the rightmost 8 bits of each through an adder, storing this quantity, observing the carry bit, forcing the carry bit and the leftmost 8 bits of one value through an adder and, finally, forcing that sum through an adder with the leftmost 8 bits of the other value.

All of this data manipulation is regular enough that it can be described through a low-level programming language. Programming in a language that actually controls the paths of signals or data within the computer is called *micropro-gramming,* and a computer that uses microprogramming to emulate its machine instructions is called a *microprogrammed instruction set* computer.

Microinstructions are called *firmware,* to show that they are somewhere between hardware and software. They are like software in that using them is like using a programming language. They are like hardware, however, because they are a tangible piece of equipment, a form of memory that cannot be accessed directly.

The microinstructions to emulate computer instructions are stored in a ROM. If a new hardware algorithm is found for supporting a particular instruction, a new circuit board or chip of ROM can be made that incorporates this new algorithm into its microprogram. This circuit board can be replaced in computers; if the new algorithm is faster, the computer will operate faster each time it performs the revised instruction. Some computer instructions may introduce an error into the computation and, depending on the algorithm, they may introduce more or less error. Thus a new, low-error algorithm might also improve the performance of a computer; these changes are possible if the computer is microprogrammed.

Microprogramming is convenient for computer manufacturers who wish to improve the speed at which their computers operate without changing any hardware components, such as adders. Given users may choose to optimize the performance of their computers on certain frequently used instructions. Another possible use for microprogramming is to support additional instructions. Suppose that for a major application a user could use an efficient single instruction to compute the average of two values. Few (if any) computers have an "average" instruction; however, by writing a new microprogram for a computer, it would be possible to create such an instruction. This creates the need for writable ROM, or ROM that can be written, but only one time.

The common technology for changable ROM involves thin bridges of a material; by sending a strong enough current across the bridge, the bridge melts, much like a fuse in a wiring circuit. A melted bridge might represent a 0, since it would not pass current, while an intact bridge might represent a 1. This type of memory is called *programmable read-only memory* (PROM), since it is possible to store values once in memory under program control; after the bridges have been burnt, however, the memory can only be read. ROM permits the user to store a number of microinstructions or an amount of permanent data in a section of memory that cannot be changed. There are even varieties of PROM that can be erased and rewritten. Their normal state is read-only; however, it is possible to eliminate all information in them and reprogram them. This is called *erasable programmable read-only memory* (EPROM).

This introduction to the internal characteristics of memory should help you to understand how bits are arranged and accessed. In the next chapter you will see how numbers are represented internally in order to be stored in binary memory devices. Following is a summary of information on memory devices.

1. Memory devices are organized into individual bits. It must be possible to set and read each bit.
2. Core memory uses small disks of ferrite material. Cores have the property that each can adopt either of two directions of magnetism. They adopt one of these directions in reaction to the direction of a current that is passed through them. The two directions represent 0 and 1 settings.
3. Core memory is a destructive read memory, meaning that in order to determine the setting of a particular bit, it is necessary to destroy the previous value in that bit by setting the bit to a particular value, either 0 or 1. The original value of the bit is determined by whether the bit

changed setting as it went to the new setting. After being set in order to be read, core memory must be reset to the original value.

4. Core is frequently stored in a rectangular grid. Individual bits are addressed by a combination of two wires, one horizontal and one vertical. To set a particular bit, 1/2 current is sent along its horizontal wire and 1/2 current along its vertical wire. This is called coincident current core.

5. To enhance performance of memory units, the bits of memory are sometimes divided into independent units, so that different words will be in different units. The two or more units can be accessed in more rapid succession than could one large unit. This process is called interleaving.

6. Another memory device is the semiconductor flip-flop. This device can be faster than core, partly because no restore is necessary in reading this kind of memory. Semiconductor memory can be fabricated in LSI circuits; thus many bits of memory can be built on a single small chip.

7. Some computers use ROM to store permanent information. This information may be in the form of a microprogram to produce the effect of executing computer instructions. A microprogrammed instruction set has the advantage of being fairly easily changed and extended.

1.3 SAMPLE MACHINES

This section contains descriptions of the architecture of three sample machines: the IBM 360-370 family, the PDP-11 series, and the Intel 8080 microcomputer. Throughout the remainder of this text, these will be the principal example machines studied.

1.3.1 IBM 360-370 Family

The IBM 360-370 computers include many machines. The 360 group were designed and announced in the early 1960s. There are about 10 different models of series 360 computers, all sharing the same apparent architecture. (That is, the machines seem the same to the user, executing the same instructions, and having the same set of hardware features.) In the early 1970s the 370 line was introduced as an "upward compatible" family of machines to the 360 line. By "upward compatible" IBM meant that programs that would run on a 360 would also run on a 370. However, because of the addition of new instructions and new hardware features on the 370s, not all programs that run on a 370 will also run on a 360. In the middle of the 1970s more products in this line—the 3031, 3032, and 3033— were announced. More recently the 4331 and 4341 have been added. The 303x and 4300 machines are structurally like 370s.

These machines are large, general-purpose machines, suited to heavy and varied computing work loads. These machines are popular in commercial installations and major academic computing centers.

The machines have 16 general-purpose registers of 32 bits each. There are also 4 64-bit registers for floating point (real number) computation. The program counter is called a PSW (for program status word), and it contains 64 bits—24 bits for the address of the next instruction and 40 bits for the machine status. There are other internal registers for computation and control.

The smallest unit of addressable memory is the 8-bit byte. The addressing structure allows over 16 million bytes of memory. Memory is grouped into words of 4 bytes each. Most computation is word oriented, although some instructions use halfwords (16 bits), doublewords (64 bits), and single bytes (8 bits).

The features of the IBM 360-370 family are summarized in Figure 1.24.

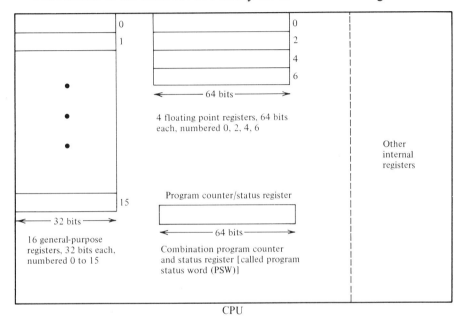

CPU

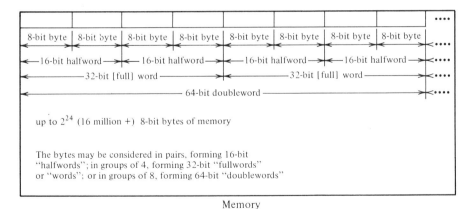

Memory

Figure 1.24 IBM 360-370 computers.

1.3.2 PDP-11

The PDP-11 was introduced in the middle of the 1960s. There are a range of PDP-11 machines that operate at a variety of speeds and prices. Larger PDP-11s (e.g.,

PDP-11/70s) are powerful enough to serve as the primary machine in a moderate computing center, while the smaller models are especially appropriate for dedicated use in a laboratory or specialized application.

There are eight scratchpad registers, each of which is 16 bits long. However, the program counter is register 7, and the stack pointer is register 6. This means that there are effectively only six registers freely available for the user. A 16-bit status register contains flags for overflow, carry, zero, and negative as well as for other purposes. There are various internal registers for control purposes.

The machine can address over 65,000 main storage locations, each of which is an 8-bit byte. Words of 16 bits are also recognized. With an extra hardware device memory may be expanded to over 260,000 bytes.

Figure 1.25 shows the details of the PDP-11 architecture.

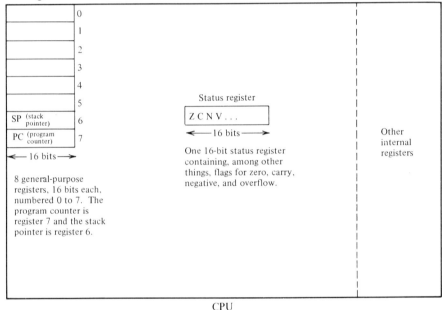

CPU

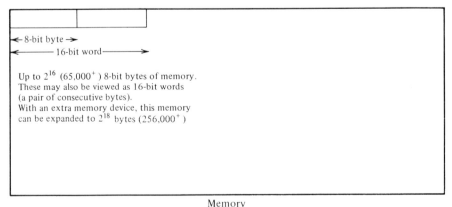

Memory

Figure 1.25   PDP-11 computers.

1.3.3 Intel 8080 Microcomputer

The third sample computer is a small, relatively inexpensive machine. (A complete computer—CPU, memory, and some I/O devices—can be purchased for under $2000.) These machines (and other similar *microcomputers*) are popular with small businesses. However, an even more active market is the computer hobbyist who uses this computer as a personal tool for recreation. Because of declining costs and increasing availability of software (programs), these machines have attracted a wide following of students, professionals, and hobbyists.

The Intel 8080, which was introduced in the early 1970s, has seven 8-bit registers. Six of these may be used in three pairs for 16-bit computation. There is a separate 16-bit program counter, a 16-bit stack pointer, and an 8-bit status register, as well as internal registers.

Memory is byte oriented, although 16-bit (2-byte) words are recognized. There may be over 65,000 bytes of memory.

The features of these machines are shown in Figure 1.26.

1.4 TERMS USED

The following terms have been introduced in this chapter. Those marked with a (*) have only been introduced; they will be defined in later chapters.

Central processing unit (CPU)
Register
General-purpose register
Scratchpad register
Accumulator
Program counter
Status register
Overflow
Carry
Flag
Stack pointer*
Base register*
Instruction decode register*
Memory address register (MAR)
Memory data register (MDR)
Arithmetic logic unit (ALU)
Positional number representation
AND
OR
Exclusive OR
NOT
Complement
Inverter
Half adder
Full adder
Parallel *n*-bit adder
Shifting

Binary number system
Shift-and-add multiplication
Core memory
Bit
Bistable storage device
Threshold current
Coincident current core
Sense wire
Destructive read memory
Fetch-restore cycle
Interleaving

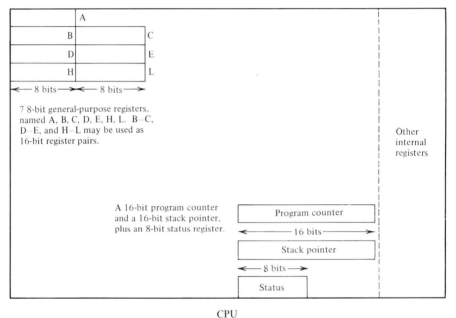

	A	
B		C
D		E
H		L

←— 8 bits —→←— 8 bits —→

7 8-bit general-purpose registers,
named A, B, C, D, E, H, L. B–C,
D–E, and H–L may be used as
16-bit register pairs.

Other
internal
registers

A 16-bit program counter
and a 16-bit stack pointer,
plus an 8-bit status register.

Program counter

←————— 16 bits —————→

Stack pointer

←— 8 bits —→

Status

CPU

←—8-bit byte—→
←————— 16-bit word —————→

Up to 2^{16} (65,000⁺) 8-bit bytes
of memory, which may also be
used as 16-bit words composed
of 2 adjacent bytes

Memory

Figure 1.26 Intel 8080 microcomputers.

Flip-flop
SR flip-flop
Metallic oxide semiconductor (MOS) flip-flop
Random access memory (RAM)
Read-only memory (ROM)
Microprogramming
Microinstruction
Programmable read-only memory (PROM)
Erasable programmable read-only memory (EPROM)

1.5   QUESTIONS

Test your understanding of the major points in this chapter by answering the following questions. (*Note:* These questions require some work on your part. Do not be surprised if you cannot answer them immediately.)

1. Name the registers of which a CPU is composed. What is the function of each?

2. A computation such as (A + B)*(C + D) can be performed easily if there are two scratchpad registers (one to hold each intermediate sum). However, it does not require three registers for a three-term multiplication, such as (A + B)*(C + D)*(E + F). The latter expression can be computed as ((A + B)*(C + D)) * (E + F), so again two registers can produce an efficient computation. Can you construct an arithmetic expression where three registers would facilitate the computation? (There are other uses for registers than just arithmetic evaluations. A general rule in computing is that the particular task you wish to perform can be done most easily with one more register than the machine has.)

3. Write a logical expression (using AND, OR, exclusive OR, or NOT) that uses two variables, A and B, and produces a 1 in every bit where the corresponding bits from A and B were not the same. All other result bits are to be 0. That is, A = 1001, B = 1100 would produce an answer of C = 0101, since A and B are the same in the first and third bits.

4. Write a logical expression that uses three variables, A, B, and C. The result is to be 1 just in case either 2 or 3 of the corresponding input bits are 1.

5. Design a function that computes A − B. (*Note:* You will see in the next chapter that a general "subtracter" is not a common piece of computing hardware. Subtraction is most often performed as a special case of addition.) Instead of a *carry*, you will probably want to produce a *borrow* output; that is, this bit should be 1 just in case B was larger than A in computing A − B.

6. Multiplication can be performed by repeated addition. Design an algorithm that computes the quotient of A/B, using only addition, subtraction, shifts, comparison, and testing a single bit.

7. Design a circuit that converts a 3-bit binary number to an 8-bit number. In three bits numbers between 000 (0) and 111 (7) can be represented. Assume that the 8 bits of the result are numbered N(0) to N(7). Bit N(j) is to be 1, and all other bits of the output are to be 0 to show that the value of the binary input was j. That is, input 000 would produce an output of 10000000, and

input 011 would generate an output of 00010000. Such a function is called a decoder.

8. Assume that a bank of memory has 64 bits. If the bank is square (8 by 8), how many wires are needed for selecting the individual bits? How many bits are needed to represent the address of any bit in this bank? Sketch a figure of this bank with all the address wires shown. Could the function designed in Question 7 be used to assist in addressing the bits of the memory bank?

chapter 2

Internal Representation of Data

As shown in the previous chapter, every data item or instruction stored in memory is represented in binary—base 2. There are a number of different encodings of the data values, depending on the internal computer design and the type of data. This chapter contains descriptions of some of the more common encodings.

2.1 THE BINARY NUMBER SYSTEM

The previous chapter introduced the binary number system. The binary number system is a positional numbering system in which the digits represent powers of 2. There are only 2 digits: 0 and 1. To interpret a binary number, simply multiply each power of 2 by its corresponding digit, as in the following example.

Position	7	6	5	4	3	2	1	0
Binary number	1	0	0	0	1	1	0	1
Powers of 2	2^7	2^6	2^5	2^4	2^3	2^2	2^1	2^0

$$1*2^7 = 128$$
$$0*2^6 = 0$$
$$0*2^5 = 0$$
$$0*2^4 = 0$$
$$1*2^3 = 8$$
$$1*2^2 = 4$$
$$0*2^1 = 0$$
$$1*2^0 = \underline{1}$$
$$141$$

Another method to convert binary to decimal works from left to right. Start with a sum of 0. At each step, multiply the current sum by 2 and add the next digit to the right. For example, converting binary 10110001 to decimal, you would use the following steps.

Sum		Digits already used	Digits not used yet
	0	—	10110001
2*(0) + 1 =	1	1	0110001
2*(1) + 0 =	2	10	110001
2*(2) + 1 =	5	101	10001
2*(5) + 1 =	11	1011	0001
2*(11) + 0 =	22	10110	001
2*(22) + 0 =	44	101100	01
2*(44) + 0 =	88	1011000	1
2*(88) + 1 =	177	10110001	—

This method works because each digit is multiplied by 2 as many times as there are digits to its right; that is, each digit is multiplied by a power of 2, where the power is the position of the digit. Consider a 5-digit binary number, abcde. The first step is

$$2*(0) + a = a$$

The following steps are

$$2*(a) + b = 2a + b$$
$$2*(2*(a) + b) + c = 4a + 2b + c$$
$$2*(2*(2*(a) + b) + c) + d = 8a + 4b + 2c + d$$
$$2*(2*(2*(a) + b) + c) + d) + e = 16a + 8b + 4c + 2d + e$$

This is just $a*2^4 + b*2^3 + c*2^2 + d*2^1 + e*2^0$. This technique works because repeated multiplication by 2 produces the powers of 2.

Converting from binary to decimal is simply a matter of determining the value associated with each digit in binary and adding the values. To convert from decimal numbers to binary, a similar process can be used, although there are easier ways. One is based on determining the largest power of 2 contained in a number and then computing the binary equivalent of the excess over that power of 2. Another process uses repeated division by 2.

The powers-of-2 method requires knowing a number of powers of 2. Since they are easy to compute (each power is twice the previous power), it is not worth memorizing them. For reference, however, a table of some powers of 2 is shown on page 51. In this listing of powers of 2 notice that 2^{10} is approximately 1000 and 2^{20} is about 1 million. These approximations can be used for quick estimates of a binary number's decimal value. The letter K is frequently used in computing to mean 1024. Memory and storage device capacities are listed as some number of K, for example, 4K of core memory or a device that can hold 300K characters. The letter K derives from the prefix *kilo* meaning 1000.

Power of 2	Decimal value	
2^0 =	1	
2^1 =	2	
2^2 —	4	
2^3 =	8	
2^4 =	16	
2^5 =	32	
2^6 =	64	
2^7 =	128	
2^8 =	256	
2^9 =	512	
2^{10} =	1024	
2^{11} =	2048	
2^{12} =	4096	
2^{15} =	32768	
2^{16} =	65536 =	65,536
2^{20} =	1048576 =	1,048,576
2^{24} =	16777216 =	16,777,216
2^{32} =	4294967296 =	4,294,967,296
2^{36} =	68719476736 =	68,719,476,736

Now suppose you need to convert the decimal number 38473 to binary. Comparing 38473 to the powers of 2, the largest power of 2 less than or equal to 38473 is 2^{15}, or 32768. By simple arithmetic, $38473 = 32768 + 5705$. Thus the binary equivalent of 38473 is 2^{15} plus the binary equivalent of 5705.

Continuing with this process, 5705 is greater than 4096, so 4096 is the largest power of 2 contained in 5705. But $5705 = 4096 + 1609$, and the process continues by trying to find the binary equivalent for 1609. Since 1609 is greater than 1024, 1609 could be written as $1024 + 585$. Then 585 could be written as $512 + 73$, and 73 as $64 + 9$, and 9 as $8 + 1$. Putting all of these pieces together,

$$38473 = 32768 + 5705 =$$
$$32768 + 4096 + 1609 =$$
$$32768 + 4096 + 1024 + 585 =$$
$$32768 + 4096 + 1024 + 512 + 73 =$$
$$32768 + 4096 + 1024 + 512 + 64 + 9 =$$
$$32768 + 4096 + 1024 + 512 + 64 + 8 + 1 =$$
$$2^{15} + 2^{12} + 2^{10} + 2^9 + 2^6 + 2^3 + 2^0 =$$

```
(15) (14) (13) (12) (11) (10) (9) (8) (7) (6) (5) (4) (3) (2) (1) (0)
  1    0    0    1    0    1   1   0   0   1   0   0   1   0   0   1
```

or the binary number

1001011001001001

This process works by breaking a decimal number into two parts: the sum of the largest possible power of 2 and a remainder. The remainder is broken into two parts: a largest power of 2 and a new remainder. This process continues until the remainder is 0. Then the powers of 2 are collected, and 1s are recorded in the corresponding positions of a binary number.

The other method to convert a decimal number to binary is nearly the reverse of this process. This works by dividing the decimal number successively by 2. The first time the number is divided, the remainder is the number of 1s represented in the decimal number (a 0 remainder means the number is even, so the number contains no 2^0 term; a remainder of 1 means the number is odd, and it contains a 2^0 term).

The next step is to divide the result of the previous division by 2 again (effectively dividing the original number by 4). If this remainder is 0 the original number was divisible by 4, which means it had no 2^1 term; if the remainder is 1 the original number did contain a 2^1 term. The next division gives the number of 4s (2^2), and so forth. At each step, the remainder tells how many of the next lower power of 2 were present in the number. The remainders are saved and written *right to left* (with the first remainder on the right). These remainders are the binary equivalent of the number. This process is now illustrated.

Convert 1348 to binary. For this example, we will perform division, writing the quotient *under* the number being divided and the remainder (rem.) to the right side.

$$
\begin{array}{rl}
2\,)\ \underline{1348} & \\
674 & \text{rem. } 0 \\[4pt]
2\,)\ \underline{674} & \\
337 & \text{rem. } 0 \\[4pt]
2\,)\ \underline{337} & \\
168 & \text{rem. } 1 \\[4pt]
2\,)\ \underline{168} & \\
84 & \text{rem. } 0 \\[4pt]
2\,)\ \underline{84} & \\
42 & \text{rem. } 0 \\[4pt]
2\,)\ \underline{42} & \\
21 & \text{rem. } 0 \\[4pt]
2\,)\ \underline{21} & \\
10 & \text{rem. } 1 \\[4pt]
2\,)\ \underline{10} & \\
5 & \text{rem. } 0 \\[4pt]
2\,)\ \underline{5} & \\
2 & \text{rem. } 1 \\[4pt]
2\,)\ \underline{2} & \\
1 & \text{rem. } 0 \\[4pt]
2\,)\ \underline{1} & \\
0 & \text{rem. } 1
\end{array}
$$

Thus

   1348 = 10101000100

It does not matter which of these two methods you use to compute the binary equivalent of a decimal number (for that matter, you can use any other algorithm you know). Some people prefer one method, while others find another easier to use.

2.2 OCTAL AND HEXADECIMAL NUMBERS

The binary numbers became rather large in the previous examples. For example, the binary equivalent of 1384 was 11 binary digits long. It is hard to remember a long string of 0s and 1s. Therefore, two shorthand versions, *octal* and *hexadecimal* notation, are used with binary numbers.

Octal numbering is a technique of grouping units of 3 binary digits and associating each such group with a single digit 0 to 7. Look at the following binary equivalents table.

Decimal		Binary
0	=	000
1	=	001
2	=	010
3	=	011
4	=	100
5	=	101
6	=	110
7	=	111

Each group of 3 binary digits matches one decimal digit between 0 and 7. The octal numbering system may be thought of as a system based on groups of 3 binary digits. For example, the binary number

   010101000100

is grouped as

   010   101   000   100

for determining the octal representation, which is

   2   5   0   4   or   2504

Note that the octal representation of a number is generally *not* its decimal representation. For example, octal 2504 is equivalent to decimal 1348. Octal is a shorthand notation for groups of 3 binary digits.

The octal equivalent of a binary number is computed by separating the binary number into groups of 3 digits, starting at the right end of the binary number. If there are not 3 binary digits in the last (leftmost) group, it is padded on the left with 0s. For example, 1111011 would be divided as 1 111 011, which then becomes 001 111 011. The octal equivalent of each 3-digit group (which is also the decimal equivalent) is then written. The octal equivalent of a binary number will be roughly one-third the length of the binary number.

There is another reason for choosing octal representation. Since $2^3 = 8$, each group of 3 digits represents a power of 8. The octal numbering system is simply the base 8 numbering system: the digits are 0 to 7, and the value of each digit is a power of 2^3, or 8. We can thus use a similar method for converting octal numbers to decimal as we used for binary. For example, 2504 octal $= 2*8^3 + 5*8^2 + 0*8^1 + 4*8^0 = 2*512 + 5*64 + 4*1 = 1024 + 320 + 4 = 1348$ decimal. It is also possible to compute the octal equivalent of a decimal number by methods similar to those outlined for converting to binary.

Another numbering system used as a shorthand for representing binary numbers is the hexadecimal numbering system, which is the base 16 system. Since the binary system uses 2 digits, 0 and 1, and the base 8 system uses 8 digits, 0 to 7, the base 16 system will need 16 distinct digits. These can be the digits 0 to 9 and the letters A to F. The binary equivalents of all hexadecimal digits are shown here.

Hexadecimal	Decimal
0 =	0000
1 =	0001
2 =	0010
3 =	0011
4 =	0100
5 =	0101
6 =	0110
7 =	0111
8 =	1000
9 =	1001
A =	1010
B =	1011
C =	1100
D =	1101
E =	1110
F –	1111

(Notice that the hexadecimal number that follows 9 is A, not 10; 10 hexadecimal is 16 decimal: $1*16^1 + 0*16^0$.)

To convert a binary number to hexadecimal, group the binary number in units of 4 binary digits, working from the right, and associate the matching hexadecimal digit with each group. For example, the binary number

1001001011101110101

is grouped as

1001   0010   1110   1111   0101

which is shown below in hexadecimal.

9   2   E   F   5   or   92EF5

The hexadecimal system is compatible with the binary system in the same way that octal was, since 16 is 2^4. The positions of hexadecimal numbers, representing powers of 16, really represent powers of 2^4 as well.

Because of the notational advantages of hexadecimal and octal numbers, they are frequently used in describing the data in a computer memory. The hexadecimal and octal number systems also can be used for arithmetic. One way to do this is to convert the numbers back to binary and compute the sum in binary. The answer will be converted back to hexadecimal or octal. Since these conversions are a matter of grouping and translating between 3 or 4 digits and 1, this is not difficult. There are other ways, however. You can construct a table of octal or hexadecimal sums: $0+0=0, 0+1=1, \ldots F+F=1E$. With a little practice, some people perform hexadecimal arithmetic directly, while others convert each pair of hexadecimal digits to decimal, add the decimal values, and convert the sum back to hexadecimal. Some examples follow that you may want to study, and there are some additional exercises at the end of the chapter.

Octal

732	3044	2101	100000	77777777	7777
+252	+2344	−0101	−034125	−12345670	+0001
1204	5410	2000	43653	65432107	10000

In the first example, working from the right, $2+2=4$, $3+5=8$ (decimal), but 8 decimal is 10 octal, so the correct value is 0 with 1 to carry. $7+2+1=10$ decimal, which is 2 with 1 to carry in octal.

In subtraction, as in the fourth example, it is necessary to convert the 10 on the left (top line) to 7 plus a digit carried to the right. (Remember that $7+1 = 10$ in octal.) The next position becomes 10, which is again converted to 7 plus a carry to the right. Carries to the right continue to the rightmost digit, so that $10-5$ can be computed (as 3). The entire computation follows.

	1	1	1	1
100000	070000	077000	077700	077770
−034125	−034125	−034125	−034125	−034125
				43653

Hexadecimal

10C4	23B5	C60A	100000	FFFFFF	FFFFFF
+3CF2	+F038	−29F3	−0C3D5A	−1C3EF6	+000001
4DB6	113ED	9D17	3C2A6	E3C109	1000000

In the first example, $4+2=6$, $C+F$ (hexadecimal) $= 12+15$ (decimal) $= 27$ (decimal) $= 16+11$ (decimal) $= 1B$ (hexadecimal) $= B$ with 1 to carry. $C+1=D$

(directly in hexadecimal), and $3+1=4$. Hexadecimal subtraction involves the same need to carry digits from left to right as in octal and decimal. For example, C60A $-$ 29F3 is computed as shown here.

```
                1        11
  C60A        C50A     B50A
 -29F3       -29F3    -29F3
 ─────       ─────    ─────
     7          17     9D17
```

Here are some summary remarks about binary, octal, and hexadecimal numbers.

1. The binary numbering system is a positional number system based on powers of 2. The digits are 0 and 1.
2. An approximation to decimal values is that 2^{10} is close to 1000, and 2^{20} is near to 1 million. K is a common abbreviation for 1024.
3. To convert from binary to decimal, multiply each digit of the binary number by the power of 2 that corresponds to its position and add the products.
4. To convert a number from decimal to binary, either:
   (a) Find the largest power of 2 not greater than the decimal number, separate the decimal number into a power of 2 plus a residue, and repeat this process with the residue until the residue becomes 0. Then collect the powers of 2 and write down a 1 in every position where that power of 2 was represented.
   (b) Repeatedly halve the decimal number and record the remainder until the number becomes 0. The remainder digits, written from right to left as they are produced, are the binary equivalent.
5. The octal number system is the base 8 system. Its digits are 0 to 7; the positions represent powers of 8: 1, 8, 64, 512, and so on. An octal number may be computed from a binary number by grouping the binary number in groups of 3 digits, from the right, and writing down the octal (which is also the decimal) equivalent of each group.
6. The hexadecimal number system is the base 16 system. Its digits are 0 to 9 and A to F; the positions represent powers of 16: 1, 16, 256, 4096, and so on. A hexadecimal number may be computed from a binary number by grouping the hexadecimal number in blocks of 4 digits, from the right, and writing down the hexadecimal (which is *not* always the decimal) equivalent of each group.

2.3 BINARY REPRESENTATION OF INTEGERS

In this section you will see how integers are represented internally. There are several different coding schemes, all of which are used on some popular computers. Positive numbers are the same under all of these representations, but the negative numbers differ. Furthermore, these descriptions are a basis for representations of other kinds of data, as will be described later.

In order to keep the examples simple, all numbers will be shown as 9-binary-digit numbers. However, each of these three representations can be used with binary numbers of any arbitrary size, such as 16, 36, or 64 digits.

2.3.1   Sign and Magnitude Representation

The *sign and magnitude representation* is the one that is closest to the common decimal representation of numbers. In sign and magnitude representation the leftmost bit of the number tells whether the number is positive or negative, and the remaining bits tell the absolute value or magnitude of the number. A positive number is represented with a 0 sign and a negative with a 1. Thus a positive number is represented as the binary equivalent of the number; a negative number is represented by a 1 for the sign, followed by the binary equivalent of the absolute value of the number.

A few examples should make this representation clear.

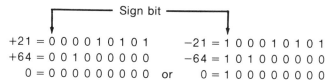

```
                   Sign bit
+21 = 0 0 0 0 1 0 1 0 1      −21 = 1 0 0 0 1 0 1 0 1
+64 = 0 0 1 0 0 0 0 0 0      −64 = 1 0 1 0 0 0 0 0 0
  0 = 0 0 0 0 0 0 0 0 0  or    0 = 1 0 0 0 0 0 0 0 0
```

Although this numbering system is convenient because of its similarity to common notation (sign + number), it has some defects. The first is a problem shared with common decimal arithmetic: addition and subtraction are two separate operations. Beginning students in arithmetic have to learn separate tables for addition and subtraction. Consequently, addition of a positive to a negative number is treated like subtraction. (For example, $+64 + -21$ must be computed as $+64 - +21$.) The use of different circuitry for addition and subtraction is tolerable, since these would be the results of different machine language instructions. However, it is much more difficult to design a computer that can either add or subtract, depending on the signs of the operands. It is more efficient if the choice of an addition or a subtraction unit depends on the instruction instead of on the data.

A second difficulty with sign and magnitude representation is that there is not a unique 0, since both 100000000 and 000000000 are 0. The circuitry is complicated if there are two possibilities to check for to determine if a value is 0.

In spite of these difficulties, sign and magnitude representation is used in some instances on modern computers. The benefits of this notation are that it is easy to compute the negative (arithmetic complement) of a number. It is also easy to read a negative sign and magnitude number and to determine its decimal equivalent.

2.3.2   Ones Complement

The *ones complement representation* of a negative number is computationally easier to manipulate than sign and magnitude. A positive number is represented in ones complement by its binary form. If x is a negative number, it is represented as

$2^n - 1 - x$, where a computer word is n bits long. In this example we are using $n = 9$. The binary representation of $2^9 - 1$ is as follows.

$$2^9 \quad = 1000000000$$
$$\underline{ -1}$$
$$2^9 - 1 = \quad 111111111$$

For any value n, $2^n - 1$ is a series of n 1s.

As an example, here is how to compute the ones complement form of -51.

$$2^9 - 1 = 111111111$$
$$\underline{-51 \ = \quad\quad 110011}$$
$$-51 \ = 111001100$$

Notice that the ones complement of -51 is a number that has a 1 in every place that $+51$ has a 0, and vice versa. This leads to a simple way of computing ones complements: reverse each bit of the binary equivalent of the number. The leftmost bit of every negative number will be 1, and it will be 0 for a positive number.

A few examples of ones complement values are shown here.

$+17 = 000010001$		$-17 = 111101110$
$+64 = 001000000$		$-64 = 110111111$
$\ 0 = 000000000$	or	$\ 0 = 111111111$

Notice that there are two different values for 0.

An advantage in using this number representation is that addition and subtraction can be performed from the same operations. That is, to subtract B from A, form the ones complement of B and add A to it.

There is, however, a difficulty in adding some numbers with unlike signs. For example, consider $+17 + -64$.

$$+17 = 000010001$$
$$\underline{-64 = 110111111}$$
$$111010000 \ = -47$$

which is correct. However, consider $-17 + +64$.

$$-17 = 111101110$$
$$\underline{+64 = 001000000}$$
$$1 \ 000101110 = +46, \quad\quad \text{which is not correct}$$

$\uparrow$
$\llcorner\!\!\rule{4cm}{0.4pt}$(carry digit)

To correct this, we add the carry digit (1), producing $+47$, which is correct.

The addition algorithm is to add the two numbers, without regard for their signs, and add the carry digit produced by the leftmost digits being added (the sign positions) to the result. This approach works, but it requires two additions.

In summary, ones complement notation has an advantage in that addition and subtraction are really one operation. However, there are two distinct representations of 0, and it is necessary to add the carry digit whenever an addition is performed on numbers of differing signs. There are a few uses of ones complement arithmetic on modern computers. The primary purpose for studying it, however, is that it forms the basis for twos complement notation.

2.3.3 Twos Complement

The final form that we will study is the *twos complement representation*. The twos complement of a positive number is the binary value of the number. For a negative number, x, the twos complement of x in n bits is

$$2^n - |x|$$

But this is

(the ones complement form of x) + 1

An example of the conversion is shown next.

Compute the twos complement of -39.

Compute $|-39|$ in binary	000100111
Compute ones complement	111011000
Add 1	+1
Twos complement of -39	111011001

A few examples of twos complement values follow.

+17 = 000010001   −17 = 111101111
+64 = 001000000   −64 = 111000000
 0 = 000000000

Notice that there is a unique 0. Trying to compute (-0) yields

−0 = ones complement of 0 = 111111111
        +1   +1
      (Carry 1)   000000000

so there is only one representation of 0. (Notice that in twos complement arithmetic any carry from the leftmost digits is discarded.)

Addition and subtraction are one operation, without having to add in the carry bit to correct the answer. Consider these examples.

−17 =   111101111   +17 =   000010001
+64 =   001000000   −64 =   111000000
      1 000101111 = +47   0 111010001 = −47
          └──────(Carry digit)──────┘

In summary, the advantages of twos complement notation are that it has a unique representation of 0, addition and subtraction can be treated as the same operation, and addition does not require an extra step (to add in the carry digit). The disadvantages are that it requires two steps to complement a twos complement number, and twos complement negative numbers are not easy to interpret in decimal. For example, -9 is represented as 111110111, which does not look much like the binary equivalent of $+9$. In spite of these problems, twos complement representation is widely used for arithmetic on modern computers.

The emphasis in this section has been on finding a representation for integers that will make addition easier. However, subtraction can also be done in the same way. That is, $A - B$ is the same as $A + (-B)$. Most computers perform subtraction by finding the negative (complement) of the second operand and adding that to the first operand. Therefore no separate circuitry is needed to subtract. Here are some important features of the three representations described.

1. In all three schemes—sign and magnitude, ones complement and twos complement—a positive number is represented as the binary equivalent of the number. Also, in all three the leftmost bit of a negative number will be 1.
2. In sign and magnitude representation a negative number is represented as a 1 (in the leftmost bit) followed by the binary equivalent of the absolute value of the number. Sign and magnitude representation requires separate circuitry for adding numbers whose signs are not the same. In this form there are also two distinct representations of 0.
3. In ones complement a positive number is represented in binary. A negative number is represented in n bits as $2^n - 1$ minus the binary equivalent of the absolute value of the number. Another way to compute this is by taking the binary equivalent of the absolute value and replacing all 0s by 1s and all 1s by 0s. Using ones complement requires a two-step addition process: add the two numbers and then add the carry that resulted from the leftmost digit. Also, this form has two different representations of 0.
4. In twos complement a positive number is represented in binary. A negative number is represented in n bits as 2^n minus the binary equivalent of the absolute value of the number. Another way to compute this is to compute the ones complement of the negative number and add 1. Twos complement arithmetic does not require a two-step addition process. There is only one representation of 0.
5. With ones or twos complement notation, subtraction can be performed by addition circuits simply by negating the number to be subtracted and adding.

2.3.4   Overflow

One final feature of integer arithmetic must be considered. The prior examples dealt with 9-bit numbers. Generally, enough 0s have been appended to the front of the number to fill it to a length of 9. All values used have been able to be represented in 9 digits. There is a limit, however, to the size of a number that can be contained in 9 digits. If 1 digit is reserved for a sign, only 8 digits remain. The largest (positive) binary number that can be represented in 8 bits is $2^8 - 1$, which is 255. (To see this, consider the largest 8-bit number. It would have a 1 in every bit, so it is 11111111, which is $2^8 - 1$, or 255.)

Consider adding 1 to 011111111 on our 9-bit machine using twos complement number representation. The straightforward answer is 100000000. The number 100000000 is negative, since it has a 1 in the sign bit. But 011111111 + 1 should be positive, since both of the values added ($+255$ and $+1$) were positive. The difficulty here is that the result obtained is larger than the storage location in which it is to be placed: 2^8 cannot be expressed in only 8 bits and a sign. This situation is called *overflow*. Overflow is the generation of a result too large to fit into its destination location.

Pencil-and-paper computation usually does not produce problems with overflow. However, an automobile odometer has only a fixed number of positions (usually five plus a "tenths" position); when the mileage on an old automobile exceeds 99999.9, this register recycles to 00000.0 and continues upward. This is an example of overflow. Overflow is not too serious on an automobile, since few people would mistake a car driven only 1000 miles with one driven 101,000 miles.

However, overflow during a computation is liable to go undetected. Therefore most computers maintain an indication of overflow or carry in the status register so that the programmer can check for this situation and take corrective action. On some computers overflow leaves the sign bit unchanged and sets the carry flag on. On other machines, an overflow bit will enter the sign bit, and the computer signals an error condition. Both of these possibilities are shown here.

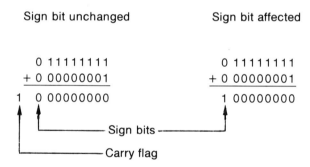

2.3.5 Binary Coded Decimal Data

Another representation of numbers will be noted briefly here. This is the binary coded decimal representation. In commercial applications, such as paycheck, statement, and invoice printing, the amount of computation is minimal. It is time consuming to convert a decimal number (as might come from an input data card) to binary, compute with the binary number, and reconvert the answer to decimal for output. The decimal to binary and binary to decimal conversions take extra time.

There are so-called "decimal" computers. These machines still perform their operations on a series of bits, and all quantities in memory are represented as a series of 0s and 1s. However, each number is not converted to a corresponding sign and magnitude or ones or twos complement number. Instead, decimal numbers are stored in a decimallike form. Each decimal digit is encoded in a number of bits, usually 4 bits per decimal digit (since all decimal digits 0 to 9 can be represented in 4 bits). The decimal number

57209

would be represented as

0101 0111 0010 0000 1001   or   01010111001000001001
  5   7   2   0   9

In 4 bits there are six other settings (1010 to 1111) that do not correspond to decimal digits. These can be used as signs.

Arithmetic can be performed on such numbers in 4-bit (1-decimal digit) groups, working from the right to the left, exactly as is done in elementary school arithmetic. Of course, since the groups of 4 bits represent decimal digits, a carry must be generated any time one of these groups exceeds 9 (1001). Although the arithmetic is slower than binary arithmetic, some time is saved by not having to convert to and from one of the binary forms. There may be an overall savings of time in using binary coded decimal numbers when few arithmetic computations are to be performed.

2.4 CHARACTER REPRESENTATION

Characters (symbols) are also types of data that must be represented internally. For example, a data card might contain digits (0 to 9), a sign, and a decimal point. However, the input to compilers (source programs) is also a form of data, so all the symbols of a program must be representable internally. These programs contain variables and keywords (composed of alphabetic characters) plus marks of punctuation (,, ;, ., ', ", etc.) and arithmetic symbols (+, −, *, /, =, (,), etc.).

The standard character set for internal representation on a computer contains all digits, all letters, and some collection of "special symbols," which are the punctuation, arithmetic, and other ($, @, %, etc.) symbols. *Control characters* such as *backspace, linefeed, tab, carriage return,* and *bell* are also stored internally in these coding schemes, since they are signals that must be received from or sent to various I/O devices. All of the printed symbols of this book were characters for input to a computer, since a preliminary version of this book was produced with the aid of a computer program to form paragraphs and pages.

Since the only possibilities in computer memory are 0s and 1s, every character must somehow be represented as a number. This is usually done by associating each character with a numeric code; a string of characters is then represented by a succession of these codes. There are three major coding schemes in common use. These are BCD (binary coded decimal), ASCII (American standard code for information interchange), and EBCDIC (extended binary coded decimal interchange code). The BCD coding is a 6-bit form, ASCII is 7 bits, and EBCDIC is 8; this means that each character is represented by a 6-, 7-, or 8-bit number, respectively. Since there are only 6 bits for BCD encodings, there are only 64 different possible characters in BCD. With 7 bits, ASCII allows 128 different characters. (There is also an 8-bit ASCII, but only 128 of the possible 256 combinations are used.) The 8 bits for EBCDIC allow 256 different characters. Tables for the BCD, ASCII, and EBCDIC characters are shown in Figure 2.1.

Character	BCD Code	ASCII Code	EBCDIC Code
blank	110 000	010 0000	0100 0000
. (period)	011 011	010 1110	0100 1011
(	111 100	010 1000	0100 1101
+	010 000	010 1011	0100 1110
$	101 011	010 0100	0101 1011
*	101 100	010 1010	0101 1100
)	010 100	010 1001	0101 1101
−	100 000	010 1101	0110 0000
/	110 001	010 1111	0110 0001
, (comma)	111 011	010 1100	0110 1011
' (apostrophe)	001 100	010 0111	0111 1101
=	001 011	011 1101	0111 1110
A	010 001	100 0001	1100 0001
B	010 010	100 0010	1100 0010
C	010 011	100 0011	1100 0011
. . .		. . .	
I	011 001	100 1001	1100 1001
J	100 001	100 1010	1101 0001
K	100 010	100 1011	1101 0010
. . .		. . .	
R	101 001	101 0010	1101 1001
S	110 010	101 0011	1110 0010
T	110 011	101 0100	1110 0011
. . .		. . .	
Z	111 001	101 1010	1110 1001
a	—	110 0001	1000 0001
b	—	110 0010	1000 0010
c	—	110 0011	1000 0011
. . .		. . .	
i	—	110 1001	1000 1001
j	—	110 1010	1001 0001
k	—	110 1011	1001 0010
. . .		. . .	
r	—	111 0010	1001 1001
s	—	111 0011	1010 0010
t	—	111 0100	1010 0011
. . .		. . .	
z	—	111 1010	1010 1001
0 (zero)	000 000	011 0000	1111 0000
1	000 001	011 0001	1111 0001
2	000 010	011 0010	1111 0010
9	001 001	011 1001	1111 1001

Figure 2.2 Arrangement of bytes in an IBM 360-370 word.

On many computers the notion of a byte and a character are synonymous. A byte is exactly the amount of space required to hold a character. On the IBM 360-370 computers, for example, a byte is 8 bits, and EBCDIC encodings are used. On other machines, a byte is used for a character, even if one bit per character is wasted this way. For example, the PDP-11 uses ASCII encodings; because it has a word of 16 bits divided into 2 8-bit bytes, two characters are stored in a word, even though this wastes 2 bits per word. On the DEC-10 there is no fixed size of a byte; ASCII encodings are used, and the word size is 36 bits, so that five 7-bit characters can be stored in 1 word.

Now we will consider how characters are stored internally. As described, different computers have different numbers of characters per word and, in some cases, a few extra bits may be left over in the computer word. Depending on the machine's instruction set, it may be difficult or easy to separate the characters stored in a word.

For example, the IBM 360-370 computers have byte-oriented instructions that can move a single byte from memory to a register, deposit a byte from a register into any byte of a word, move 1 or more bytes from one place in memory to another, and compare two strings of bytes. There are exactly 4 bytes (characters) per word, and they occupy bits 0 to 7, 8 to 15, 16 to 23, and 24 to 31, as shown in Figure 2.2.

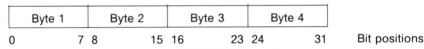

Figure 2.2 Arrangement of bytes in an IBM 360-370 word.

On a 360-370 computer using machine language, it is relatively easy to operate on characters. Some higher-level languages—such as PL/I and FORTRAN-77—give the user direct character manipulating instructions, and these languages can execute efficiently on such machines.

By contrast, the DEC-10 allows the user to define a byte as any contiguous series of bits within a word. In one case a user might want to manipulate bits 3 to 17 as a byte and later call bits 14 to 16 a byte. (This may be in the same or a different word.) An instruction that allows this much variability will be slower to execute than one that works on fixed places in a word. On the DEC-10 the time to execute a byte-oriented instruction depends on how many bits constitute the byte and how close they are to the left end of the word; in any event, they are slow instructions.

In all machines, characters are encoded as sequences of binary digits. Thus characters are indistinguishable from numbers or instructions. In fact, few machines tag a piece of data in memory to indicate that it contains characters instead of numeric information. Just as programs and data reside in memory together, different types of data may sit in adjacent memory locations. You must apply arithmetic operations only to arithmetic data.

Do not confuse character form data with binary numbers for computation. The character string 41 would be represented in 2 8-bit ASCII bytes as

00110100 00110001

which is *not* the binary equivalent of 41; 41 in binary is 00000000 00101001. A character string is used principally for input and output, while a binary number is used for computation.

Some higher-level-language users have devised complicated arithmetic operations to manipulate characters. Characters are encoded as a series of bits, and those bits can be interpreted as a number. Then, for example, multiplying a number by 2 has the effect of shifting all bits one position to the left, while dividing by 2 will shift all bits one position to the right. (There are some problems in dealing with overflow and accounting for the "sign" of this number; even though the number is a series of encoded characters, for arithmetic purposes it will be treated as a signed number, and this sign will not move left or right as the other bits do.) Multiplication and division can be used to move characters to any desired position (such as the right end or the left end) of a computer word. Recall the complexity of the multiplication algorithm (shift and add) in Chapter 1. Although this is not the only algorithm, all multiplication algorithms are fairly slow, and division is even slower. In some cases, only arithmetic "tricks" can be used to move characters within a word; however, it is preferable, where possible, to use higher-level language forms that will translate directly into efficient machine language instructions.

Characters are usually packed as densely as possible in computer words. For example, in EBCDIC, the string of 11 characters would be represented on an IBM 360-370 as follows.

```
String:         GOOD GRIEF!
Representation: C7D6D6C4    40C7D9C9    C5C65A40
                G  O  O  D   ƀ G  R  I    E F ! ƀ
```

(Here ƀ represents the character "blank space.") The characters have been shown in hexadecimal, with a break between the separate words. Since IBM has a 32-bit word, with 8-bit EBCDIC encodings, four character encodings can fit in 1 word. To represent 11 characters, 3 words are needed, with one character left over. The extra character has been filled in as a blank in the preceding example.

Here are some summary comments about character representations.

1. Characters are represented internally by a code; each character matches with a particular sequence of bits.
2. There are three major coding schemes for characters: BCD, which uses 6 bits per character; ASCII, which uses 7; and EBCDIC, which uses 8.
3. Characters are frequently packed as densely as possible in a word. Some computers have machine instructions to extract each character from a word, while on others a series of operations must be performed to shift a single character to a particular position in order to extract it from the word.

2.5   REAL NUMBERS

The last form of data to be described will be floating point or real number data. Floating point numbers are used as an approximation to fractions, since the representations shown so far apply only to integers (numbers that have no decimal point).

2.5.1   Fixed Point Numbers

In terms of computational speed, the most efficient form of real number is one where the decimal point appears in the same place in each word. (The term "decimal point" actually should be "binary point," since the numbers will be represented in binary.) Consider adding 3.752 + 1004.9 + 0.000837 + 306.299418 in decimal. The first operation needed is to write these down with the decimal points lined up, as shown.

```
   3.752
1004.9
   0.000837
 306.299418
```

Then the columns of digits can be added. It would be easier to add these numbers if they were padded with enough 0s to make them all of the same length.

```
0003.752000
1004.900000
0000.000837
0306.299418
```

In all of these numbers there are the same number of digits before the decimal point; the same is true after the decimal point.

Recall that computer words are of fixed size. Therefore all numbers in computer words will be of the same length (counting leading 0s on the left end). In *fixed point representation* of fractional numbers we assume there is an invisible "binary" point at some fixed place in each computer word. For example, with a 36-bit word, one might assume a binary point in the middle, so that there are 17 binary digits plus a sign to the left of the binary point and 18 binary digits to the right of the binary point.

Digits to the right of the point represent powers of 1/2: 1/2, 1/4, 1/8, 1/16, and the like. These are just the negative powers of 2: 2^{-1}, 2^{-2}, 2^{-3}, 2^{-4}, and so on. A fraction such as 45/64 is represented in binary as shown.

$$\frac{45}{64} = \frac{32}{64} + \frac{8}{64} + \frac{4}{64} + \frac{1}{64}$$

$$= \frac{1}{2} + \frac{1}{8} + \frac{1}{16} + \frac{1}{64}$$

$$= 2^{-1} + 2^{-3} + 2^{-4} + 2^{-6}$$

$$= 0.101101$$

This fraction could be represented exactly as a sum of fractional powers of 2. Not all fractions can be represented exactly, however. The fractions 1/3, 1/10, and 1/25, as well as many others, do not have an exact binary representation.

However, there is one binary fraction that is closer to 1/3 than any other binary fraction; this value is used for the internal representation of 1/3.

The "real" numbers used in computers are actually a restricted set of rational numbers: the fractions whose denominator is a power of 2, where the power of 2 is less than or equal to the number of bits to the right of the binary point. With 18 binary fractional digits, numbers as small as 2^{-18} (about 0.0000038) can be represented. With 17 digits to the left of the point, numbers as large as 2^{17} (about 128,000) can be represented.

The point in a fixed point number can be located anywhere; the point is in the same position in each real number, so the point does not actually have to appear in the words of memory. This scheme is efficient in its use of storage and in the ease with which such data values are manipulated. However, there is a strict limit on the magnitude of numbers that can be represented; in scientific applications, numbers much smaller than 2^{-18} or larger than 2^{+17} occur frequently. (The value of 2^{-18} is not even as small as 0.000001, and 2^{17} is only slightly over 100,000.) For this reason few computers use fixed point representation for real numbers. The representation shown next overcomes some of these problems.

2.5.2 Floating Point Numbers

The binary point in a *floating point number* does not appear in a fixed position in all words; instead, it can float to various places in the computer word, so more digits can be assigned to the left of the point (in order to permit the representation of larger numbers) or more digits can be located to the right of the point (in order to obtain more digits for the fraction). In fact, the point can effectively be located somewhere beyond the computer word, either to the left or to the right.

Consider so-called "scientific notation." In this form a value is represented as a fraction multiplied by a power of 10, such as $6.23*10^{-18}$ or $2.945*10^{+23}$. The two components of such numbers are a *fraction*, or *mantissa* and an *exponent*, or *characteristic*. The exponent is a scaling factor applied to the fraction. Usually numbers are represented with one or no digits to the left of the decimal point. Any number for which this is not so (such as $245.68*10^{7}$) can be "scaled" by moving the decimal point and adjusting the power of 10 accordingly ($.24568*10^{10}$ in this case). The decimal point can be moved either left or right by increasing or decreasing the power of 10, respectively.

A similar notation can be used internally in binary. A computer word is broken into three parts: sign, characteristic, and mantissa. Examples from the two manufacturers will be shown.

The DEC-10 uses a 36-bit word. For floating point numbers, the sign occupies 1 bit, the exponent occupies 8 bits, and the fraction occupies the remaining 27 bits. The fraction is assumed to have its binary point immediately to the left of its leftmost digit, so that the fraction is between 0.0 and 1.0. The exponent is represented in *excess 128* notation; this means that the exponent internally is 128 larger than the true exponent. Use of excess 128 notation avoids having to represent a sign in the exponent field. With 8 bits, exponents can range between 0 and 255; since these are 128 high, the true exponents range from -128 to $+127$.

With 27 bits for fractions, it would seem as if the smallest real value that could be represented is 2^{-27}. However, since this fraction is also multiplied by 2 to the power shown in the exponent, real numbers range from about 2^{-145} to 2^{+144}, or about 10^{-38} to 10^{+38}. The range of real numbers is large; however, the fraction is only 27 binary digits long, so the equivalent of only about 8 decimal digits of a fraction can be kept. The *magnitude* of a real number is an indication of its relative size; the magnitude of DEC-10 real numbers ranges from 10^{-38} to 10^{+38}. The *precision* of a real number is the number of digits of fraction that are retained; DEC-10 real numbers are precise to only about the eighth (decimal) digit.

For example, the value of 0.625 would be represented on a DEC-10 as follows. Since $0.625 = 1/2 + 1/8$, it would be 0.101 in binary. That is, $0.101 * 2^0$, so the exponent would be 0 and the fraction 101. Since exponents are represented in excess 128 notation, the binary value in the exponent field would be $128 + 0 = 10000000$ (binary). The sign would be 0 for positive. The value of 0.625 as a real number on a DEC-10 would be

    0   10000000   101000000000000000000000000000

DEC-10 real numbers are represented using twos complement for negative numbers.

PDP-11 real numbers are represented similarly. Each number is represented in 2 16-bit words. The first bit is the sign (0 for positive, 1 for negative). The next 8 bits are the exponent, which is represented in excess 128 form. The remaining 23 bits are the fraction. Each fraction is stored so that its first bit is 1. (This can be accomplished by shifting the fraction and adjusting the exponent.) However, since the first bit of each fraction is 1, this bit is not stored internally, so that in reality a 24-bit fraction is stored in 23 bits. (Exact powers of 2 are represented specially.)

IBM 360-370 and similar machines use a 32-bit word for real numbers. The sign uses 1 bit, 7 bits are taken for the exponent, and the remaining 24 bits are available for the fraction. With only 24 bits of fraction, IBM machines can achieve only about 7 (decimal) digits of precision. However, by a trick in the representation, IBM machines can achieve a wider range of magnitudes than DEC-10 machines with fewer bits for the exponent. The exponent is excess 64, meaning that the exponent is stored internally as 64 larger than the true exponent. In 7 bits values from 0 to 127 can be represented, indicating true exponents of -64 to $+63$. However, this exponent is a power of 16, unlike the DEC-10, where the exponent is a power of 2. Thus the magnitude ranges from approximately 16^{-64} to 16^{+63}, which is approximately 10^{-78} to 10^{+75}.

The example of 0.625 on an IBM machine would be represented as follows. The fraction is 0.101 multiplied by 16^0, so the exponent is 0. Since $64 + 0 = 64$ or 1000000 binary, the exponent field contains 1000000. The sign is 0 for positive. The value of 0.625 is thus

    0   1000000   101000000000000000000000

Negative numbers are represented using sign and magnitude form.

A more complicated example is representing -25.75 in binary. In binary this would be 11001.110 (since $25 = 11001$ and $.75 = 1/2 + 1/4 = .11$). That is, $11001.110 * 2^0$, but the binary point of the fraction must be just left of the leftmost digit. To achieve this, move the point left (which has the effect of dividing the number by 2); to compensate, increase the exponent by 1 for each position the point is shifted. The fraction becomes .11001110 * 2^5. However, IBM exponents are powers of 16, not 2, so the point must be shifted further until the characteristic is a power of 16. This produces .00011001110 * 2^8 = .00011001110 * 16^2. The exponent field is in excess 64 form, so it will be 66, or 1000010 in binary. The sign is 1 for negative. Thus the value of -25.75 would be

```
1   1000010   00011001110000000000000000
```

When two floating point numbers are to be added, they must be aligned so that the binary points line up. This is done in decimal when adding 0.4839 to 1046.73, for example. With floating point numbers the binary points must be aligned. Since the binary point in a floating point number immediately precedes the fraction, it would seem they are already aligned. However, adding

```
0.4839   *10¹ to
0.104673*10⁴
```

requires adjusting the numbers until the exponents match, as follows.

```
0.0004839 * 10⁴
0.1046730 * 10⁴
0.1051569 * 10⁴
```

The operation here was to shift the value with the smaller exponent until both exponents match.

A similar process occurs in binary. If two numbers are to be added, the one with the smaller exponent is shifted until its exponent matches the larger one. Then the two fractions can be added directly. There are only a fixed number of bits allocated to the fraction. In the process of aligning to make exponents match, bits from the one fraction may be shifted out of the right end of the number and lost. Thus, when adding an extremely large number (large exponent) to an extremely small number (small exponent), there may be no effect on the larger number (if all significant digits of the fraction of the smaller number are shifted out of the register a situation called *underflow*).

After an addition it may be necessary to readjust exponents to obtain a result in proper form. This can be shown in decimal. Suppose 0.738*10^4 is to be added to 0.622*10^4.

```
    0.738 * 10⁴
+   0.622 * 10⁴
    1.360 * 10⁴
=   0.136 * 10⁵
```

In this case a carry forced a digit to the left of the decimal point. The fraction and the exponent need to be adjusted so that the decimal point will precede all digits of the fraction.

The opposite situation is true for subtraction. After subtracting two values, there may be leading 0s in the fraction portion. A real number is said to be *normalized* if the first digit of the fraction is nonzero, or if the fraction is 0. On the DEC-10, since the exponent is a power of 2, normalization can be achieved by shifting and adjusting the exponent. On IBM 360-370 and similar machines, the exponent is a power of 16, so a normalized real number is one where the first 4 digits of the fraction are 0000 only if the whole fraction is 0. [Since the exponent is a power of 16, the binary point must be moved 4 binary digits ($2^4 = 16$) each time the exponent is changed.] Normalized fractions are unique. There is only one normalized version of each floating point number, while there are a number of unnormalized versions ($0.1234*10^5$, $0.01234*10^6$, $0.001234*10^7$, etc.).

This concludes the information on real numbers. The following points are keys to understanding floating point numbers on computers.

1. Most real numbers are approximated by a series of fractional powers of 2. Common decimal fractions such as 1/3 and 1/10 cannot be represented exactly in most real number schemes on computers. In fact, the real numbers of computers are a restricted set of rational numbers.
2. Real numbers may be represented in fixed point form. In this form each number has an imaginary binary point located at some fixed position within the word. The disadvantage to this type of representation is that even with a machine with a moderately large word size, only a small range of magnitudes can be represented.
3. The floating point format represents each real number as a fraction and an exponent. The fraction is between 0.0 and 1.0, and the exponent is a power of 2 (or a power of 16 for IBM 360-370 computers).
4. Floating point numbers must be aligned for addition. To do this, if two floating point numbers have different exponents, the one with the smaller exponent is shifted and the exponent is adjusted until the two exponents are equal.
5. A floating point number may be normalized. This means that the first digit (or the first 4 digits for IBM 360-370 computers) of the fraction is 0 only if the entire fraction is 0. There is a unique normalized representation of a real number.

2.6 TERMS USED

The following terms have been introduced in this chapter. Before moving on, you should understand the meaning of each word.

Binary number system
Positional number system
K
Octal number system
Hexadecimal number system
Sign and magnitude representation
Ones complement representation
Twos complement representation
Overflow
Binary coded decimal representation

Character
Special symbol
Control character
BCD characters
ASCII characters
EBCDIC characters
Byte
Real number
Fixed point number
Binary point
Floating point number
Magnitude
Precision
Fraction
Mantissa
Exponent
Characteristic
Underflow
Normalization

2.7 QUESTIONS

Following are questions by which you can test your understanding of the material in this chapter.

1. What is the decimal equivalent of each of the following binary numbers (assume all are positive)?
   (a) 010001
   (b) 01111011
   (c) 011011000
   (d) 011111111
   (e) 010000000

2. Show the following decimal numbers in binary notation.
   (a) 42
   (b) 123
   (c) 257
   (d) 329
   (e) 1067

3. Show each of the following binary numbers in octal notation.
   (a) 10111110101101
   (b) 11111111111111
   (c) 00001001101110111
   (d) 10001001101110111

4. Show each of the numbers in Question 3 in hexadecimal notation.

5. Show each of the following numbers as a 9-bit binary number in sign and magnitude notation.
   (a) +45
   (b) +117

    (c) −45

    (d) −117

    (e) +512

    (f) +255

    (g) −256

6. Show each of the numbers in Question 5 as a 9-bit binary number in ones complement notation.

7. Show each of the numbers in Question 5 as a 9-bit binary number in twos complement notation.

8. Show how each of the following character strings would be represented in BCD notation.

    (a) STR1

    (b) $1.00

    (c) +117

    (d) (A+B)*C

9. Show how each of the character strings in Question 8 would be represented in ASCII notation.

10. Show how each of the character strings in Question 8 would be represented in EBCDIC notation.

11. Show how the number $0.1234*10^{-6}$ would be represented as a decimal fraction without the 10^{-6} term (i.e., show it as simply a fraction). What is the magnitude of this fraction? What is its precision?

12. Show how each of the following floating point numbers would be represented on a DEC-10.

    (a) 1/8

    (b) −1/8

    (c) 37/128

    (d) +10.625 (= 10-5/8)

    (e) −10.625

13. Show how each of the numbers in Question 12 would be represented on an IBM 360-370.

chapter 3

Machine Language Instructions

This chapter contains information on three major characteristics of machine language instructions—kinds, formats, and addresses. First, it is important to know what the typical machine operations are. The chapter begins with a description of some common machine instructions. It is also important to know the various forms of machine instructions, since these are so closely related to the internal structure of a computer. The chapter contains descriptions of the standard machine instruction formats: zero-, one-, one-and-a-half-, two-, three-, four-address instructions. Finally, different machines use different addressing modes, and concepts such as indexed, indirect, immediate, and register relative addressing are defined. The chapter concludes with descriptions of the instruction sets and addressing modes of three popular machines: the Intel 8080, the PDP-11, and the IBM 360-370 family. When you finish this chapter, you will know enough machine organization to understand simple machine language programs for real computers.

3.1 TYPICAL MACHINE INSTRUCTIONS

Every computer has a different machine instruction set. Some computers are designed for specific uses, such as mathematical computation, commercial use, or control of a complex machine. We will, however, consider the so-called *general-purpose computer;* this means that the computer has a wide enough variety of instructions that it can be used for most kinds of scientific and business computing.

Arithmetic instructions will be considered first. Standard ADD and SUBTRACT instructions are available on all general-purpose computers. These instructions, of course, use two inputs (which we will call A and B for reference) and compute $C = A + B$ and $C = A - B$, respectively. Some variations are available.

The ADD WITH CARRY instruction computes A + B + (the contents of the carry flag). The carry flag is 1 if the last operation produced a carry and 0 if it did not. This instruction would be used for multiple-word arithmetic. Consider a machine that has only 8-bit registers and, therefore, all arithmetic is 8-bit arithmetic. In 8 bits the largest unsigned number that can be represented is $2^8 - 1$ or 255 and, if 1 bit is reserved for a sign, the limit is $2^7 - 1$ or 127. This is too small for most meaningful computing.

Look at the following example of binary addition. (An artificial break for readability has been inserted between the first 8 and the last 8 digits.)

			(carry from A0 + B0)	
	A1	A0	1	
A:	00101101	10110010	00101101	10110010
B:	00100110	10010011	00100110	10010011
	B1	B0	Sum: 01010100 1	01000101

The normal way to do this addition would be to work from right to left, adding each pair of digits and combining any carry digit with the next pair of digits. In fact, the same result can be obtained by adding the rightmost 8 digits as a block, observing any carry that results from that block, and adding the carry with the sum of the leftmost block of 8 digits. ADD instructions set the carry flag. Thus the key to obtaining large results on a computer that performs only short-length arithmetic is to perform any carries between words yourself. For example, the preceding computation could be performed by using a conventional ADD on the rightmost 8 digits of A and B and then executing an ADD WITH CARRY to combine the leftmost 8 bits. This same method can be used for producing results that are as long as desired; simply work from the right, 1 byte at a time, using ADD WITH CARRY for all bytes but the rightmost. This technique is shown next, where two 3-byte quantities are added.

```
          2          1          0
    A:   00011010  00101101  10110010
   +B:   01001110  00100110  10010010
```

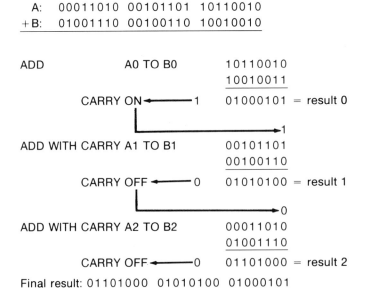

Final result: 01101000 01010100 01000101

The SUBTRACT WITH BORROW instruction is used in the same situations as ADD WITH CARRY. This instruction subtracts two quantities and then subtracts 1 from the result if the carry flag was set before the instruction was executed. Furthermore, it sets the carry flag if a borrow was necessary in the high-order digit (i.e., if the number being subtracted was larger than the number from which it was subtracted).

Not all computers contain hardware MULTIPLY and DIVIDE instructions. As pointed out in Chapter 1, multiplication can be very time consuming. Furthermore, many computer applications, particularly those run on small computers, have no need for multiplication.

The computers that do have multiplication need an extra space for the results. Consider the multiplication of two 3-digit decimal numbers. For some of these (such as 012 * 034) the result is still a 3-digit number. However, most results are longer than 3 digits (e.g., 012 * 345 = 4140), and it is possible to reach 6 digits (999 * 999 = 998001). Similarly, the product of two 1-word values (regardless of the size of the word) may exceed 1 word in size, but the product can always be contained in 2 words. Computers with hardware multiplication circuitry usually have either an extension to the accumulator or there is a way for two registers to work together as one long register for multiplication. For example, single-accumulator machines may have an MQ (multiplier quotient) or AX (accumulator extension) register. The IBM 1130 has such an extension to the accumulator. The IBM 360-370 machines use a pair of registers—an even numbered register and the next higher odd-numbered one—to receive the result of a multiplication.

Division is another operation not available on all computers. Although the larger machines have divide instructions, few microcomputers do. While multiplication can produce a result twice the size of the inputs, division can produce two results: a result (quotient) and a remainder. On the IBM 1130 the accumulator and the MQ register are used for the dividend (the number being divided), and the result and remainder are left there. On IBM 360-370 computers the number to be divided must be in an even-odd pair of registers, and the result will go back to these.

Two additional useful instructions are INCREMENT and DECREMENT. These add 1 and subtract 1, respectively, from a specified register. For counting and for control of repetition, adding and subtracting 1 are common operations, so special instructions facilitate these.

Another instruction that is similar to an arithmetic instruction is the COMPARE instruction, which shows its entire result in the status indicators. COMPARE instructions operate like SUBTRACT instructions, *without* changing any data values. That is, if A and B are compared, it is as if A − B were computed. If A and B are equal, the status flags are set to *zero* or *equal*. If A is larger than B (the result of the subtraction would have been positive), the status flags are set to show a *high* or *positive* result. If A is smaller than B (A − B would turn out negative), the status flags are set *low* or *negative*. Later instructions can test the status flags. Comparisons are shown in Figure 3.1.

There are three important instructions for data movement. Data can be moved from main memory into a register. Transferring data from memory to one of the registers is called a LOAD instruction. A STORE instruction is the opposite; it moves data from a register to main memory. The MOVE instruction can be

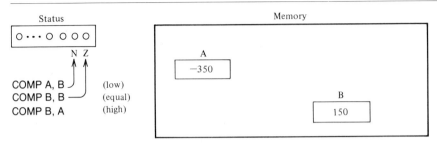

Figure 3.1 Examples of the COMPARE operation.

used to move data from one memory location to another. (Some machines stream-line the machine architecture by treating the registers as if they were memory locations. On these machines—including the PDP-11 and the INTEL 8080—a MOVE instruction is also used to load a value into a register or to store it from a register into memory.) Figure 3.2 shows the differences among STORE, LOAD, and MOVE instructions.

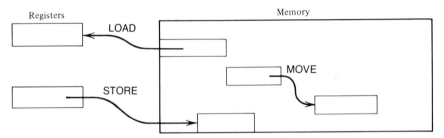

Figure 3.2 STORE, LOAD, and MOVE instructions.

The SHIFT instructions have been alluded to previously. These instructions move each bit of a data value 1 bit or more to the left or right. For example, if we take the quantity

00110110

and shift it 2 digits left, it becomes

11011000

Shifting the original value 1 digit right produces

00011011

There are two kinds of shifts. In a *logical* SHIFT all bits participate in the SHIFT; the sign position is not treated as a special bit. Vacated bit positions are filled with 0s, and bits moving off the right or left end of the register are simply lost. Some examples of this are shown in Figure 3.3.

In an *arithmetic* SHIFT the sign position bit is maintained. Bits vacated on the left end of the register (from right shifts) are filled with a copy of the sign bit.

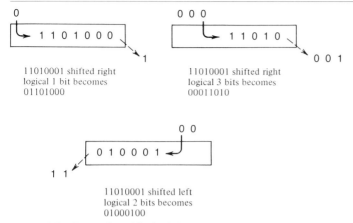

Figure 3.3   Examples of logical shifts.

Bits shifted to the left do not move into the sign position. Some examples of this are shown in Figure 3.4.

Shifts can be used for separating two quantities stored in one computer word. For example, two 8-bit characters may be stored in one 16-bit word. If that word is loaded into a register and the register is shifted right 8 bits, only the first (leftmost) character remains in the register; the remaining half of the word is filled with 0s. In order to isolate the second character (i.e., to discard the leftmost character), load the word into a register and shift the register 8 bits left and then 8 bits right. All of these shifts should be logical shifts. For example, a word might contain the letters AB in ASCII. It would look like this.

0100000101000010   or   01000001 01000010

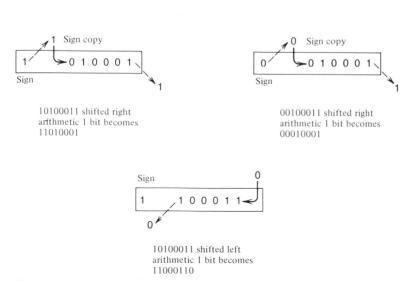

Figure 3.4   Examples of arithmetic shifts.

After being shifted right 8 bits, the value is

0000000001000001   or   00000000 01000001

Instead, shifting left 8 and then right 8 produces

0000000001000010   or   00000000 01000010

More (shorter) values may be packed in 1 word, and shifting is one means of separating these values.

Arithmetic SHIFTs are useful for multiplication and division by powers of 2. To multiply by 32 (2^5), shift the value left 5 bits. Dividing a number by 8 (2^3) can be achieved by shifting the number 3 bits to the right. Arithmetic SHIFTs are also used in some arithmetic algorithms to perform other computations, such as the Shift-and-Add multiplication technique.

A variation on the SHIFT is the ROTATE or the END-AROUND-CARRY SHIFT. In this type of SHIFT any bits shifted out of the right end (in a right SHIFT) are circled around and reinserted in vacated positions on the left end. Similarly, bits dropped from the left are put in the right end of the register. For example, the value

00111001

rotated right 1 bit becomes

10011100   →1 0 0 1 1 1 0 0→1

The 1 from the right end is moved into the left end of the register.

Logical operations AND, OR, exclusive OR, and NOT are also standard computer instructions. These are computed bit by bit, as defined in Chapter 1. Tables for the AND, OR, XOR (exclusive OR), and NOT functions follow.

AND	0	1		OR	0	1		XOR	0	1		NOT	0	1
0	0	0		0	0	1		0	0	1			1	0
1	0	1		1	1	1		1	1	0				

The logical operations can be used to set certain bits to 0 or 1. For example, the previous section contained one method for zeroing out the left half of a computer word containing two characters. This method was to shift left and then right. The same result can be achieved in only one step by ANDing the word with 00000000 11111111. This operation is as follows.

```
    01000001  01000010
AND 00000000  11111111
    ────────────────────
    00000000  01000010
```

Notice that ANDing any bit with a 0 produces a 0 (from the first row of the AND table), but ANDing a bit with a 1 preserves the bit. Therefore the AND instruction can be used to make certain bits 0s while leaving others intact.

Similarly, ORing a bit with a 0 leaves the bit unchanged, while ORing it with a

1 changes the bit to 1. The OR instruction is used to make certain bits 1s while leaving others intact.

A bit may be reversed (a 0 changed to a 1 and a 1 changed to a 0) by use of either the XOR or the NOT instruction. A 0 xored with a 1 produces a 1, while a 1 xored with a 1 produces a 0. Any bit xored with 1 is reversed, and any bit xored with a 0 is unchanged. In order to reverse some bits, xor them with a 1. In order to reverse all bits of a word, negate it (by the COMPLEMENT or NOT instruction).

One final class of instructions that will be described here are the BRANCH, JUMP, or SKIP instructions, which are used to control the order in which other instructions are executed. In order to achieve the effect of the higher-level-language statement

IF (A<B) THEN C: = B ELSE C: = A;

several machine language instructions would be used. One possible translation of this statement would be as follows.

```
        COMPARE    A , B          ; determine if A<B
        JUMPLO     L1             ; if A<B go to instruction L1
        MOVE       A , C          ; if NOT (A<B) replace C by A
        BRANCH     L2             ; go to instruction L2
L1 :    MOVE       B , C          ; if A<B replace C by B
L2 :    -- next instruction       ; executed whether or not A<B
```

The JUMPLO and BRANCH instructions alter the flow of execution. The JUMPLO instruction indicates that if the low (negative) flag is set (from the previous COMPARE), execution is to skip to the machine instruction at label L1. The BRANCH instruction causes execution to proceed to the instruction at label L2.

BRANCH, SKIP, and JUMP instructions are all called *transfer instructions.* Transfer instructions can be either *unconditional* or *conditional.* Unconditional transfers (such as BRANCH, JUMP, or SKIP) are effective any time they are executed. Conditional transfer instructions (such as JUMPLO or SKIPEQ) are effective only if a particular status condition exists (e.g., jump if the 0 flag is set, or branch if a carry occurred in the last arithmetic operation). If the tested condition is not true, the transfer causes no other action.

SKIP instructions usually cause execution to skip just one instruction; that is, they pass over the instruction immediately following. JUMP or BRANCH instructions may have two forms: a short form, which is used to jump to a nearby instruction, and a long form, used for jumping to an instruction many instructions away.

There are a number of other more esoteric instructions available on computers, but this is a basic set. Large computers, such as the IBM 360-370, have instruction sets of over 100 machine instructions. Even the Intel 8080 microcomputer has over 50 instructions in its repertoire. The following list is enough for our present discussions, however.

1. All general-purpose computers have ADD and SUBTRACT instructions. There may also be other forms of ADD and SUBTRACT that interact with carries in order to permit arithmetic involving more than 1 word.
2. MULTIPLY and DIVIDE instructions are uncommon on smaller machines (such as microcomputers). Where present, they may need an extra register to hold the long result that can be generated from a multiplication or division.
3. COMPARE instructions set status flags to show which of two operands is larger than the other.
4. LOAD instructions transfer values from main memory to registers. STORE instructions transfer values from registers to memory. MOVE instructions transfer data within memory. On some computers, MOVE instructions can also be used to load and store registers.
5. SHIFT instructions move each bit of a value either right or left one or more positions. Logical SHIFTs ignore signs, while arithmetic SHIFTs preserve the bit in the sign position. SHIFTs can be used for multiplying and dividing by powers of 2. ROTATE instructions are SHIFT instructions that take the bit moved out of one end of a register and cycle that bit into the other end of the register.
6. Instructions performing logical operations are AND, OR, XOR, and NOT. AND can be used to force certain bits to 0 while leaving others unchanged. OR can be used to force certain bits to 1 while leaving others unchanged. XOR can be used to reverse certain bits while leaving others unchanged. NOT can be used to reverse all bits of a word.
7. Transfer instructions include SKIP, JUMP, and BRANCH. These can be unconditional or conditional. Unconditional transfers always cause execution to transfer to the listed location. Conditional transfers test the setting of the status flags and may cause execution to move to another point in the program.

3.2 MACHINE INSTRUCTION FORMS

In previous sections you have seen concepts applicable to all computers. Each computer has a CPU, memory, and some complement of I/O devices. Each computer manipulates binary numbers in one of the forms described in Chapter 2. This section contains information on the forms of instructions. However, the forms of instructions are closely related to the internal form of each specific computer, as you will see. A given computer may have instructions of any of the following forms. The kinds of instructions are classified by the number of addresses contained in the instructions. Some instructions have four addresses; others have three, two, one, or no addresses. We will consider these in that order: four, three, and so on. The instructions to be considered are arithmetic or logical instructions, such as ADD, SUBTRACT, or AND. Other instructions, such as MOVE, JUMP, and COMPLEMENT, have somewhat different formats, although they will be consistent with the internal structure.

3.2.1 Four-Address Instructions

This instruction will appear like Figure 3.5.

Op code	Source 1	Source 2	Destination	Next instruction

Figure 3.5 Four-address instruction format.

Let us take an example of an ADD instruction and assume that we wish to compute the value of

C := A+B;

The assignment would be evaluated by one single instruction, which would be represented as in Figure 3.6.

ADD	Address of A	Address of B	Address of C	Address of next instruction

Figure 3.4 Examples of arithmetic shifts.

This instruction form specifies the addresses of two input operands (A and B) and the address of the one result operand (C). Furthermore, each instruction in the program contains the address of the instruction to be executed next.

One of the first assembler programs, the Symbolic Optimizing Assembler Program (SOAP), was designed for use with the IBM 650 computer in the middle of the 1950s. That computer had a limited memory, so programs were stored on a drum, not in main memory. Each instruction was executed from the drum. The drum revolved at a relatively slow speed. If the next instruction to be executed had just passed the read/write head on the drum, there would be a considerable delay waiting for the drum to revolve once before the next instruction could be fetched. The optimizing in SOAP involved scattering the instructions around the surface of the drum so that as one finished execution, the next would be ready to pass under the read/write head. Each instruction would then indicate which instruction should be executed next. In Figure 3.7 INST1 points to INST2 as the next instruction to be executed.

Instructions in the four-address format fully specify the current operation; they also tell where the next instruction is located. Although the four-address

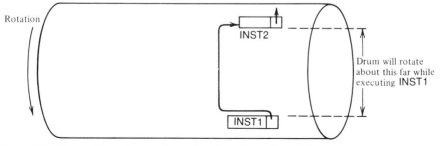

Figure 3.7 Four-address instructions placed on drum for efficient computation.

format is not used at the machine language level of most machines today, some microprogrammed computers do use this format for the microinstructions that interpret the instructions.

3.2.2 Three-Address Instructions

Three-address instructions are identical to four-address ones, except they do not give the address of the next command. Three-address instructions have the format shown in Figure 3.8.

Op code	Source 1	Source 2	Destination

Figure 3.8 Three-address instruction format.

If this were used to represent C : = A+B; the instruction would be a numeric encoding of the form in Figure 3.9.

ADD	Address of A	Address of B	Address of C

Figure 3.9 Example of a three-address instruction.

Of course, some machines may reorder these operands; that is, on some machines the destination may come before the two source addresses. Notice that order does make a difference: C : = A+B; is not the same as A : = B+C; even though they have the same instruction format. Furthermore, even the order of the source operands sometimes makes a difference: C : = A−B; is not the same as C : = B−A.

3.2.3 Two-Address Instructions

Two-address instructions have only two addresses for operands. This is shown in Figure 3.10.

Op code	Source 1	Source 2 / Destination

Figure 3.10 Two-address instruction format.

Since operations such as addition require two inputs and produce one output, one of these addresses must identify both an input and an output address; that is, one of the operands must be both input and output. Suppose that we need to compute C : = A+B; again. Since the value of C is being replaced in this operation, C can be used to hold a temporary result. The value of C : = A+B; would be computed as in Figure 3.11.

MOVE	Address of A	Address of C
ADD	Address of B	Address of C

Figure 3.11 Examples of two-address instructions.

In this example the value of A is copied into C and the value of B is added to C to yield A + B . In general, this form requires use of a number of temporary storage locations to hold intermediate results during a computation.

3.2.4 One-and-a-Half-Address Instructions

These instructions are really two-address instructions in that they contain two operand addresses. However, in this form the address of one operand, usually the destination operand, is a register designation, not a full memory address.

IBM 360-370 computers have instructions of this form. The destination field is the Source 1 field; it is a register number into which (for most instructions) the data moves. Figure 3.12 shows an example of instructions that would compute C : = A + B; on a one-and-one-half-address computer.

LOAD	Register 1	Address of A
ADD	Register 1	Address of B
STORE	Register 1	Address of C

Figure 3.12 Examples of one-and-one-half-address instructions.

3.2.5 One-Address Instructions

These instructions have only one address; thus the address of the second source operand and the destination must be implicit. This sort of instruction is frequently used on machines with just one accumulator, so the instruction ADD really means "add to the accumulator." The form of these instructions is shown in Figure 3.13.

Op code	Source

Figure 3.13 One-address instruction format.

The example of C : = A + B; would be coded as in Figure 3.14, using one-address instructions.

LOAD	Address of A
ADD	Address of B
STORE	Address of C

Figure 3.14 Examples of one-address instructions.

Notice that three instructions are needed just to do the same thing that could be done in one instruction on a three- or four-address machine.

3.2.6 Zero-Address Instructions

Machines of this sort really have two kinds of instructions: one address and zero address. The one-address instructions are called *operand fetch* or *store instructions;* the zero-address instructions cause computation. The heart of this kind of machine is called a *stack*. A stack is much like the English interpretation of a stack: you put items on the top of the stack, and this makes all other items in the stack that much further from the top. When an item is removed, it comes off the top, and that makes all other items that much nearer the top. Items are inserted and deleted only at the top of the stack. Figure 3.15 shows the use of a stack.

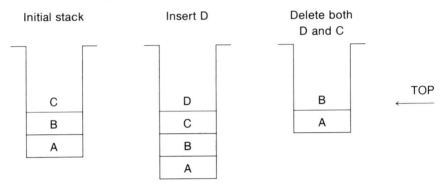

Figure 3.15   Use of a stack.

Computationally, zero-address machines use a stack to hold operand values before they are combined arithmetically. Each arithmetic operation applies to the top two (or one, or three, or more) operands on the stack. The number of operands depends on the operation: addition requires two operands, while square root requires only one, and some more complicated functions may require three or more. Enough operands are removed from the stack to complete the operation; the result of a computation is returned to the stack.

The example of C : = A + B; would be computed on a stack computer as shown in Figure 3.16.

FETCH	Address of B
FETCH	Address of A
ADD	
STORE	Address of C

Figure 3.16   Computing C: = A + B on a stack computer.

The operation of the stack in computing C : = A + B is shown in Figure 3.17.

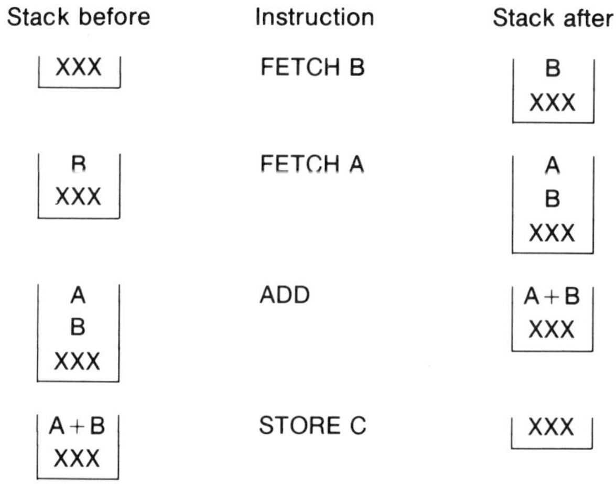

Stack before	Instruction	Stack after
| XXX |	FETCH B	| B | | XXX |
| R | | XXX |	FETCH A	| A | | B | | XXX |
| A | | B | | XXX |	ADD	| A + B | | XXX |
| A + B | | XXX |	STORE C	| XXX |

Figure 3.17 Stack operations in computing C: = A + B.

Any machine may have a combination of these instruction types, although each machine has one primary architecture. For example, the IBM 360-370 computers are basically one-and-a-half-address machines, although there are some two-address instructions. The PDP-11 is largely a two-address machine, and the Intel 8080 is primarily a one-address machine. Each machine has instructions of one or more other types, however.

It is tempting to conclude that four-address machines are in a sense "better" than zero-address ones, since four-address machines can do in one machine instruction what zero-address machines require four instructions to do. That is not a fair comparison, however. The machine language instructions are much longer on a four-address machine than on a zero-address one. That fact should be obvious; a four-address instruction must be the encoding of five different pieces of information: an operation and four different addresses. The zero-address instructions have, at most, one address (on the FETCH and STORE instructions), and most instructions have no addresses; on these latter instructions the only piece of information is an operation code.

There is no general rule for how long the encoding of a machine language instruction will be; this varies between different models of computers. For example, the IBM 360-370 family allows for up to 256 operations, so 8 bits are reserved for the op code (since $2^8 = 256$). The Intel 8080 does not use any fixed number of bits for an op code, and the op codes range from 2 to 8 bits. The PDP-11 op codes vary between 4 and 10 bits.

There are also differences in the ways addresses are expressed. For example, most machines permit *absolute addressing,* which means that the instruction specifies exactly which location number in memory contains the operand. For a machine with 64K memory locations, 16 bits are needed to identify any address, since $2^{16} = 65,536 = 64K$. (That is, the largest unsigned number that can be expressed in 16 bits is $2^{16} - 1$ or 65,535; addresses on such a machine range from 0 to 65,535.) For microcomputers, 64K of memory is a reasonable quantity of memory. For large computers where many users will be sharing the computer resources at one time, however, memory sizes are much larger than that. The IBM 360-370 family address space exceeds 16 million locations. To address this amount of space directly would require 24 bits per address, since 2^{24} is approximately 16 million. There are other ways to specify an address in fewer bits.

The length of a machine language instruction depends not only on the number of addresses, but also on the encoding scheme, the memory size, the number of registers, and the addressing modes of a particular computer. Thus it is not fair to say that one machine having a four-address format machine instruction will necessarily have shorter (or longer) machine language programs than another.

3.3   ADDRESSING MODES

As noted, to address the full memory of a computer directly in the machine instructions would require a large number of bits for machines having large memories. Also, it is not always convenient to use absolute addressing; there are some applications where another form of addressing is more appropriate. In this section we will consider different addressing modes.

3.3.1   Register Addressing

Machine instructions can be very long if they need to cover a large range of possible addresses. As shown, it requires 24 bits to address a 16 million location address space. However, machines seldom have more than 8 or 16 registers. Thus, to indicate any one of the registers requires only 3 ($8 = 2^3$) or 4 ($16 = 2^4$) bits. Machine language instructions may permit the address of an operand to come from a register. In such a form, an instruction such as

    MOVE   R2,R4

might mean *move the value in register 2 into register 4* . However, an instruction such as

    MOVE   R2,(R4)

might mean *move the value in register 2 into the memory location whose address is in register 4* . Then, if register 2 contained the value 100 and register 4 contained the value 38475, the first of these instructions would replace the contents of register 4 by 100, while the second would place the value 100 in location number 38475. In the latter case, the value in register 4 is not the operand itself, but the *location* of the operand. This distinction is shown in Figure 3.18.

    MOVE   R2,R4   ; (move contents of register 2 into register 4)

Before		After	
R2	R4	R2	R4
100	xxx	100	100

Figure 3.18a   Register containing an operand.

MOVE R2,(R4)   ; (move contents of register 2 into the memory location
                   ; whose address is in register 4)

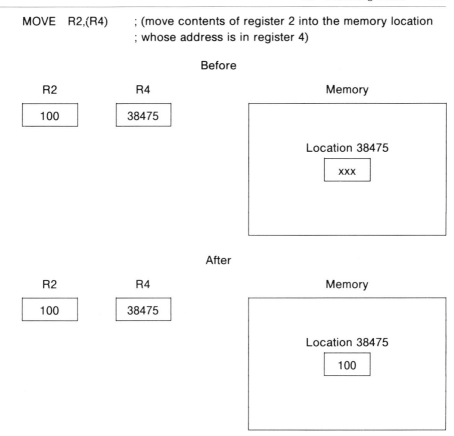

Figure 3.18b   Register containing an operand's address.

There is an additional advantage to using register addressing. Suppose you are creating machine language for a CASE statement. A CASE statement is one having a number of blocks of code. Only one of these blocks is executed, however; the one to be executed is determined by the value of the CASE index, which is an expression identified in the CASE statement. (The PASCAL language has a CASE statement. FORTRAN has a computed GOTO construct that can be used to achieve the effect of a case. In PL/I, subscripted labels can be used to achieve the effect.)

An example of a CASE statement is shown in Figure 3.19. The CASE is interpreted as follows. If the index, INX, has value 1, the one statement after the constant 1 : is executed. If the value of INX is 2, the block (which contains two executable statements) after the constant 2 : is executed. If INX is 3, the single statement that follows the 3 : is executed. Finally, if INX is 0, only one statement, the one following 0 : , is executed. The CASE operates by evaluating the case index expression (INX in this example) and executing the one block following the constant that matches the value of the index expression.

```
CASE (INX) OF
  1: (* CREDIT *)
     BAL := BAL - AMOUNT;
  2: (* DEBIT *)
     BEGIN
       BAL := BAL + AMOUNT;
       IF (BAL > MAXBAL)
         THEN WRITE (OUTPUT, ' ACCOUNT # ',
              ACCTNO, ' EXCEEDS CHARGE LIMIT OF ',
              MAXBAL);
     END;  (* DEBIT *)
  3: (* BALANCE INQUIRY *)
     WRITE (OUTPUT, ' ACCOUNT # ', ACCTNO,
         ' BALANCE IS ', BAL);
  0: (* ILLEGAL *)
     WRITE (MSGOUT, ' ERROR; CASE INDEX VALUE IS 0')
END;  (* CASE *)
```

Figure 3.19   Example of a CASE statement.

In generating code for a CASE statement you might create a table of the addresses of the blocks of code for all the possible case index values. This table might look like the following one.

Word	Contents
0	Address of code for error message
1	Address of code for BAL:=BAL−AMOUNT statement
2	Address of code for BAL:=BAL+AMOUNT and WRITE statements
3	Address of code for WRITE statement

It would be easy to compute the value of the index and use that as an offset into the table. From the table you load a register with the address of the statement group to be executed. That register could then be used for a register mode address in a JUMP instruction to perform the right block of code. This idea is shown in the following code.

```
MOVE   index to R2     ; put index value into R2
ADD    #TABLE,R2       ; add table address to get
                       ; address of correct word
MOVE   (R2),R3         ; put table contents (= address
                       ;     of right code section) in R3
JUMP   (R3)            ; jump to correct location
```

Register mode addressing can be used to reduce the number of bits needed in a machine language instruction to specify an address, or it can be used to combine computation in the program with addresses. Next we will show another form of addressing that uses values computed in a program.

3.3.2 Indexed Addressing

Consider the following simple computation involving subscripts.

```
SUM := 0;
FOR I := 1 TO 100 DO
  BEGIN
    SUM := SUM + A[I]
  END;
WRITE (OUTPUT, ' SUM IS ', SUM);
```

Reference to the array element A[I] requires two components to the address: a fixed part (A) and an increment for the current value of I. Arrays are usually stored as a block of consecutive words. If A[1] is stored at location 4031, A[2] will be at 4032, and A[100] will be at 4130. Thus any reference to an element of A can be composed of a fixed part (4030) plus the value of the subscript.

This can be conveniently achieved at the machine language level by using a register as an *index register*. This is a register whose value is added in the calculation of an operand's address. This might be specified in machine language as

```
ADD A(R3),SUM     ; add I-th element of A to SUM; I in R3
```

A is the address of a fixed word in storage. The notation A(R3) means *the address of* A, *plus the current contents of register* 3. If register 3 contains the value of I, this expression will select that word that represents the Ith element of A.

Indexed addressing can be used in CASE statements, as just described. It can also be used for array references and for working one-by-one with adjacent items.

3.3.3 Autoincrement and Autodecrement Addressing

A special form of register addressing is the *autoincrement* or *autodecrement indexed address*. In this form, the value of the index register is either increased or decreased by 1 before or after the address is generated. Assume that register R3 already contains the address of the first element of A. Then an instruction such as

```
ADD   (R3)+,SUM     ; add A[I] to SUM, increment I
```

would mean that after register R3 is used in this computation, its value is to be increased by 1, causing it to point to the next element of A. Similarly,

```
ADD   -(R3),SUM     ; decrement index and add A[I] to SUM
```

would mean that before register R3 is used for address computation, its value is to be reduced by 1; the value would be the address of the previous element of A.

Recall the example using indexed addressing: a loop to sum elements 1 to 100 of A. Autoincrement indexed addressing can be used to select one element of A and then to update the index. Computers can be profitably used to perform a similar operation many times. The autoincrement and autodecrement feature takes care of a lot of the changing to be done between one repetition and the next. Autoincrement and autodecrement are ways to reduce the number of separate machine language instructions needed to accomplish a task.

3.4   IMMEDIATE ADDRESSING

Immediate addressing is a means of building constants directly into a program. In the previous examples we showed the autoincrement address mode, which automatically increases the value in a register by 1. On the IBM 360-370 the standard word is four memory locations long, and on the PDP-11 it is two locations long. Thus, incrementing by 1 is not sufficient if array elements occupy 1 word each. The ADD IMMEDIATE instruction can be used to add a fixed constant value to a value. For example, the instruction

```
ADDI  4,R3
```

might add the constant value 4 to register R3 . This is not the same as adding the contents of memory location 4 to register R3 ; that instruction would be

```
ADD  4,R3
```

The ADD IMMEDIATE instruction uses its first operand as a *constant* (the value to be added) instead of the *address* of the value to be added. Certain instructions expect an immediate operand, while with other instructions you may specify an immediate operand as one of a number of possible operand types.

For small constants the immediate instructions have two advantages. First, they are self-contained; that is, they "say" exactly what they are going to do (whereas

```
ADD  INCR,R3
```

does not give any clue as to what the value of INCR is.) A second advantage of immediate instructions is that they are frequently shorter and faster than comparable memory reference instructions because the constant value is obtained when the instruction is fetched. Other instructions may require an extra memory fetch to obtain the value of the operand.

3.5   INDIRECT ADDRESSING

The *indirect* form of addressing is another means of selecting the actual operand address during execution. An address such as

```
JUMP  @ADDR
```

would mean to transfer control *not* to address ADDR itself but to whatever address is currently contained in the word ADDR . That is, ADDR does not contain the operand; instead, it contains the *address of* the operand.

This form of addressing is especially convenient for subroutine calls and for passing arguments to subprograms. Both topics will be discussed later.

There are also combinations of these addressing modes. It is possible to have a direct, indexed, autoincrement address. Not all of these addressing modes are possible on each instruction or on every machine. For example, the IBM 360-370 families have no general autoincrement, autodecrement, or indirect mode addresses. Immediate operands are usually restricted to selected instructions, known as *immediate instructions*.

When you have a choice, you should select the simplest type of addressing you can. For example, direct addresses are preferable to indirect addresses, since indirect addresses require one memory reference that direct addresses do not.

Here are some major points of addressing modes to remember.

1. *Absolute addressing* uses the full address of the operand directly in the machine language instructions without needing any additional computation to decide the address.

2. In *register mode addressing* the address of the operand is contained in a register, and the register is identified in the machine language instruction.

3. *Indexed addressing* is a form of addressing containing two components: a fixed memory address and a register number. The actual operand address is the sum of the memory address and the contents of the register.

4. *Autoincrement* and *autodecrement* apply to indexed references, meaning that the specified register is to be incremented or decremented by 1 as a part of the execution of the instruction. Either type may be done before the value in the register is used or after it is used in forming the operand address.

5. *Immediate address* instructions use an actual piece of data as the operand in the machine language instruction.

6. In *indirect addressing* the operand address in the instruction specifies not the address of the operand, but the address of a word that contains the address of the operand. The computer must fetch the indirect word in order to determine the actual address of the operand.

3.4 EXAMPLES OF INSTRUCTION SETS AND INSTRUCTION FORMATS

This chapter concludes with summaries of the instructions available on three model computers: the Intel 8080, the PDP-11, and the IBM 360-370 families.

3.4.1 Instructions on the Intel 8080

Before you can appreciate the instruction set on the Intel 8080, you should be familiar with the hardware features of that machine. Recall that it is primarily an 8-bit machine: the memory is organized into 8-bit bytes, and the registers are 8 bits wide. There are seven registers: A (the accumulator), B, C, D, E, H, L. Memory addresses are 16 bits long. For certain addressing purposes, the H and L registers act together, identifying one 16-bit address. (Note that this device can keep instructions short; it requires only a few bits to indicate that an operand address is in the H-L register pair, while it would require 16 bits to code the actual operand address in the instruction itself. For example, adding a value in memory to the accumulator is a 1-byte instruction.) Registers B and C can also be used as a 16-bit pair, as can D and E.

The program counter is a 16-bit independent register. There is also a 16-bit stack pointer that is used for subprogram calls and returns.

Most instructions reference a register and either a memory address or another register. Most arithmetic instructions implicitly use the accumulator (register A) as the source of one operand and as the destination. The arithmetic and logical instructions are listed below.

ADD	r	Add contents of register r to the accumulator (A)
ADC	r	Add contents of register r and the carry flag to A
ADD	M	Add contents of memory location whose address is in registers H-L to A
ADC	M	Add with carry, memory location address in H-L
ADI	byte	Add the value of byte (the second byte of the instruction) to A

A similar set of instructions exists for SUBTRACT, AND, OR, XOR, and COMPARE. There are also instructions to INCREMENT or DECREMENT any register or memory location. There are no MULTIPLY or DIVIDE instructions.

The MOVE instructions can move data between any two registers, from a memory location whose address is in H-L to any register, and from any register to the memory location whose address is in H-L. The MOVE IMMEDIATE instruction will move one constant byte (the second byte in the instruction) to any register or any memory location.

There are no SHIFTs. Instead, the machine has both right and left ROTATE instructions. In a left ROTATE, bit 7 (the leftmost) of the accumulator circles left into the carry flag and the carry flag moves into the rightmost bit (bit 0). By manipulating the carry flag, it is possible to achieve the effect of a straight shift. The ROTATE instructions move only one bit at a time.

There is only one form of transfer instruction: the conditional JUMP. This instruction specifies its target address as the second and third bytes of the instruction. JUMPs can test any of the status flags, such as JM (jump if minus—the sign bit of the most recent result was 1) or JNC (jump if not carry—if the carry flag is off, meaning that the most recent arithmetic instruction did not cause a carry from the leftmost bit). An interesting feature is that CALL and RETURN instructions (for subprograms) are also conditional: you can, for example, call a subprogram if the zero flag is on or return if the carry flag is off.

3.4.2 PDP-11 Instruction Summary

The PDP-11 is a 16-bit word machine. There are eight 16-bit registers, numbered 0 to 7. Register R6 is also the stack pointer, and register R7 is the program counter. Memory is addressed in 8-bit bytes. Most instructions use either a 16-bit word or an 8-bit byte as an operand. There is no single register designated as the accumulator; therefore many arithmetic instructions specify both a source and a destination register. The registers are addressed as if they were memory locations 0 to 7.

There are eight addressing modes, including indexed, autoincrement and decrement, indirect, and absolute. Since the program counter is also a general register, it can be used as an index for relative addressing. Thus most instructions can reference a word or byte in memory just as easily as they can address a register.

Arithmetic and logical instructions include ADD, SUBTRACT, (for some models MULTIPLY and DIVIDE), COMPARE, AND (called *bit test*), OR (called *bit set*), and XOR.

There are a series of one-operand instructions: set a byte or word to 0 (CLEAR), COMPLEMENT, INCREMENT, DECREMENT, NEGATE, ADD THE CARRY FLAG, and SHIFT RIGHT or LEFT.

There is a series of conditional branch instructions that test various settings of the status flags, such as BRANCH IF NOT OVERFLOW or BRANCH IF HIGH OR EQUAL. There is a single subroutine CALL and a RETURN instruction.

3.4.3 IBM 360-370 Instructions

The IBM 360-370 is both word and byte oriented. The 16 registers, numbered 0 to 15, are 32 bits long. However, they can also accept 8- or 16-bit operands. There are four 64-bit floating point registers and a separate 64-bit program counter and status register.

Memory addresses are generally computed by using a base register, one of the 16 general-purpose registers. Thus 16 bits in an instruction suffice to address a memory of 2^{24} bits. Some instructions have two register operands, others have one register and a memory address, and others have two memory addresses.

Most instructions reference 32-bit fullwords, although some reference 16-bit halfwords or 8-bit bytes. Variable-length, binary-coded decimal data is used in some operations. Floating point instructions reference either 32-bit words or 64-bit doublewords.

The instructions denotes the type and the length of the operands. For example, there are six different ADD instructions: 32-bit integer, 16-bit integer, variable-length binary-coded decimal, 32-bit, 64-bit, and 128-bit floating point. (Not all models have floating point instructions, and some have only a subset for using short or medium operands.) There are also a variety of SUBTRACT, MULTIPLY, DIVIDE, COMPARE, LOAD, and STORE instructions.

Data movement occurs both to and from registers (LOAD and STORE) and between two memory locations (MOVE). The logical operations and shifts access only the general-purpose registers. There are a full set of logical operations and shifts.

There is essentially one conditional BRANCH instruction, although it has two forms, and different operands test various conditions. There are instructions for loop control and for subprogram calls.

This chapter has reviewed the typical kinds of machine language instructions. In the next chapter you will see how these instructions are used in assembler language programs. You will then be ready to consult documentation for the computing system you will use and write your own assembler language programs.

3.5 TERMS USED

The following terms have been used in this chapter. Be sure that you know what they mean before you move on.

instructions
>   ADD, SUBTRACT
>   ADD WITH CARRY, SUBTRACT WITH BORROW
>   INCREMENT, DECREMENT
>   LOAD, STORE, MOVE
>   arithmetic SHIFT
>   logical SHIFT
>   ROTATE (END-AROUND CARRY)
>   BRANCH, SKIP, JUMP

Conditional transfer
Unconditional transfer
Instruction formats
>   four-address
>   three-address
>   two-address
>   one-and-a-half-address
>   one-address
>   zero-address

Stack computer
Operand fetch instruction
Addressing modes
>   register addressing
>   indexed mode addressing
>   autoincrement, autodecrement addressing
>   immediate addressing
>   indirect addressing

3.6 QUESTIONS

The following questions are for your review to check your understanding of the material in this chapter.

1. Suppose you wanted to perform multiword arithmetic (as was described earlier in this chapter), but you had no ADD WITH CARRY instructions on your computer. Show how you could perform this task with just conventional ADD instructions and testing the carry flag.
2. Why do arithmetic right shifts propagate the sign bit? (*Hint:* Consider the value of a negative number in twos complement notation. What is $-14/2$, for example? Recall that shifts can be used for division by powers of 2.)
3. Assuming a 6-bit register, what is the result produced by each of the following instructions?
    (a) 110101 shift right arithmetic 2.
    (b) 000001 shift right arithmetic 2.

(c) 110101 shift left arithmetic 1.
(d) 110101 shift left arithmetic 1.
(e) Same as parts a to d, using logical shifts.
(f) 100110 rotate right 1.

4. Write a piece of code using three-address instructions to compute A = ((B+1) * (C−5))/22. Do the same thing with two-address and with one-address instructions. Which do you prefer? Why?

5. Explain the difference between LOAD R2,A and LOAD R2,@A (where the @ indicates indirect addressing).

6. Explain the difference between an instruction that uses an absolute operand and one that uses an immediate operand. For example, distinguish between LOAD R3,4 (absolute) and LOADI R3,4 (immediate).

7. Suppose you have register addressing [e.g., LOAD R6,(R2) meaning load R6 from whatever memory address is in R2], but there is no indexed addressing. Write a program that sums the 100 values of an array named LIST1 using register addressing. Write the same program for a machine that has indexed addressing. Which is easier to write? Why? Which is easier to read and understand? Why?

chapter 4

Characteristics of Assembler Languages

Most programmers who write machine language programs use assembler language. An *assembler* is a computer program that translates assembler language into machine language. Assembler language statements are converted one for one to machine language statements; in contrast, one higher-level-language statement (such as a FORTRAN, PL/I or PASCAL statement) may translate into several or even hundreds of machine language statements.

This chapter contains information on writing programs in assembler language. It will be easier to study the characteristics of a real assembler, so this chapter includes references to assemblers for IBM 360-370 and PDP-11 computers. The end of this chapter contains specific instructions and examples from programs for these two machines.

4.1 ASSEMBLER LANGUAGE INSTRUCTIONS

Instructions in assembler language have five basic fields. These are the label, the mnemonic op code (also called the operation code), operands, comments, and a sequence number.

The *label* associates a name (meaningful to the programmer) with a location or a value in the machine. In higher-level languages a label or statement number is used as the target of BRANCH and CALL statements, such as GO TO 100 or CALL SUB1 . This is one important feature of labels in assembler language programs. Some higher-level languages are rich in statement types, and the use of GO TO statements is seldom necessary. In assembler language programming, however, DO WHILE or IF THEN ELSE statements are seldom found. These logical constructs must be simulated, often using labels and branches.

Another important use of labels is to create and identify storage space for constants, variables, arrays, and other program data. In a higher-level language the programmer can allocate space for data items by declaring them, as shown.

VAR   ARR: ARRAY [1..100] OF INTEGER;

Some higher-level languages will also reserve storage for simple variables, even if the variables have not been declared.

In assembler language the programmer must explicitly declare all storage locations to be used for data in a program. A programmer may label any storage location to refer to later. A label then associates with a location number, which is its position within the program. It is also possible to use expressions to refer to other locations in a program. For example, if NUM is a label in a program, NUM + 1 is the first memory address after NUM.

A *mnemonic op code* is an abbreviation of the function of an instruction. For example, ADD, SUBTRACT, MULTIPLY, DIVIDE, LOAD, and STORE instructions may have mnemonic op codes A, S, M, D, L, and ST. The mnemonic makes it easy for the programmer to code programs: it is far easier to associate L with LOAD than a numeric op code such as 81. Of course, there is just one acceptable mnemonic for an instruction; L, LD, LOAD, and LDA would all be logical mnemonics for a LOAD instruction, but only one of these will be accepted by an assembler. In most assembler languages there is a card for the programmer's reference that lists all instructions and their mnemonics. Such a card is shown in Figure 4.1.

There may be none, one, or more *operands*. The operands specify data locations and other information that detail exactly what the instruction is to do. Each instruction will have a set of possibilities for operands. Some instructions will have one or more identifiers of storage locations (as in ADD A , B), registers (LR R1,R2) , constant data items (COMP X, # 1 2 3) , or specific keywords (LIST ON) . You must check each instruction to determine what operands it must have and what forms the operands may take.

An important part of an assembler language instruction is the *comment field*. Unlike higher-level-language instructions, it often takes a number of assembler language statements to perform a single task. The programmer or someone who reads a program may lose track of what is to be done and how an individual instruction contributes to that goal. It is important, therefore, to use meaningful, expressive comments to describe the relationship of each statement to the whole program.

Most assemblers allow the use of a *sequence number field*. This can be used to reorder the statements if they should be shuffled or to identify any statement that needs to be changed or replaced. This field may also be used by a program, called a *text editor,* that can be used to aid in the typing of a program. This portion of assembler language statements will be ignored from now on.

Some assembler languages are *free-format* languages, meaning that the fields may start in any column and a delimiter character is used to separate one field from the next. Between the label and the mnemonic there must be a colon and at least one space (there may be more than one). Between the mnemonic and the operands there must be one or more spaces. The operands may not have any spaces (except strings of characters enclosed in apostrophes), since the first space

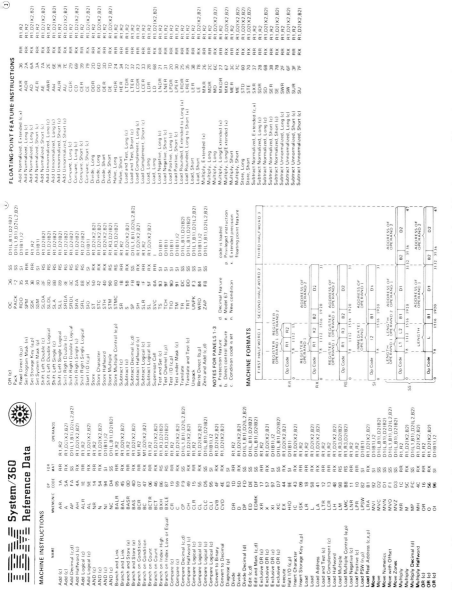

Reprinted by permission from IBM System/360 Reference Data, © by International Business Machines Corporation.

Figure 4.1 Instruction reference card.

after the operands marks the beginning of the comment field. Other languages use *fixed fields,* meaning that each field must begin in a specified column.

In IBM assembler language there are three fixed fields. Labels begin in column 1. A continuation is signaled by a nonblank character in column 72. The line to be *continued* must have a continuation mark. The sequence field occupies columns 73 to 80. Although the op code, operand, and comment fields may vary, most programmers choose some standard, as in the following table.

Field	Begins in Column
Label	1
Op code	10
Operands	16
Comments	36
(Continuation	72)
(Sequence	73)

The op code, operand, and comment fields are free format, while the label, continuation, and sequence fields are fixed to certain columns.

Some examples of assembler language statements follow. The various items—labels, mnemonics, operands, and comments—have been aligned for easier reading. This is a wise habit for you to adopt in your assembler language programming.

Label	Op Code	Operands	Comments
FIRST	START	256	BEGIN PROGRAM AT LOC. 256
	USING	FIRST,15	RELOCATE PROG. BASED ON REG. 15
	L	1,CON20	PLACE CONSTANT 20 INTO REG. 1
	SR	5,5	SUB. REG 5 FROM ITSELF; REG 5 <-- 0
	SPACE	1	LEAVE BLANK LINE SOURCE LISTING
LOOP	AR	5,1	REG 5 <-- REG 5 + REG 1
	S	1,CON1	REG 1 <-- REG 1 − 1
	BNZ	LOOP	IF REG 1 NOT = 0, REPEAT LOOP
	ST	5,ANS	STORE ANSWER AT "ANS"
	BR	14	RETURN TO MONITOR
	SPACE	1	LEAVE BLANK LINE IN SOURCE LIST.
ANS	DS	F	RESERVE 1 FULL WORD FOR ANSWER
CON1	DC	F'1'	CONSTANT HAVING VALUE 1
CON20	DC	F'20'	CONSTANT OF VALUE 20 (DECIMAL)
	END	FIRST	END OF FIRST EXAMPLE PROGRAM

This example has been taken from IBM 360-370 assembler language, and the form of the statements corresponds to its rules. Other assemblers differ slightly, for example, by using a colon after the label or by separating the comment from the body of the statement by a semicolon.

The assembler converts an assembler language program into machine language. There is no choice in what statements it selects, since each assembler language statement corresponds to a unique machine language command (except for directives to the assembler itself, which are not translated to machine language). The assembler does two things to help the programmer.

1. It performs conversions to binary. For example, the assembler has a table of mnemonics and the corresponding machine language op codes. The assembler composes a statement using the appropriate op code. It also converts constants and expressions from one number system to another. In the preceding example, it would convert the decimal values 20 and 1 to the binary equivalents.

2. It converts symbolic addresses to machine addresses. On the IBM 360-370 computers, for example, each operand representing an address is either a fixed (constant) memory location or an address relative to some point (e.g., the top) in the program. In the preceding example, ANS is some number of bytes past the top of the program. Coding in machine language, you would have to compute the lengths of all instructions that precede ANS and sum these lengths to figure the address of ANS relative to the start of the program. Say, for example, that ANS is 60 bytes from the top of the program. Any statement referring to ANS would have to be coded as 60 *bytes from the base of the program.* If the instructions in the program are changed, ANS may move closer to or farther from the start of the program. Any machine language statements referencing ANS would then have to be changed.

If you use symbolic addresses (labels within a program) the assembler will recompute the displacement of each label each time the program is assembled, so changes in the program are easily handled (on your part, at least). The second task of the assembler is to convert all addresses to the proper internal form.

4.2 ADDRESS TYPES

Instructions may use a variety of address types, depending on the individual instruction. This section contains information on the most common address types.

4.2.1 Absolute Addresses

An *absolute* address is one that refers to a fixed machine location. The IBM 360-370 and PDP-11, like many other machines, have tables and pointers in fixed memory locations that help to control use of the machine: which programs are currently sharing use of the machine, what instruction each program should execute next, and what routines should be invoked in the event of an error. These are at fixed memory locations. For example, location 104 on an IBM 360-370 machine contains the address of a routine that is to be executed if an error occurs during execution of the current program.

The programmer can inspect and use these values by referring directly to the desired location numbers. For example, the instruction

    MVC   MYLOC,104

says to move (copy) the contents of memory location 104 to the place called MYLOC. The value 104 is a reference to an absolute location. Memory address 104 is a fixed address that does not change, regardless of the size or position of the current program. (This does not say that the *value at* location 104 is fixed. The contents of a location are *not* related to its address.)

4.2.2   Relative Addresses

Many user programs share a medium or large computer facility. A program called an *operating system* allocates the resources of the computer—including memory, the CPU, and the I/O devices—to the requesting user programs. Most user programs are *location independent;* that is, they will execute successfully in any block of memory to which they are assigned.

Suppose a program named EXAMPL contains a label LOOP1 that is 20 bytes away from the start of EXAMPL. At one time, EXAMPL may be placed in the block of memory beginning at address 4000. In that case LOOP1 would be at location 4020. Another time, however, EXAMPL may be placed at location 9000, in which case LOOP1 would refer to address 9020. Label LOOP1 is called a *relative* or a *relocatable address,* since its actual location in memory shifts as a program is placed in different machine addresses. This situation is shown in Figure 4.2. Although the address of LOOP1 changes, it is always at the same position within EXAMPL (assuming, of course, that EXAMPL is unchanged). We say then that LOOP1 is a *relative address.*

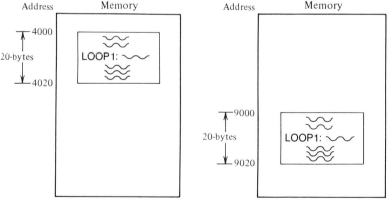

Figure 4.3   Sample IBM 360-370 assembler language program.

While assembling a program, the assembler can determine the constant part of each relocatable address: the distance between the address and the relocation point (e.g., the start of the program or the address of the current instruction). The assembler encodes this constant part (called the *displacement*) and the manner for relocating the address. When the program is readied for execution, the operating system must relocate all relative addresses.

4.2.3 Register Operands

One-and-a-half-address instructions use a register as one of the operands. Instructions of this kind must include an operand that designates which register is to be used in the instruction. Some machines, such as the IBM 360-370 and the PDP-11, use numbers to refer to the registers, while other machines, such as the Intel 8080, use labels such as A, B, C, D, H, L to refer to the registers. A register operand is either a number or a label specifying the register to be used in the instruction.

4.2.4 Deferred Operands

Sometimes it is convenient to be able to defer the choice of the address of an operand until execution time. For example, a subprogram that is designed to sort the elements of an array will be of limited use if it can work on only one array. To overcome this problem, most assemblers and machine languages permit the choice of an exact address to be postponed until the program is executed. Then the address is supplied in a register.

This form differs from the previous one. A *register operand* is one in which the value for the computation is in a register; for example, the instruction

```
A       5,LOC1
```

might add the values in register 5 and memory location LOC1 . Thus the contents of register 5 is a value used in executing the instruction. By contrast, a *deferred operand* does not say that its value is to be used in the computation but, instead, that its value is the *address* of a value to be used in the computation. On a PDP-11 the instruction

```
ADD     (R7),R5
```

says that the value in register 5 is to be added to the value whose *address* is in register 7 . The distinction here is that in the first case the value added is the *number* in register 5 , while in the second case the value added is the one at the memory location whose *address* is in register 7 .

You may have observed that the direction of data movement is different between the IBM and PDP machines. On an IBM machine the destination operand of most instructions is the first operand; for example

```
AR      R5,R3
```

causes the contents of register 3 to be added to register 5 . However, on a PDP-11, the second operand is usually the destination; for example

    ADD   R5,R6

would add the value in register 5 to register 6 .

4.2.5 Immediate Operands

Sometimes a particular constant value is needed as an operand in an instruction, such as *examine the contents of memory location* A *to see if it contains the value* 40 , or *place the encoding of the character* '*' *at location* CH1 . In both cases the constant 40 or the character encoding for '*' are represented as a part of the instruction. This is called an *immediate operand,* and the operand itself is called a piece of immediate data, because the data are immediately available—no memory reference is needed to obtain the data.

Most machines limit the size of the immediate data. IBM 360-370 machines, for example, restrict the immediate data to one byte (8 bits); the PDP-11 permits an immediate field up to one word.

4.2.6 Indexed Operands

Assembler language permits the processing of arrays in much the same way that they are processed in higher-level languages. Array references in higher-level languages consist of two parts: an array name and an expression denoting an element of the array. *Indexed operands* use an *address* (usually a relocatable label) to designate the beginning point of the array, and a *register* is then used as an index telling where the desired data item is relative to that beginning point. The index is in terms of machine addresses. Thus a machine using a 2-byte word would probably use index values of 0, 2, 4, 6, etc., to designate the first, second, third, fourth, etc., words of an array. The index values need to match the size of an element in the array. Arrays having 4-byte entries would need index values that are multiples of 4. Similar to higher-level languages, indexed operands are usually formed by a label followed by a register designation in parentheses, as in the following instruction.

    ST   R5,TABLE1(R3)

In this instruction the current value of register R3 would be added to the address of TABLE1 ; this sum will be the address at which register R5 is to be stored. If, for example, register R3 contains the value 18, this statement is equivalent to

    ST   R5,TABLE1 + 18

where the second operand is the 18th address past the starting address of TABLE1 .

On the PDP-11 the autoincrement and autodecrement addressing modes are convenient for use with indexed operands. In the autoincrement mode, when a register is used, the value in the operand address register is increased by 1 (for an instruction that operates on 1-byte data) or by 2 (for an instruction that operates on 2-byte data). The autodecrement mode works similarly. Suppose that register 2 initially contains the address of a table of 100 1-word (2-byte) values. The following loop could compute the sum of all entries in the table.

```
           CLR   R3            ; set R3 to zero
           MOV   #100,R4       ; set R4 to 100, count table entries
LOOP:      ADD   (R2)+,R3      ; add next table entry to reg. 3
                               ; also increment table pointer by 2
           DEC   R4            ; decrement count of entries
           BPL   LOOP          ; loop till all values added
```

In this example, after register R2 is used as an address, the value in it is increased by 2, so that it will point to the next word in the table. At the end of the loop, R4 will contain the address of the word after the last entry in the table. This "side effect" of executing the ADD instruction reduces the number of instructions needed to code a particular task.

Although there are other addressing modes for operands, this set is comprehensive enough for many programming applications. The next topic to be considered will be the components of assembler language programs: directives to the assembler and machine language instructions.

4.3 ASSEMBLER DIRECTIVES

The assembler produces a *source listing*. This is a listing of all of the statements in the program, along with their machine code and locations in the program. If there are any errors, they are flagged in the assembler listing. The assembler *listing* is different from the *output* produced by the program. If the program is to print the values of the first 10 prime numbers, these values will be printed during the execution of the program. The source listing is produced during assembly, before the program begins to execute.

There are statements, called *assembler directives* or *pseudo-instructions,* that the assembler recognizes and acts on during program assembly. Some of these directives affect the appearance of the source listing, others control the allocation of storage in the assembler language program, and others are cues for the assembler, such as an indication of a new subprogram or the end of the entire assembly. All of these directives are used by the assembler; only the ones that allocate memory in the program are passed from the assembler to the program's execution.

4.3.1 Source Listing Controls

Good program documentation often separates a mature programmer and a beginner. Experienced programmers recognize the need to explain their code, both for themselves and for any others who may read the program. Documentation is especially important in assembler language programming, since it may take 5 to 10 machine instructions to represent one thought or one higher-level-language construct. In order to identify the motivation behind a series of instructions, mature programmers provide comments before each group of instructions and on nearly every individual instruction. Any program also needs a block of header documentation to explain what the program does, what its inputs are, and what output it can produce.

In assembler language each individual statement may have a comment. After the operand field, you code a delimiter, such as a blank or a semicolon, and the remainder of the statement may be comments. Also, an entire statement may be a comment if it begins with a comment symbol, often a semicolon or an asterisk. IBM 360-370 assembler language uses the blank as a delimiter between the last operand and the comments, and a whole comment statement begins with an asterisk. In PDP-11 assembler a semicolon is used both to separate operands from comments and to begin a statement that is entirely comments.

The appearance of the source program on a printed listing is also important as documentation. Fixed-field assembler languages will read in even columns. Even with free-format statements, readability is dramatically improved by using consistent columns. The program is also easier to follow if it is divided into major sections, separated from other sections by blank lines. Major sections should begin at the top of a new page. Listing techniques to support these ideas are available in all assembler languages.

To assist in documenting a program, blank lines can be inserted in the source listing. These can visually block the program into separate sections.

On the IBM 360-370 this is done with the SPACE command. The SPACE command (where SPACE is the op code) has one operand, a constant telling how many blank lines to leave. For example,

```
SPACE  3
```

inserts three blank lines in the source listing at this point. (Remember that these blank lines are in the source listing; this statement has no effect on the output of a program during execution.)

For both the PDP-11 and the IBM 360-370, comments can be used to block a program and place blank space in a program listing. Comments that have only the comment identifier (asterisk or semicolon) can provide an amount of blank space to a program.

The TITLE statement can be used to label the source program listing with an identifying heading. On an IBM 360-370 the one operand to TITLE is a string of any characters (including letters, marks of punctuation, digits, and spaces), enclosed in apostrophes. When this statement is found in a source program, the assembler skips to the top of a new page in the source listing, and it prints the message in the operand field at the top of that and succeeding pages. For example, the statement

```
TITLE  'SAMPLE PROGRAM — ADD VALUES 1 TO 20'
```

would cause the source listing to move to the top of a new page and print the message SAMPLE PROGRAM — ADD VALUES 1 TO 20 at the top of that page and all succeeding pages until another TITLE statement was found. On the PDP-11 the operand of the .TITLE directive is a title that is to appear at the top of all pages.

One statement can be used to turn off the listing of statements in the program and to turn it on again at other points. Listing only part of a program is especially useful when some sections of the program have already been tested. Using these listing controls can conserve the amount of paper used for the source listing of a program. (Again, remember that the source listing is *not* the output from the program; these controls affect only the listing of the source statements. There is no effect on output produced during the program's execution. Statements not listed are still assembled.)

On the IBM 360-370 the form of the statement is

    PRINT   ON

or

    PRINT   OFF

where PRINT is the op code and ON or OFF is the operand. PRINT OFF suppresses listing of the source statements from the point where it appears until a PRINT ON is encountered. These may appear anywhere within a program, and as many PRINT ON or PRINT OFF statements may be used in a program as desired. On the PDP-11 the directives to perform these same tasks are .LIST and .NLIST.

4.3.2 Allocating Storage

In assembler language programs you must specifically allocate space for all constants, variable locations, or arrays that are used in the program. IBM 360-370 assembler language has two statements for doing this: DC to define a constant and DS to allocate storage. The DC statement may have one or more operands, having the form

    DC   <repeat><type><value>

where <repeat> is an optional count of the number of constants of this type to be generated; if the repeat count is omitted, one constant is assembled. To generate an entire line of blanks, you could code

    C' '

with 132 blanks between the apostrophes. To save unnecessary counting, you could also code

    132C' '

<type> specifies what kind of constant is to be generated. A character constant is different from a decimal constant, which is different from a hexadecimal constant.

C type constants are for strings of characters, where the <value> is a string of any characters, enclosed in apostrophes. If the character apostrophe (') or ampersand (&) is to be generated, it must be coded twice; for instance,

    C'+ ISN''T &&'

is coded to represent the character string

    + ISN'T &.

F type constants are for 1-word, 4-byte, twos complement integers. The operand is a signed or unsigned decimal integer. The assembler reserves one fullword (32 bits) per constant, computes the twos complement binary form of the constant, and places that value in the fullword. The $<value>$ is any signed or unsigned decimal integer, enclosed in apostrophes.

X type constants are hexadecimal values. The $<value>$ is any string of hexadecimal digits (0 to 9 and A to F), enclosed in apostrophes. The assembler computes the binary equivalent of the hexadecimal constant, determines the size (in bytes) of the constant, allocates that number of bytes of memory, and places the binary constant in those bytes.

$<value>$ is the constant value, as described previously for each constant type.

The following are examples of DC statements.

```
DC    C'THIS IS A CHARACTER STRING'
DC    F'200',F'0'
DC    F'-1',X'FFFFFFFF'
DC    3X'00'
DC    5C'*',C' ERROR ',5C'*'
```

The DS statement is similar to the DC statement. It is used to define or allocate an amount of storage for data values. The op code is DS, and the operands are of the form $<repeat><type>$, where $<repeat>$ is an optional repetition factor, as with DCs and $<type>$ is a letter telling how to reserve the space; the types are the same as for DC. The statement DS 1F reserves one fullword (4 bytes at a fullword address) in memory. The statement DS 12C reserves 12 bytes of space, since a character occupies 1 byte. A DS statement may also have a $<value>$ field, although this field is used only to determine the length of the DS; no value is placed in the space reserved by a DS. For example, DS 2C' HELP ' reserves enough space to hold two copies of the string ♭HELP♭, or 2*6 = 12 bytes, but the characters themselves are not placed in memory.

The PDP-11 has a similar set of directives. For character strings, the .ASCII or .ASCIZ statements are used. The operand of either of these is a string of characters. The delimiter for the beginning and end of the string is the first character. That is, any character can be used as a delimiter; you inform the assembler what the delimiter for the current string is by placing it at the start (and also at the end) of the string. For example,

```
.ASCII  /A STRING/
.ASCII  "STRING #2"
.ASCII  ?YOU DON'T DUPLICATE APOSTROPHES?
```

are all acceptable strings. The .ASCII command reserves as many bytes as there are in the string and places the characters of the string in memory. (For example, the first string would set aside 8 bytes, filled with the characters A♭STRING.)

With the .ASCIZ directive, the assembler reserves 1 more byte than with .ASCII. This extra byte is located after the last character of the string; it is set to the binary value 0. This 0 is used by some programs during execution that need to be able to find the end of the string without knowing its length.

Twos complement binary values are reserved with the .BYTE and .WORD directives. The operands of these statements are octal or decimal constants. The assembler will reserve 1 byte or word per constant, compute the binary equivalent of the constant, and place the value in the storage reserved. Octal numbers are preceded by # ; decimal values may be indicated by a decimal point. Examples of use of .BYTE and .WORD are:

```
.BYTE  #277
.WORD  100,200,300
.BYTE  0
```

To reserve a block of memory (e.g., to be used for an array), the PDP-11 assembler uses .BLKB and .BLKW. The operand of each of these is a number, which tells how many bytes (.BLKB) or words (.BLKW) to allocate. There is no predictable value placed in these bytes or words.

4.3.3 Other Assembler Directives

There are two essential assembler directives that have not yet been covered. On the IBM 360-370 these are START or CSECT and END ; on the PDP-11 they are .CSECT and .END .

As you might expect, START marks the beginning of the program for the assembler. START is the mnemonic. It may have a label, which is the label of the program unit. (Each program unit—main program or subprogram—is called a *control section,* or a CSECT.)

The END or .END statement marks the physical end of a program assembly. There is only one END statement, and it must be the last line of the assembly program. The END statement may have an operand, which is the point at which execution is to begin; this would normally be the label on the START or first CSECT statement.

4.4 MACHINE INSTRUCTIONS

Now we can turn to the machine instructions of IBM 360-370 and PDP-11 computers. This section will not contain *all* the machine instructions of these machines; the goal is to show how some simple assembler language programs are written. You should obtain complete information on the instructions available on the computer to which you have access so that you can write programs on it.

4.4.1 IBM 360-370 Instructions

You may remember that the IBM 360-370 is mainly a one-and-a-half-address computer, which means many of its instructions are of the form

<mnemonic>   <register number>,<memory location>

The IBM 360-370 has 16 general-purpose registers, which are referred to by a number between 0 and 15. All of these registers are available for the programmer's use.

The normal direction of data movement is from the second operand to the first. Therefore an instruction such as

    A   5,X

means to add the contents of X *to* the value in register 5, leaving the result in register 5. Similarly,

    S   5,X

means to subtract the value at X *from* that in register 5, leaving the result in register 5.

Many instructions are one-and-a-half-address instructions, meaning that they reference a register number and a memory location. There are also some one-half-plus-one-half-address instructions, which reference two register numbers. For example,

    AR   5,2

adds the value in register 2 to that in register 5, placing the result in register 5. The subtract register (SR) instruction operates similarly. The one-and-a-half-address instructions are called RX or RS instructions, and the one-half-plus-one-half-address ones are called RR instructions. The R in all cases stands for register, and the S and X stand for storage and indexed storage, respectively. Frequently there will be two instructions: one an RR form and the other an RX form; the mnemonic of the RR form will be that of the RX form with an R on the end (e.g., AR is the RR form of A).

The following table lists some popular machine instructions.

Operation	RR Form	RX Form
ADD	AR	A
SUBTRACT	SR	S
LOAD	LR	L
STORE	—	ST
COMPARE	CR	C
BRANCH	BR	B

Recall from Chapter 3 that LOAD implies data movement *into* a register, while STORE implies movement *out of* a register. The L and ST instructions imply fetching data from memory and placing data in memory, respectively. The LR instruction is used for transferring data from one register to another. There is no RR counterpart for ST.

The following program would compute the sum of the values 10 and 15, storing the result at the location named X.

```
FIRST    START                      begin sample program 1
         USING  FIRST,15            declare base register
         L      4,C10               load first value (10)
         A      4,NUM15             add second value (15)
         ST     4,X                 save sum at X
         BR     14                  return to operating system
C10      DC     F'10'               constant of value 10
X        DS     F                   storage space for a full word
NUM15    DC     F'15'               constant of value 15
         END
```

This program has five pieces: the *header* (START, USING), the *computation* (L, A, ST), a *return* (BR 14), *data storage* (DC and DS), and an *end*. Your programs will probably have a similar structure.

The forms and uses of the ADD and SUBTRACT instructions have been described previously. The LOAD instructions, L and LR, again imply right to left data movement, copying the value of the second operand into the first register. The compare instructions do not change either registers or storage; they simply show whether the first operand is less than, equal to, or greater than the value at the second operand (in the second register or in the specified memory address).

The status register on an IBM 360-370 is called the *condition code,* and it has four possible settings.

Condition code setting	Letter
0: zero, equal	Z, E
1: low, negative, minus, less than	L, M
2: high, positive, plus, greater than	H, P
3: overflow	O

Arithmetic and compare instructions set the condition code. The condition code always has one of the preceding four values, whichever it was last set to.

The condition code can be tested by the conditional BRANCH instructions. There are a number of these to test the four possible settings of the condition code. All branches start with the letter B, have a letter to indicate the condition (or N and a letter to indicate the negation of a condition) and, optionally, the letter R to indicate an RR form. For example, BE means *branch if the condition code is set equal (0);* BNE represents *branch if the condition code is any value not equal (1, 2, 3);* BER and BNER are the RR counterparts of these two. The operand of an RX form is a label in the program to which you want to branch if the condition code is set as you test. The RR operand is a register containing the address to which to branch. If the condition code is set to a different value, the test fails, and execution continues with the next statement in the program.

A sample IBM 360-370 assembler language program is shown in Figure 4.3.

4.4.2 PDP-11 Instructions

The PDP-11 has eight 16-bit registers. There are eight addressing modes used in the instructions. The first word of most instructions includes the operation code

```
LOC   OBJECT CODE   ADDR1 ADDR2   STMT   SOURCE STATEMENT

                                    3    *===============================================================*
                                    4    * THIS PROGRAM READS CARDS CONTAINING A CODE AND A NUMBER.       *
                                    5    *   IF THE CODE IS 'A' THE NUMBER IS ADDED TO A RUNNING SUM       *
                                    6    *   IF THE CODE IS 'S' THE NUMBER IS SUBTRACTED FROM A RUNNING SUM*
                                    7    *   IF THE CODE IS 'P' THE SUM IS PRINTED AND RESET TO ZERO       *
                                    8    *   IF THE CODE IS 'H' THE PROGRAM HALTS                          *
                                    9    *                                                                *
                                   10    * ALGORITHM:                                                     *
                                   11    *   THERE ARE TWO LOOPS.  THE OUTER LOOP PRINTS A HEADING, RESETS *
                                   12    *   THE RUNNING SUM TO 0, PERFORMS THE INNER LOOP, AND PRINTS     *
                                   13    *   THE SUM WHEN THE INNER LOOP HAS TERMINATED.                  *
                                   14    *   THE INNER LOOP READS AN INPUT CARD, DETERMINES IF AN ADD,     *
                                   15    *   A SUBTRACT, OR A PRINT IS CALLED FOR, AND BRANCHES TO THE     *
                                   16    *   POINT WHERE ADD, SUBTRACT, OR PRINT IS DONE.                 *
                                   17    *                                                                *
                                   18    * DESCRIPTION OF CODE:                                           *
                                   19    *   REGISTERS USED:                                              *
                                   20    *     R3 = RUNNING TOTAL                                          *
                                   21    *     R4 = NUMBER FROM CARD                                       *
                                   22    *   INSTRUCTIONS USED:                                            *
                                   23    *     AR  - ADD REGISTER TO REGISTER                              *
                                   24    *     B   - UNCONDITIONAL BRANCH                                  *
                                   25    *     BE  - BRANCH IF CONDITION CODE SETTING IS "EQUAL"           *
                                   26    *     CLI - COMPARE IMMEDIATE (1 BYTE) TO STORAGE ADDRESS         *
                                   27    *     SR  - SUBTRACT REGISTER FROM REGISTER                       *
                                   28    *   PSEUDOINSTRUCTIONS USED                                       *
                                   29    *     XDECI - CONVERT TO BINARY, PUT IN REGISTER                  *
                                   30    *     XDECO - CONVERT TO DECIMAL FROM REGISTER TO STORAGE         *
                                   31    *     XPRNT - PRINT LINE FROM STORAGE FOR GIVEN LENGTH            *
                                   32    *     XREAD - READ INPUT CARD, PLACE IN STORAGE                  *
                                   33    *                                                                *
                                   34    *   PROGRAMMER: C. PFLEEGER         DATE: 1 MAY 1981              *
                                   35    *===============================================================*
```

Figure 4.3 Sample IBM 360-370 assembler language program.

FIGURE 4.3   EXAMPLE ASSEMBLER LANGUAGE PROGRAM.

```
LOC     OBJECT CODE       ADDR1 ADDR2  STMT  SOURCE STATEMENT
001000                                  37   EXAMPLE  START X'1000'        BEGIN ASSEMBLY AT LOCATION HEX 1000
001000                                  38            USING EXAMPLE,15     DECLARE BASE REGISTER

                                        40   *        OUTER LOOP: RESET AND PRINT HEADING
001000  1B33                            41   OUTER    SR    3,3            RESET RUNNING SUM TO ZERO
001002  E020 F05A  0018  0105A          42            XPRNT HEADER,24

                                        44   *        INNER LOOP: READ CARD AND SELECT NEXT ACTION
001008  E000 F080  0028  01080          45   INNER    XREAD CARD,40        READ COLUMNS 1-40 OF NEXT INPUT CARD
00100E  E020 F072  0036  01072          46            XPRNT ECHO,54        ECHO COPY OF CARD JUST READ

                                        48   *        SPLIT FOUR WAYS DEPENDING ON VALUE OF FLAG
001014  95C8 F080        01080          49            CLI   CARD,C'H'      IS CODE HALT?
001018  4780 F052        01052          50            BE    ENDPROG        IF YES, TERMINATE PROGRAM
00101C  95C1 F080        01080          51            CLI   CARD,C'A'      IS CODE "A" FOR ADD?
001020  4780 F030        01030          52            BE    ADD            IF YES, ADD TO RUNNING SUM
001024  95E2 F080        01080          53            CLI   CARD,C'S'      IS CARD "S" FOR SUBTRACT?
001028  4780 F03A        0103A          54            BE    SUBTRACT       IF YES, SUBTRACT FROM RUNNING SUM
00102C  47F0 F044        01044          55            B     RESET          NONE OF ABOVE, PRINT SUM AND RESET

                                        57   *        CODE "A": GET VALUE FROM CARD AND ADD
001030  5340 F081        01081          58   ADD      XDECI 4,CARD+1       GET NUMBER AFTER COLUMN 2
001034  1A34                            59            AR    3,4            ADD TO RUNNING SUM
001036  47F0 F008        01008          60            B     INNER          REPEAT INNER LOOP

                                        62   *        CODE "S": GET VALUE FROM CARD AND SUBTRACT
00103A  5340 F081        01081          63   SUBTRACT XDECI 4,CARD+1       GET NUMBER AFTER COLUMN 2
00103E  1B34                            64            SR    3,4            SUBTRACT FROM RUNNING SUM
001040  47F0 F008        01008          65            B     INNER          REPEAT INNER LOOP

                                        67   *        CODE "R": PRINT AND RESET SUM
001044  5230 F0BC        010BC          68   RESET    XDECO 3,OUTSUM       CONVERT SUM FOR PRINTING
001048  E020 F0A8  0020  010A8          69            XPRNT OUTMSG,32      PRINT OUTPUT LINE
00104E  47F0 F000        01000          70            B     OUTER          REPEAT OUTER LOOP TO RESET

                                        72   *        CODE "H": HALT PROGRAM
001052  E020 F0C8  0011  010C8          73   ENDPROG  XPRNT ENDMSG,17      PRINT ENDING MESSAGE
001058  07FE                            74            BR    14             HALT PROGRAM

                                        76   *        DATA STORAGE: CONSTANTS AND TEMPORARY LOCATIONS
00105A  F0C2C5C7C9D5D5C9                77   HEADER   DC    C'0BEGINNING NEW INPUT SET'
001072  404040C3C1D9C440                78   ECHO     DC    C' CARD READ: '   TITLE BEFORE CARD ON OUTPUT LINE
001080                                  79   CARD     DS    40C              SPACE FOR FIRST 40 COLUMNS OF CARD
0010A8  40E3C8C540D9E4D5                80   OUTSUM   DC    C' THE RUNNING SUM WAS'
0010BC                                  81   OUTSUM   DS    12C
0010C8  F0D7D9D6C7D9C1D4                82   ENDMSG   DC    C'0PROGRAM FINISHED'
                                        83            END
```

Figure 4.3 *cont'd*

113

```
*** NO  STATEMENTS FLAGGED  -   NO  WARNINGS,  NO  ERRORS
*** DYNAMIC CORE AREA USED:     2928 LOW +    892 HIGH, LEAVING  174356 FREE BYTES.  AVERAGE:          45 BYTES/STMT ***

*** CROSS-REFERENCE:  VALUE(HEX)  LOCATION REF REF ... (- SHOWS MODIFY) ***
ADD      001030   52   CARD     001080   -45   49   51   53   58   63   ECHO     001008   001072   46   ENDMSG   0010C8   73
ENDPROG  001052   50   EXAMPLE  001000   -38   HEADER   00105A          INNER    001044   60   65   OUTER    001000   70
OUTMSG   0010A8   69   OUTSUM   0010BC   -68   RESET    001044   55     SUBTRACT 00103A   54
*** ASSEMBLY TIME =  C.118 SECS,   711 STATEMENTS/SEC ***
*** PROGRAM EXECUTION BEGINNING - ANY OUTPUT BEFORE EXECUTION TIME MESSAGE IS PRODUCED BY USER PROGRAM ***


BEGINNING NEW INPUT SET
  CARD READ: A 10
  CARD READ: S  5
  CARD READ: P
THE RUNNING SUM WAS              5

BEGINNING NEW INPUT SET
  CARD READ: A   200
  CARD READ: A   100
  CARD READ: A    50
  CARD READ: P
THE RUNNING SUM WAS            350

BEGINNING NEW INPUT SET
  CARD READ: S   5
  CARD READ: S   5
  CARD READ: S   5
  CARD READ: S   5
  CARD READ: S  -12
  CARD READ: P
THE RUNNING SUM WAS             -8

BEGINNING NEW INPUT SET
  CARD READ: P
THE RUNNING SUM WAS              0

BEGINNING NEW INPUT SET
  CARD READ: A   3
  CARD READ: S   3
  CARD READ: P
THE RUNNING SUM WAS              0

BEGINNING NEW INPUT SET
  CARD READ: H

PROGRAM FINISHED

*** EXECUTION TIME =   0.073 SECS.        200 INSTRUCTIONS EXECUTED -    2739 INSTRUCTIONS/SEC ***
*** AM004 - NORMAL USER TERMINATION BY RETURN ***
*** TOTAL RUN TIME UNDER ASSIST =    0.248 SECS ***
```

Figure 4.3   *cont'd*

and one or two register designations; there may be an extra piece of data after the instruction. There are eight different addressing modes, most involving a register. The addressing modes are as follows.

Mode 0: Register.   In this mode the register itself is the source or destination of the data *Example:* MOV R2 , R3 meaning to copy the data currently in R2 to R3 .

Mode 2: Autoincrement / Mode 4: Autodecrement.   In this mode the register contains the address of operand. In the autoincrement address mode the address register is increased by 1 (for byte instructions) or by 2 (for word instructions) after the operand address is calculated. In the autodecrement mode the register is decreased by 1 or 2 *before* the operand address is calculated. *Example:* ADD (R5)+ , R3 adds the value at the word in memory pointed at by register 5 to register 3 . Furthermore, register 5 is increased by 2, so that it now points 1 word higher.

Mode 6: Indexed.   This mode has two components: a base address and a register. The base address and the contents of the register added together form the operand address. (This form is especially useful in array processing, where the base address is the beginning of the array; the register "steps through" the array, identifying one element at a time.) *Example:* INC ARR1 (R4) . Assuming that ARR1 begins at address 017040 and register 4 contains 100 , the operand address is 17040 + 100 = 17140 . The word at location 17140 is incremented by 1.

Mode 1: Deferred Address.   In this mode the address of the operand is supplied in a register. *Example:* CLRB (R3) clears (sets to 0) the byte whose address is shown in register 3 .

Mode 3: Autoincrement Deferred / Mode 5: Autodecrement Deferred.   In this mode the register contains the address of a word in memory that contains the address of the operand. That is, if register 4 contains 010452 and word 010452 contains the value 003460 , the operand is located at address 003460 . The register is incremented or decremented as in direct autoincrement or autodecrement mode. *Example:* MOV @(R4)+ ,R6 moves into register 6 the value stored at the word pointed to by the word identified in register 4 . For example, register 4 might point to a list of addresses of parameters to a subprogram. This instruction would move one parameter *value* into register 6 and move the pointer in register 4 to the next parameter *address.* Autodecrement deferred mode is denoted MOV @ − (R4) , R6 .

Mode 7: Indexed Deferred Mode.   In this mode the contents of a register and a base address are summed to form the address of the operand. *Example:* ADD @TBL (R3) , R0 adds to register 0 the contents of the word whose address is contained in the word at the address of TBL plus the current contents of register 3 . This mode is useful with a table of addresses of values. The table is the base address, and the index register identifies the desired word.

When these modes are combined with the program counter (register 7), additional addressing modes, such as immediate and relative, can be produced. The modes and the addressing forms are now summarized.

Mode	Name	Example	Interpretation
0	register	MOV R3,R5	operand is in register
1	register deferred	MOV (R3),R5	operand address is in register
2	autoincrement	MOV (R3)+,R5	address in register; register increased by 1 or 2
3	autoincrement deferred	MOV @(R3)+,R5	operand address in word pointed to by register; register increased by 1 or 2 after use
4	autodecrement	MOV −(R3),R5	address in register; register decreased by 1 or 2 before use
5	autodecrement deferred	MOV @−(R3),R5	operand address in word pointed to by register; register decreased by 1 or 2 before use
6	indexed	MOV adr(R3),R5	address plus contents of register is operand address
7	indexed deferred	MOV @adr(R3),R5	address plus contents of register is address of word pointing to operand

The PDP-11 instructions are both byte and word oriented. Many operations have two forms: the mnemonic ending in -B uses a 1-byte operand, while the mnemonic not ending in -B uses a 1-word operand. Several of the more common instructions are shown here.

ADD	src,dst	add contents of src to contents of dst
SUB	src,dst	subtract contents of src from contents of dst
MOV (B)	src,dst	move contents of src to contents of dst
CMP (B)	src,dst	compare contents of src to contents of dst, setting negative flag if src less than dst and zero flag if both equal
BIC (B)	src,dst	("bit clear") sets dst to contents of src AND contents of dst
BIS (B)	src,dst	("bit set") sets dst to contents of src OR contents of dst
CLR (B)	dst	sets contents of dst to 0
INC (B)	dst	adds 1 to contents of dst
DEC (B)	dst	subtracts 1 from contents of dst
BR	loc	branch to loc (where loc is within 128 bytes past current instruction and 127 bytes before current instruction)

conditional branches: BCC (carry clear), BCS (carry flag set), BEQ (equal zero), BNE (not zero), BGE (greater or equal zero), BGT (greater than zero), BLE / BLT (less than or equal/less than zero), BHI (higher), BLO (lower)

> JMP   *dst*   unconditional jump to *dst; dst* may be any address

4.5 WHAT CAN (AND WILL) GO WRONG?

As with every other programming language, there are numerous little flaws that can prevent a program from executing properly. This section contains some hints to some of the difficulties that can occur and their probable causes and solutions.

There are two kinds of errors: assembly and execution errors. Assembly errors are errors in the syntax of statements so that the assembler refuses to accept them. Most of the time the assembler will give some clue as to the cause of the error, although the message "operand error" can be cryptic. There are fewer execution time errors, although this is not always a benefit: each error can arise from many different causes. Following are some interpretations and suggestions for handling some of the more popular errors.

4.5.1 Assembly Errors

The (easy) explanation of an assembly time error is that the statement is improperly formed. It is not so easy to catalog the corrections. Here, however, is a list of error messages and their suggested remedies.

Missing Operand. This message implies that an instruction that was supposed to have two (or more) operands had fewer than required. *Probable Cause:* Inadvertent space between operands. (Remember that the first space after the start of the operand field marks the start of the comments. That is,

> L   5, X

may be attractive, but the space before the X means that the operand field stops at the comma—the X is a part of the comments.)

Invalid Operation. This means that the mnemonic as entered is not a legal mnemonic. *Probable Cause:* Spelling or copying error in entering mnemonic. For example, LOAD is a logical but incorrect mnemonic; the only correct one is L on an IBM 360-370.

Address Error. This means that the address of the operand is beyond the limits of the program or that the address mode is not legal. *Probable Causes:* Reference to a memory location instead of a register number. This can come from using an RX instruction instead of an RR one. For example,

> L   5 , 4

means to place the contents of *memory location* 4 into register 5 . More likely what was intended was

> LR   5 , 4

in order to copy *register* 4 into register 5 . This sort of error will be detected by using START 256 or some other nonzero value on the START .

Alignment Error. This is the result of trying to perform a fullword operation on a piece of data that is not as large as the operation requires. For example, A , L , S , ST , and C all perform 32-bit operations. That is, 32 bits are added (loaded, etc.) to a register at a time. The following example will not work.

```
        A           5 , ONE
                . . .
ONE     DC          C ' 1 '
```

because C ' 1 ' is a 1-*byte* constant (one character = 8 bits = 1 byte). The addition requires 32 bits. The only way to achieve this is to use a fullword constant (DC   F ' 1 '). The IBM 360 requires fullword operands to be at addresses on "fullword boundaries," that is, addresses that are multiples of 4. The assembler will take care of alignment for F type DC and DS operands. However, C and X type operands are not aligned. Thus, although F ' 1 ' and X ' 00000001 ' have the same value, the first will always be at a fullword boundary, while the second may or may not (with a three out of four chance not). *Probable Cause:* Base or index register error or operand incorrect.

Label Error. This results from a malformed or duplicate label in the program. One label may be used only once in an assembly. There are syntax rules controlling how labels may be formed. For example, labels usually must begin with a letter. They may contain only letters, digits, and a few special characters. The length of a label is usually limited to five to eight characters. For example, on the IBM 360-370, a label begins with a letter and is composed of up to eight letters, digits, or @ , $, and # . For the PDP-11 a label must end with a colon (:). *Probable Cause:* Typing errors.

Undefined Symbol. This error comes from using an operand in an instruction but never defining that label in the program. *Probable Cause:* Misspelling or forgetting to include a statement to define the storage area.

There are other errors that can be detected during assembly of a program, but these are the most common ones. Others, such as *Invalid Delimiter* and *Invalid Constant,* say what they are. When correcting the syntax of an assembler language program, it is helpful to have a model of each statement at hand for reference.

4.5.2   Errors During Execution

A running program responds only to exceptional conditions. On the IBM 360 an *interrupt* is used to halt execution of a user program and to transfer to a routine to handle an exceptional condition. The interrupt causes the CPU to cease what it was doing and to begin executing another program, called an *interrupt handler.*

Depending on the cause of the interrupt, the CPU may or may not later return to the program that was in progress at the time of the interrupt. Conditions that prevent successful execution of an instruction cause an interruption. There are 15 reasons for a program interruption. (There are also reasons for interruptions due to other causes, such as completion of an I/O activity.) Fortunately, only a few of these causes show up in beginning programs. These are now summarized.

> *Operation Exception, Privileged Operation Exception.* These errors come from the CPU attempting to execute an operation code (the first byte of an instruction) that is not a legal instruction on this machine or that is not legal for this programmer. Remember that there is no difference between a piece of data and an instruction in memory; that is, a value could be a piece of numeric or character data, an address, or an instruction. The CPU simply fetches each value from memory in order and tries to execute it as an instruction. Some pieces of data will not resemble valid instructions and will cause operation exceptions if you try to execute them. *Probable Causes:* Omitting a STOP or BR 14 or RETURN at the end of the executable code of a program (in which case the CPU flows into the data area, seeking the next instruction). Another cause is putting a storage statement (DC, DS, .ASCII, .BYTE, .WORD, .BLKB, or .BLKW) with executable machine instructions. This can be done only if there is a branch to cause the CPU to skip over these data items. Another cause is branching to an incorrect address. The trace of recent instructions will reveal the point of the error.

> *Protection Exception.* A multiprogrammed machine like an IBM 360-370 may have a number of users occupying memory at one time. There is a mechanism to prevent one from inadvertently (or maliciously) modifying part of another person's program. Attempting to access part of memory outside your own program will cause a protection exception. *Probable Cause:* Base or index register in error. You should not modify the value in the base register (the one declared in the USING statement). Inspect the value in that register at termination to verify that it does contain the address of the start of your program. If your last instruction used an index register or an explicit base displacement operand, verify that the value in the index register or the base register is correct.

> *Addressing Exception.* This error is caused by trying to access an address that is larger than the highest address in the machine. *Probable Causes:* Error in base or index register. See the suggestions under *Protection Exception.*

> *Specification Exception.* This occurs from an incorrect form of an operand. As noted previously, instructions such as LOAD, ADD, SUBTRACT, and STORE require their operands to be located at fullword boundaries, that is, at addresses that are multiples of 4. *Probable Cause:* Incorrect base and/or index register. See suggestions under *Protection Exception.* Remem-

ber that an index register being used to sequence through fullwords of storage must change by 4 each repetition.

There are a few other causes for error terminations that you are not likely to run into with your first programs. The list of possibilities should help you to interpret some of the problems you encounter. You will probably also want to check with your instructor to get advice on your particular program. In some environments, such as an IBM 360-370, you will have a comprehensive program termination *dump* from which to work in the event of an error. A dump is a printed listing of the contents of each register and each memory location at the time of termination. With single-user machines you may have the luxury of being able to debug at the computer: inspect the contents of any relevant memory locations directly by supplying the memory address in the front panel registers. You have probably already done a fair amount of debugging in higher-level languages. Debugging at the assembler level is easier, from one perspective, because you have access to all memory locations and you can examine all values for their reasonableness.

4.6   TERMS USED

The following terms have been used in this chapter.

Label
Mnemonic operation code (opcode)
Operand
Comment field
Sequence number
Free-format language
Fixed-field language
Absolute address
Relative address
Register operand
Deferred (indirect) operand
Immediate operand
Indexed operand
Assembler directive
Pseudo-instruction
Source listing control
DC (define constant) or .BYTE, .WORD, .ASCII, .ASCIZ
DS (define storage) or .BLKB, .BLKW
Operand error
Operation error
Address error
Alignment error
Undefined symbol
Protection error

4.7   QUESTIONS

The following questions will test your facility with the material in this chapter.

1.   In IBM 360-370 or PDP-11 assembler language write a program to compute the sum of all values in a table **TAB** of 100 words.
2.   Write a program to count the number of times the value 3 appears in a table of fullword values.
3.   Write a program to compute the Fibonacci numbers. The first two numbers in the sequence are 1 and 1. After that, each term in the sequence is the sum of the immediately preceding two numbers. For example, the first few terms are 1, 1, 2 (1 + 1), 3 (1 + 2), 5 (2 + 3), 8, 13, 21. Write the program so that it accepts a value n in a register or a word in memory and determines the value of the nth Fibonacci number.
4.   Multiplication can be simulated by repeated addition. Write a program that takes 2 words from registers or from memory and computes their product, without using a MULTIPLY instruction.
5.   Write a program that computes factorials. Your program should take a word from memory or from a register and compute that value times all other integers less than it, down to 1.
6.   Write a program that takes 10 values in a table and rearranges them so they are in increasing order by value.

chapter 5

Program Execution

This chapter contains a description of how a program is executed. After a program has been written, translated (e.g., by an assembler) into binary machine language, and placed in memory ready for execution, the CPU executes the program instructions. The CPU performs a sequence of operations to execute each instruction. This chapter describes the way the CPU acts on a program.

5.1 NORMAL INSTRUCTION EXECUTION

Execution of a single machine instruction involves five separate CPU activities.

1. Fetch the instruction at the address specified in the program counter (PC). The PC contains the address of the next instruction to be executed, so the CPU uses it as a pointer to keep track of where execution is in the program. To fetch an instruction, the CPU puts the contents of the PC into the MAR, reads memory, and moves the value in the MDR into an internal instruction decoding register. Depending on the size of the MDR and the size of an instruction, it may take more than one memory read to obtain an entire instruction.

2. Update the PC. On some machines this simply involves adding a constant to the PC. Other machines, such as the PDP-11 and the IBM 360-370, have instructions of different lengths, so it may be necessary to analyze the instruction to determine its length. On the IBM 360-370 the operation code (first byte) tells the length of the instruction. On a PDP-11 it is necessary to examine the addressing modes for the operands, since different addressing modes imply different instruction sizes. In any event, the PC is updated so that it contains the address directly after the current instruction.

3. Decode the instruction and compute operand addresses. In this phase the CPU analyzes the fields of the instruction to determine which operation is to be performed and what the addresses of the operands are. The CPU often performs some arithmetic to determine the operand addresses. For example, if an index register is being used, the current value in the register must be added to the address shown in the operand part of the instruction. Instructions with indirect address operands require a memory fetch just to determine the operand address. (Remember that an indirect address operand shows the *address* of a word in memory that contains the actual operand address.)

4. Fetch operands. It is easier to execute an instruction if the operands are in predictable locations, such as a particular register or memory location. The CPU copies operand values into internal registers in order to have the operands in standard places. Sometimes, too, fetching the operands requires changing the forms of the operands; for example, a small value may be padded on the left with 0s so that it will fill all bits of a register.

5. "Perform" the operation. In this phase the CPU does what the operation indicates. For example, with ADD instructions the CPU activates an adder unit to compute the sum of two operands in internal registers; in performing a subtraction, the CPU complements the internal register to be subtracted and then activates an adder [A − B is computed as A + (−B)]. A BRANCH, SKIP, or JUMP instruction is performed by modifying the address in the PC, since this will alter where the next instruction is taken from.

The CPU performs these steps for each instruction to be executed. As an example, consider the following program. It compares the values of A, B, and C and places the largest of them into the memory location identified by label BIG. We will assume that the example is a fragment of a larger program. Each statement is identified by a location counter value (in hexadecimal) and a letter for reference.

Reference	Location Counter		Instruction		
			. . .		
(a)	000140		L	5 , A	take first value
(b)	000144		C	5 , B	is B larger?
(c)	000148		BNL	TRYC	no, compare to C
(d)	00014C		L	5 , B	B is larger; save it
(e)	000150	TRYC	C	5 , C	is C larger?
(f)	000154		BNL	DONE	no, present value is largest
(g)	000158		L	5 , C	C is largest; save it
(h)	00015C	DONE	ST	5 , BIG	store largest value
			. . .		

As we trace through this program, notice the value of the program counter (which will be shown at the left). Assume the values of A, B, and C are 7, 18, and 9, respectively. A picture before each step shows the values of relevant registers before the step is performed.

PC	MAR	MDR	R5
000140	?	?	?

(a) 000140 (1) The CPU fetches the instruction at location 140. (2) Since this is a 4-byte instruction, the PC is increased by 4, to 144. (3) The instruction is decoded, and the address of A is determined and placed into the MAR. (4) Memory is read, and the value at A moves into the MDR. (5) This is then transferred to register 5.

PC	MAR	MDR	R5
000144	addr of A	7	7

(b) 000144 (1) The instruction at location 144 is fetched into the instruction decode register. (2) Since the instruction is of length 4, the PC is raised by 4, to 148. (3) The address of B is computed and transferred to the MAR. (4) Then a memory fetch puts B into the MDR. This value is transferred to an internal register for the comparison to the value in register 5. (5) Since 5 (A) is less than 18 (B), the status register is set to *low.*

PC	MAR	MDR	R5
000148	addr of B	18	7

(c) 000148 (1) The instruction at location 148 is fetched into the instruction decode register. (2) Since that instruction has a length of 4, the PC is raised by 4, to 14C. (3) The address of the operand, label TRYC, is computed and retained internally. (5) Since the status register is set *low* and the instruction is BNL *(branch if the status is not low),* no branch occurs. Execution of the instruction is completed.

PC	MAR	MDR	R5
00014C	addr of B	18	7

(d) 00014C (1) The instruction pointed at by the PC is fetched into the instruction decode register. (2) This is decoded, and 4 is added to the PC, making it 150. (3) The operand address, B, is computed and placed into the MAR. (4) The LOAD instruction causes a value to be fetched from memory, and (5) transferred to register 5.

PC	MAR	MDR	R5
000150	addr of B	18	18

(e) 000150 (1) The next instruction (at location 150) is fetched into the instruction decode register, and (2) 4 is added to the PC, yielding

154. (3) The operand address is computed, and that value, the address of C, is placed into the MAR. (4) The value is fetched from memory and moved from the MDR into an internal register. (5) The value in register 5 (18) is compared to the value obtained (9), and the status register is set *high.*

PC	MAR	MDR	R5
000154	addr of C	9	18

(f) 000154 (1) The next instruction is fetched. (2) The PC is incremented by 4 from 154 to 158. (3) The operand address, the address of label DONE, is computed. (5) The status register is examined; since it is set *high,* and the branch requires any setting other than *low,* the branch is taken. The address calculated as the operand, 15C, is placed into the PC. Notice that this causes an alteration in the normal flow of execution, since the PC indicates the address of the next instruction. Thus instruction (g) is skipped.

PC	MAR	MDR	R5
00015C	addr of C	9	18

(h) 00015C (1) The instruction identified by the PC (15C) is fetched and placed in the instruction decode register. (2) Since the length of this instruction is 4, the PC is incremented by 4, to 160. (3) The operand address, the address of BIG, is calculated and placed in the MAR. (4) The value in register 5 is placed in the MDR. (5) A STORE transfers that value to memory location BIG.

PC	MAR	MDR	R5
000150	addr of BIG	18	18

The actions performed in executing each instruction are now summarized.

1. Fetch the instruction pointed at by the program counter.
2. Update the program counter so it points to the next instruction.
3. Decode the instruction and compute operand addresses.
4. Obtain the values of the operands.
5. Perform the action requested by the instruction.

This same sequence of operations is performed for each arithmetic or logical instruction executed. For all instructions the program counter is incremented by a length so that it contains the address of the next instruction to be executed. Beyond that, most instructions do not change the program counter. Transfer of control instructions (BRANCH, SKIP, JUMP), however, cause a transfer by putting a new address into the program counter. In the next section, we will examine two kinds of BRANCH instructions and see how both operate.

5.2   TRANSFER OF CONTROL INSTRUCTIONS

Some machines have only one type of transfer of control: branch. (In this section, the term *branch* will mean both the unconditional BRANCH—always branch—and the conditional BRANCH—branch only if the machine status is as specified in the branch instruction.) The operand of a BRANCH instruction is the address to which to transfer. Execution of that instruction causes the address shown in the operand to be placed in the program counter. The IBM 360-370 machines have only one BRANCH instruction: BRANCH ON CONDITION (although this one instruction has two forms, depending on whether the branch address is located in a register or in the instruction).

By contrast, machines such as the PDP-11 have two different instructions, a *long* BRANCH and a *short* BRANCH. (On the PDP-11 these are called JUMP and BRANCH, respectively.) A long BRANCH contains the full address that is to go into the program counter; a short BRANCH contains only a displacement that is to be added to or subtracted from the program counter. For this reason, the machine code for a long BRANCH (which contains a full address) is larger than that for a short BRANCH (which has only a displacement). Because it requires computation of a full address, a long BRANCH may also take longer to execute than a short one.

The form of a long branch would resemble Figure 5.1.

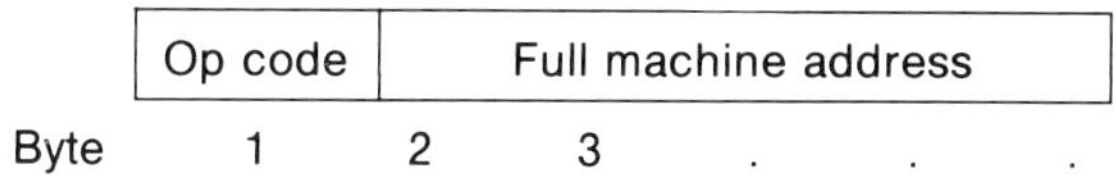

Op code	Full machine address

Byte   1   2   3   .   .   .

Figure 5.1   Long branch instruction.

Since this instruction contains an entire machine address that is to be placed in the program counter, the address part of the instruction must be as large as the program counter. For example, if the program counter is 16 bits long, a long BRANCH will have 16 bits devoted to the address. However, machines such as the IBM 360-370 use 24-bit addresses, so the address portion of this instruction would be 24 bits long. (*Note:* On the PDP-11, different addressing modes permit some economy, since a machine address may be held in a register, in which case only the register number is encoded in the instruction.) When this instruction is executed, the entire operand value is moved into the program counter.

A short BRANCH instruction contains only a displacement, as shown in Figure 5.2.

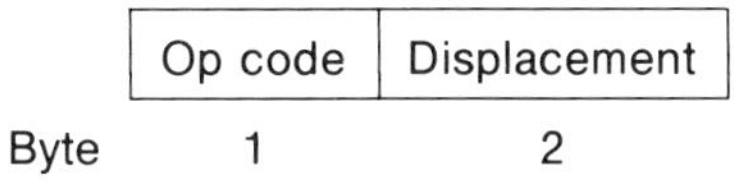

Op code	Displacement

Byte   1   2

Figure 5.2   Short branch instruction.

When this instruction is executed, the displacement (which is taken to be a signed number) is *added* to the program counter. If an 8-bit byte is used for the displacement, displacements of -128 to $+127$ can be represented.

Recall the example from the last section on finding the largest of three values. The two BRANCH instructions were merely used to skip over an instruction if the larger of two values was already in the correct register. Instead of using two long conditional branches (BNL), this could be done in PDP-11 assembler language (using short branches). See the example shown on page 129. Note that the branches in statements 3 and 6 are only 1 word long; these contrast to the move and compare instructions (1, 2, 4, 5, 7, 8), which are 2 words long. Frequently the target of a BRANCH instruction is within a few instructions of the branch. In these cases the use of short branches can reduce the program length.

5.3 SUBPROCEDURE CALLS AND RETURNS

This section describes the mechanism for calls to and returns from procedures. The basic mechanism used in procedure calls is the *stack*. A stack was described in Section 3.2.6. Remember that a stack is a data storage structure that resembles a tube with one end closed; items are inserted and removed from the open end. Items are removed in reverse order from that in which they went in; that is, the latest item inserted is the first one removed.

A stack can be represented using a single array and a pointer. The bottom (closed end) of the stack may be the first or the last element of the array. The pointer will always show the item most recently inserted in the stack. Initially, the pointer has a value 0, showing that no entry is yet in the stack. Each time an item is placed in the stack, the pointer is increased by one, and each time an item is removed, the pointer is decreased by one. (This description assumes that the bottom end of the array is used as the closed end of the stack; the logic is, of course, reversed if the top of the array is used as the closed end.)

Several operations on a stack are shown in Figure 5.3, in which the closed end of the stack is shown on the left; the position of the pointer is indicated by an arrow.

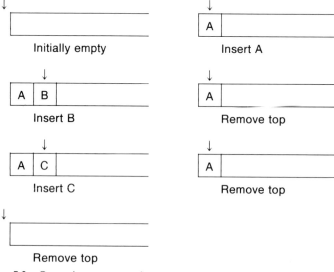

Figure 5.3 Operations on a stack.

State-ment	Location Counter	Object Code	Source Statement			
1	000000	016705 000036		MOV	A,R5	; ASSUME A IS LARGEST
2	000004	020567 000036		CMP	R5,B	; COMPARE TO B
3	000010	103402		BHI	TRYC	; IF R5 HIGHER, SKIP
4	000012	016705 000030		MOV	B,R5	; B WAS LARGER—INTO R5
5	000016	020567 000026	TRYC:	CMP	R5,C	; COMPARE TO C
6	000022	103402		BHI	DONE	; LARGEST FOUND—KEEP IT
7	000024	016705 000020		MOV	C,R5	; C IS NEW LARGEST VALUE
8	000030	010567 000010	DONE:	MOV	R5,BIG	; KEEP BIGGEST VALUE
		. . .				
9	000040		A:	.WORD		
10	000042		BIG:	.WORD		
11	000044		B:	.WORD		
12	000046		C:	.WORD		

You may already have observed that procedure calls and returns are handled in stack order. For example, assume that procedure A calls B, B calls D, D returns and B returns, then A calls C, C calls D and, finally, D returns, C returns, and A halts. The active procedures (ones that have a procedure call in progress) are reflected in Figure 5.3 using stacks. The process of procedure calls and returns is shown in Figure 5.4.

The address in a calling procedure where execution is to resume after a procedure call is called the *return address*. Notice that D has two different return addresses because it is called by two separate routines. The return address must be provided at the time one routine calls another. There are also two levels of calls: A called B, which called D. Thus two different return addresses must be maintained, one for D to return to B, and one for B to return to A.

A computer memory is effectively a single array, with the elements being the individual words of memory. Some computers provide a *stack pointer* register so that a portion of memory can record active procedure calls.

When one procedure calls another, several things must be done.

1. Save the return address, the address to which the called procedure should return when it is finished.
2. Save the value of the status register and other general registers so that the called procedure will not alter values needed by the calling procedure.
3. Arrange for any needed parameters to be passed to the called procedure.
4. Provide a mechanism for the called procedure to return any arguments and results.
5. Branch to the called procedure.

The rest of this section describes instructions and conventions that do these things.

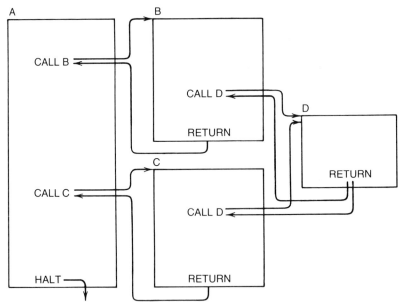

Figure 5.4 Sequence of procedure calls.

5.3.1 Saving the Return Address

A called subprocedure must know the address to which it should return when it is finished. The return address is readily available in the program counter just before the branch to call the procedure. For example, if A calls B using an instruction as shown,

```
000132        CALL B
000136        . . . next instruction
```

where 1 3 2 is the address of the CALL instruction, a part of the execution of the call is for the program counter to be incremented to 1 3 6 , the address of the next instruction. A CALL is a form of a BRANCH, so to complete execution of the CALL, the address of B is put into the program counter.

Computers have an instruction that saves the updated program counter value before replacing it with the branch address. This instruction goes under different names, such as BRANCH AND LINK (BAL) , JUMP AND SAVE RETURN (JSR) , JUMP TO SUBROUTINE (JSUB) , and CALL . These instructions copy the updated program counter value into some predefined location before loading the branch address into the program counter.

For example, on an IBM 360-370, the instruction

```
BAL   14,SUB
```

causes the updated program counter to be moved into register 14, and the address of SUB is placed into the program counter. On the Intel 8080 the stack is implicitly used, where

```
CALL   SUB
```

causes the updated program counter to be pushed onto the stack, the stack pointer is decremented, and the address of SUB is placed into the program counter. (On the Intel 8080 the stack grows "in reverse," from high-numbered memory locations to low ones. Thus, decrementing the stack pointer makes it point after the new insertion.)

5.3.2 Saving Register Values

A program usually has certain values held temporarily in the registers. After one routine calls a subprogram, the calling routine should receive the registers back as they were at the time of the call. However, the called subprogram also needs to use registers. Fortunately, the caller's values can be stored in memory and reloaded before the called subprogram returns.

Usually a convention is established between a calling procedure and its called procedure regarding who should save registers. Often the called procedure has this responsibility. That way, if the called procedure needs to use only a few registers, it need not save the full set, thereby saving unnecessary instructions. The stack frequently is used for this.

The IBM 360-370 computers have no stack *per se,* so saving registers becomes a bit more involved. Each procedure establishes what is called a "save area"; this is 18 words of storage in which all 16 general-purpose registers can be saved, along with certain pointers. A calling procedure provides a save area, but it is used by the called procedure. Lowest-level procedures, those that call no others, need not establish a save area. By convention, one of the general-purpose registers (register 13) contains the address of the current save area.

5.3.3 Passing Arguments To and From Procedures

There are a variety of techniques for passing arguments. Each has advantages and disadvantages; in a certain situation one may be preferred to another.

The simplest method of passing arguments to and from called procedures is to put the values of the arguments themselves in the registers. Of course, the calling procedure and the called procedure need to agree on which argument will go in which register.

This technique is obviously limited to the number of registers available on the machine. The PDP-11 has 8 registers, but register 7 is the program counter, and register 6 is the stack pointer. Thus only six arguments could be passed this way. The IBM 360-370 has 16 registers, but one of these must be used for the save area pointer, one for the return address, and one for addressing; thus, at most, 13 registers are available for arguments. Few procedures have more than this many arguments, but many procedures pass arrays as arguments. If registers were used to pass parameters, only 13 elements of an array could be transmitted on an IBM 360-370, fewer on other machines. For an array as an argument, usually just the address of the first element of the array is passed; from that the called procedure can calculate the addresses of elements that it wants.

Passing arguments in registers can be efficient if there are few arguments (relative to the number of registers). For large numbers of arguments, however, considerable time is lost loading the registers and, in the called procedure, saving the values in certain registers in order to have free registers in which to perform computation.

A second method for passing arguments is to place them in memory, immediately after the call instruction. Thus, a CALL would look like this.

```
        CALL   SUB
        DC     (arg1 value)
        DC     (arg2 value)
NEXT    . . .    next instruction
```

The DC instructions define the values of the two arguments. In the called procedure the register containing the return address will point to the first of the DCs, since it contains the address immediately after the CALL. In order to obtain argument 1, the called procedure fetches the value whose address is contained in the return register. To obtain the second argument, the called procedure fetches the value whose address is 1 word higher than the address in the return register. The actual return point is 2 words higher than the address in the return register.

The PDP-11 often passes argument addresses directly after the call. Code for this would look like the following fragment.

```
JSR     R5,SUB        ; call subprogram
.WORD   argument      ; first argument address
.WORD   argument      ; second argument, etc.
. . . next instruction ; return point
```

The subprogram accesses these arguments as follows.

```
MOV    (R5)+,R1    ; put first argument in reg 1
MOV    (R5)+,R2    ; put second argument in reg 2 , etc.
```

The autoincrement addressing (indicated by the plus in the MOV instructions) changes R5 so that it points to the next word. By the end of this sequence, R5 points to the return point in the calling program.

With this technique, an unbounded number of arguments may be passed. Of course, it will still be desirable to pass the address of an array, instead of all the individual elements. It is necessary to copy the values of the arguments each time the call occurs; the arguments cannot be permanently stored immediately after the call. Arguments cannot be stored permanently after the call because one variable might be used as an argument in calls to a number of different procedures. For example, a program might contain the following two statements.

```
CALL   SUB1,(A,B,C)
CALL   SUB2,(B,A,D)
```

where (A , B , C) and (B , A , D) are the lists of arguments. The first requires the value of B immediately after that of A , while the second requires the value of A immediately after that of B . This is impossible, and so the alternative is to copy the values of A , B , and C or D immediately before the call is executed.

This argument-passing mechanism is time consuming for large argument lists. Furthermore, there is duplication if the same argument list is passed to a number of called procedures. For example, if (X , Y) is a common argument list in a number of calls, it would be convenient to have one copy of the values of X and Y and simply pass this to each called procedure. However, the argument list is required to be immediately after the call, so this would require the one list to be in more than one place at a time.

To overcome this last difficulty, a third argument passing mechanism uses a *remote argument list*. This is a list of addresses of arguments, and the list may be located in any convenient place, not necessarily after the call. By passing the addresses of the arguments, it is not necessary to copy the argument values each time a call occurs. If the called procedure is passed the address of A , it will obtain the current value of A when it fetches from that location. Furthermore, it does not matter if A is stored before or after B , since all that need to be consecutive are 2 words containing the addresses of A and B . Finally, one list containing the addresses of X and Y could be used as the argument list for any number of calls to different procedures. This is shown in Figure 5.5.

This last mechanism has the defect that it can be cumbersome to acquire the values of the arguments. The IBM 360-370 computers use this method almost exclusively. The address of the argument list is passed in register 1, and the called procedure must retrieve the arguments. However, the IBM 360-370 computers have no direct means of fetching a value whose address is in a given memory location; it is necessary to load the argument address into a register and then fetch, using the register as an address pointer. These two operations are inconvenient. For efficient access, the argument value is usually copied into the called procedure, so that it can be manipulated directly.

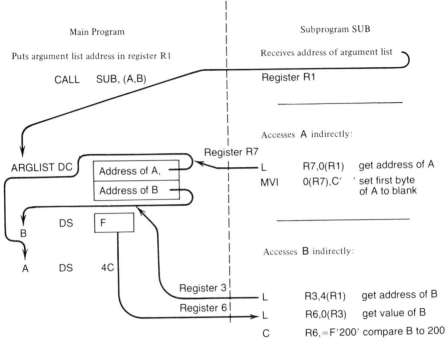

Figure 5.5   Using a list of Argument addresses.

5.3.4 Return from a Called Procedure

As noted, the return address is preserved as a part of the call. Therefore, in order to return, it is only necessary to arrange for any arguments to be passed back and to reload the program counter with the return address. Returning arguments in registers is easy. For arguments passed through an argument list, it is necessary to copy the current value of the argument into the address provided.

On the IBM 360-370 the return address is passed directly in a register, so that address is forced directly into the program counter by means of a register mode branch instruction. On the Intel 8080 the return address is pushed onto the stack; a RETURN instruction removes this return address from the stack and forces it into the program counter.

5.3.5 Summary of Procedure Calls

1. For procedure calls, it is necessary to save the return address before branching to the called procedure. This return address can be saved in a stack.
2. If the called procedure needs to do computation, registers must be saved so as not to alter values kept there by the calling procedure.
3. Arguments may be passed in a number of different manners: in the registers, in a list immediately after the call, or in a separate list. The first of these is the simplest, but it is limited to a small number of arguments. The last is very effective, but it can be cumbersome to use.

4. On returning it is necessary to send back any arguments, to reset any changed registers or the status indicator, and to place the return address in the program counter.

5.4 INTERRUPTS

So far we have considered the operation of only the CPU and memory. The CPU and memory operate at approximately the same speed, so the CPU simply waits when it has requested a piece of data from memory. However, other devices may run at a speed much different from that of the CPU and memory. Furthermore, there may be times when a device wants control of the computer. It can be time consuming to have the CPU constantly ask the device "Do you want control of the computer now?" if the answer is often "no."

An *interrupt* is a means for an external device to assert a desire to be recognized by the CPU. When an interrupt is recognized, the CPU stops executing instructions from the program it was performing, and it turns to execute a different segment of code, called an *interrupt handler* routine. The interrupt handler is like a called procedure because it performs some self-contained task and, when it is finished, it "returns" to what the computer was doing at the time of the interruption.

There are a number of possible sources of interruptions. They include:

1. I/O devices requiring service. These devices often run substantially slower than the CPU. After the CPU issues a request for data from, for example, a video/keyboard terminal, it may take a long time for the human operator of the terminal to respond. In this interim time the computer can constantly monitor the device, using a loop like the following instructions.

   ```
   LOOP1   TEST   KSR,DONE
           BZ     LOOP1
   ```

   This loop continually tests the keyboard status register (KSR) to see if it is done transferring a character. If not, it branches to LOOP1 and tests again. This approach keeps the CPU busy, but it is doing nothing productive.

   Some computers permit I/O activity to go on in parallel with computation. When the I/O operation is done, the device causes an interrupt to inform that CPU that the desired I/O operation has been completed. The CPU can then be engaged in productive computation (on other programs).

2. External event requiring attention. Computers can be used to monitor experiments, collect data, and control machinery. In these situations an attached device needs to notify the CPU that a piece of information is available or an unusual condition has arisen. The attached devices can cause interrupts in order to have service from the computer. When used in these kinds of applications, computers can do double duty: they can be involved in computation that is not time dependent (e.g., performing

some statistical analysis) but, any time a high-priority attached device needs attention, the CPU can attend to it.

3. Internal malfunction. A computer contains checking circuitry to guarantee that hardware malfunctions are detected. For example, there are checking codes used with external I/O devices and internal devices, such as memory and registers. These codes check the validity of values stored and read back so that any incorrectly recorded values can be detected. If any checking code indicates an error, the hardware responsible (in the I/O device, the memory module, or the CPU) can generate an interruption in order to suspend normal CPU activity until the damage can be assessed.

4. Operator intervention. The computer supervisor must be able to regain control of the machine if necessary. Sometimes, for example, a piece of erroneous data submitted may cause a useless or impossible computation. If a program is in error, it may cause an unending loop, which the operator may detect and want to break. For these reasons, there is a method by which the operator can interrupt the normal flow of execution.

We will now analyze what occurs in order to handle an interrupt. An interrupt handler is like a procedure call in that it is an independent piece of code to perform one task (identify and deal with the interrupt cause). In fact, the interrupt handling mechanism resembles a procedure call and return. However, an interrupt is generated by a hardware cause, so invoking the interrupt handler is a hardware, not software, activity. The following section will describe how the hardware of several popular machines responds to interrupts.

On the IBM 360-370 there are five basic interrupt causes: program (exceptional condition in a program, e.g., illegal operation or reference to a nonexistent memory location); supervisor (program requesting a service from the supervisor program); machine check (hardware malfunction detected in the machine); I/O (termination of an assigned I/O activity); and external (request for service from an external source, such as a timer, the operator, or a connected piece of equipment).

For each source there are 2 reserved words of memory. One of the reserved words must contain a PSW, which has the address of the interrupt handler routine; this word is called the *new PSW* for the interrupt source. The other word is called the *old PSW* for the interrupt. In the event of an interrupt, the current PSW is stored in the old PSW location, and the PSW register is loaded from the appropriate new PSW location. Since the PSW register is the program counter, loading a new PSW causes a branch to the address contained in the new PSW. This is done entirely by hardware, beyond the programmer's control.

For example, the external old PSW location is 24, and the external new PSW location is 88. The supervisory program provides an external interrupt handler routine and places the address of that routine in location 88. Suppose, during execution of your program, an external interrupt occurs, perhaps from the operator having pushed the STOP button on the console. As soon as the current instruction is completed, the computer hardware stores the current PSW at location 24, and the word at location 88 is put into the PSW register. This causes execution to transfer to the address at location 88, which will contain the address of the external interrupt handler.

The external interrupt handler will analyze the precise cause of the interrupt and take some action. After it has been completed, the external interrupt handler will return to the program that was in control when the interrupt occurred. (This is similar to returning from a called procedure.) The interrupt handler returns by loading the PSW register with the contents of the old PSW word. When the interrupt occurred, the current PSW was stored there, so this contains the address of the next instruction to be executed in the original program. The interrupt mechanism is shown in Figure 5.6.

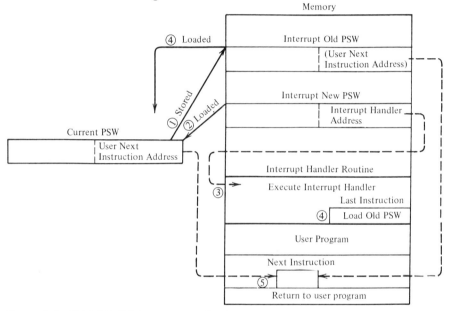

Figure 5.6 IBM 360-370 interrupt mechanism.

On the Intel 8080 there are eight levels of interrupts; the programmer can assign different levels to different sources. Each interrupt number is associated with one memory address, 16*n, where n is the interrupt number. When an interrupt occurs, the hardware sends the CPU an RST (restart) instruction, specifying the interrupt number. The CPU saves the current program counter in the stack and branches to location 16*n to begin the interrupt handling. After the interrupt handler has completed, it issues a RTI n (return from interrupt n) instruction. This causes the program counter to be restored as it was when the interrupt occurred.

This interrupt mechanism is more flexible than the IBM system, since different levels of interrupts can be assingned to different devices. Thus the user could assign different priorities to different devices and provide preferential service to certain ones.

This concludes the material on interrupts. The next chapter describes I/O service, where the motivation for interruptions will become more apparent. The interruption process is summarized now.

1. An interrupt is a means for a hardware device to break the normal flow of execution. (Interrupts can also be generated by software.) There may be a number of sources of interruptions, such as different I/O devices or external signals.
2. An interrupt is much like a subprogram call because a new instruction address must be forced into the program counter, and the return address (the point at which execution was in progress) must be saved for eventual return from the interrupt. This saving of the current program counter and branching to a new address is handled by the hardware.
3. Most computers have a set of predefined fixed memory addresses associated with interrupt service. In the event of an interrupt, these locations contain the addresses where interrupt service programs reside in memory.

5.5 TERMS USED

The following terms have been used in this chapter.

Instruction fetch-decode-execute cycle
Transfer of control
Short BRANCH instruction
Long BRANCH instruction
Subprocedure CALL
Subprocedure RETURN
Stack
Stack pointer register
Return address
Argument passing
Remote argument list
Interrupt
Interrupt handler

5.6 QUESTIONS

1. Trace the order of execution of the program earlier in this chapter assuming values 8 , 4 , and 12 for A , B , and C , respectively. That is, make a list of all instructions executed, in the order they were done, and show the values of register 5 and the PC after each instruction was executed.
2. Trace the order of execution of the program earlier in this chapter assuming values of 8 , 4 , and 8 for A , B , and C , respectively.
3. Why should the value of the program counter be updated *before* an instruction is executed? (*Hint:* What instructions change the value of the program counter as part of their execution? Would it make a difference if the program counter were updated *after* these instructions had been "performed?")
4. Why is it necessary to fetch operand values and hold them in an internal register before an instruction is executed? Consider an instruction such as

```
ADD  R5,R5
```

5. Examine the first instruction from the program using short branches earlier in this chapter:

    016705 000036   MOV A,R5

    01 is the operation code, 67 and 05 are the operand addresses. In the operand addresses, 6 and 0 are the addressing mode (see Section 4.4.2), and they represent autoincrement and direct, respectively. Register 7 is the program counter; it was 0 when this instruction was assembled. Explain how this instruction generated an operand address of 40 for the first operand. (This is not an easy question. Remember that the arithmetic is in octal.)

6. A stack is an important data structure in computing. Can you think of other instances where one activity is placed on a stack while a second is performed and the first is then removed from the stack when the second is done?

7. What addressing mode would you use if you wanted to implement a stack in machine language? Why?

8. In what instances would it be appropriate to pass arguments to a subprocedure using registers? In what instances would it be more appropriate to use an argument list or the stack for passing arguments?

9. Suppose procedure A calls procedure B and procedure B calls procedure C. Assume that register R5 is used for linking; that is, register R5 contains the address by which any called procedure returns to its calling procedure. What must procedure B do so that it can send a return address to C without losing the return address it needs to return to A? Indicate machine instructions by which B could do this.

10. Interrupts on most machines reference certain fixed memory addresses. For example, on the PDP-11, memory address $16*n$ contains a few instructions to execute in order to process interrupt n. Likewise, the five interrupts on an IBM 360-370 machine each have a pair of reserved locations that effectively branch to the interrupt handler. Why do these locations not contain the full interrupt handlers? That is, why do these locations only contain a couple of instructions, followed by a branch to the interrupt handler code itself? Why is it not a good idea to build the absolute addresses of the interrupt handlers themselves into the hardware?

chapter 6

I/O Devices and Operation

The first chapters of this book have described the internal structure of a computer system. In fact, they have concentrated strictly on the computational aspects, ignoring the process of transmitting data to the computer and receiving results. This chapter contains information on I/O activities. The chapter begins with a survey of I/O devices and data formats. You are probably already familiar with some of these devices, such as card readers, printers, and terminals. Storage devices such as tapes and disks are also described. The chapter concludes with information on how these devices are programmed and used in a computing system.

6.1 I/O DEVICES

In this section you will learn more about I/O devices. Some of the devices described here you have used before, so they will be familiar to you. Others may have been used as your programs were executed, but you may have been oblivious to their use. It will not be possible to present information on every type of I/O device available, but you will see some of the more popular ones.

6.1.1 Card Readers

Depending on the type of computing you have done, you may be familiar with card readers; regardless, you have certainly received the standard "computer punched card" with utility bills, questionnaires, and registration forms. This item, about 3 1/4 by 7 3/8 inches in size, has room for 80 columns of information, with 12 punches possible per column. A typical punched card is shown in Figure 6.1.

The cards are fed into a machine called a *card reader*. There the information

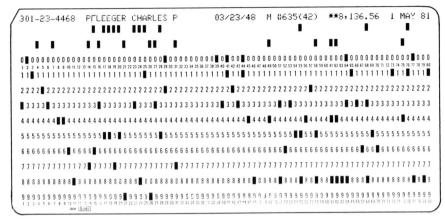

Figure 6.1 A punched card.

encoded in the punches of each column is sensed using a variety of sensing devices. One way is to use wire brushes that make electrical contact with a metal plate below the card wherever there is a hole. Another means is to use a series of lights that shine through the holes and can be sensed by photoelectric sensors on the opposite side. Typical card readers range in speed from 600 to 1200 or more cards per minute.

A punched card system is reasonably inexpensive, with cards costing less than 1 cent apiece. Cards are fairly sturdy and can withstand a little dust, a slight amount of bending, and a wide range of temperature and humidity conditions. Furthermore, card tabulating equipment can imprint the contents of a punched card on it, so that this I/O medium can be read by people as well as by computers. This is one of the original I/O media of computers, and it will probably not be replaced soon. A diagram of a common card reader is shown in Figure 6.2.

6.1.2 Printers

Another I/O device with which you may be familiar is the *printer.* These are heavily used in the computing industry, and there are many different types of printers.

One form of printer resembles a typewriter. Like a standard office typewriter, these printers have a mold of each character that strikes an inked ribbon against a paper, leaving an outline of the character printed on the paper. These print one character at a time. Because of the time required to position the print mechanism, strike it against the paper, and move to the next print position, these types of printers tend to be slow. Typical speeds are 10 to 50 characters per second.

A variation on the typewriterlike printer is the *dot matrix printer.* Probably the most widely available of these is the DECWriter manufactured by the Digital Equipment Corporation, although many other manufacturers make similar devices. These use an inked ribbon, but the mechanism striking the ribbon is a set of small needles. These needles are arranged in a rectangular grid, and each is individually controlled to force it forward and to withdraw it. Each needle makes a dot on the paper, and each character is composed of a unique combination of

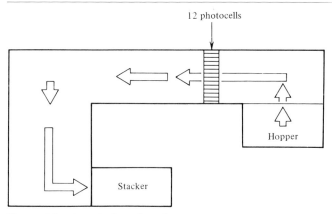

Figure 6.2 A typical card reader.

these dots. Because there is no rotation to position a unit to a particular character, dot matrix printers are somewhat faster than those just described. A typical speed for dot matrix printers is 125 characters per second. The formation of dot matrix characters is shown in Figure 6.3.

Another single-character printer has a small memory to "remember" two lines to be printed. After the first has been printed and the carriage is at the right end of the paper, most character printers send the carriage back to the left end to start printing the second line. Some printers instead start the second line at the right edge of the paper and print its characters in reverse, from right to left. This eliminates the wasted time during which the carriage simply returns to the left edge.

All of the printers described so far are low-speed printers, but they are suitable for a small computing system, such as a micro- or minicomputer. Their cost, from $500 up to several thousand dollars, makes them especially attractive to owners of small computer systems.

Another style of printer is called a *line printer* because it prints an entire line

```
XXX        XXXX        XXX            X          XXX
X   X      X    X      X     X       XX          X   X
X   X      X    X      X              X               X    XXX      X
XXXXX      XXXX        X              X              X              XXX
X   X      X    X      X              X             X     XXX       X
X   X      X    X      X     X        X            X
X   X      XXXX         XXX          XXX          XXXXX
```

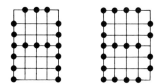

Figure 6.3 Dot matrix characters.

at a time. Two important kinds print by mechanical means: either a chain or a drum of characters striking against an inked ribbon. A faster, more expensive line printer "prints" an image by a photographic/electronic technique, similar to a photocopier. Line printers are substantially faster than single-character printers.

A *drum printer* has a cylinder with a mold of each character duplicated many times across its surface. There is one copy of each character for each print column on a line, and there is also one hammer for each print position of the line. Suppose that the character A is to be printed in position 1 of the current line. When the cylinder in position 1 is positioned with the A character directly opposite the paper, a hammer in back of the paper moves the paper against the ribbon which, in turn, hits the printing cylinder. This prints the letter A in position 1. Since there is a hammer for each print position, each hammer fires when the character for that position is directly opposite. If the whole line consists of the same character (e.g., a line of dashes), all the hammers will act at once. The characters of the line may be printed out of sequence, depending on when each character appears in the position in which it is to be printed. After all the characters desired on a line have been printed, the paper advances one line, and the next line is printed in the same way.

These printers are substantially faster than single-character printers, offering print speeds up to 1200 lines per minute or more. However, they require much more logic circuitry (to decide when to fire each hammer), and the timing requirements on these machines are more stringent. Therefore they cost much more than single-character printers. A diagram of a drum printer is shown in Figure 6.4.

Another faster form of line printer is the *train* or *chain printer*. On this printer

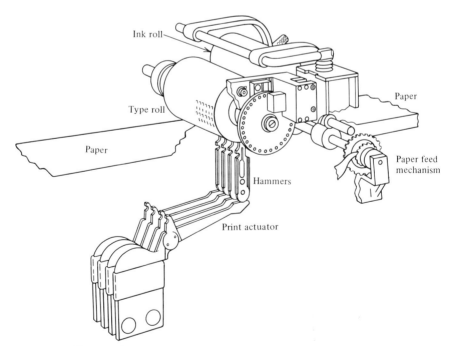

Figure 6.4   Drum printer.

a continuous loop chain, similar to a bicycle chain, has the image of each character molded on it. The chain revolves in front of an inked ribbon, which is in front
of the paper. As the chain moves and a character is in front of a print position in
which it is desired, a hammer strikes the character against the ribbon, which
contacts the paper. This causes an image of the character to be transferred to the
paper. As with drum printers, the characters of one line may be printed whenever
they are in the right position, so a line may not be printed directly left to right.
The paper advances on this model whenever the full line has been printed. Typical
speeds of these printers range up to 3000 lines per minute.

An advantage of a chain printer over a drum printer is that the chain is
removable. It is possible to replace one chain with another having a different set of
characters. Although these printer trains would not be changed on a line-by-line
basis, they might be changed for different jobs. A print train can be made with
more than one copy of a particular character on it. If, for example, the character
E is used more often than the character Q, it might be desirable to put two Es and
one Q on the train. This will halve the time for the E to revolve around to a print
position where it is desired. A print train can be made containing only digits, a
decimal point, and perhaps plus, minus, comma, and dollar sign. For printing
strictly numeric information, this train would give extremely good performance.

Figure 6.5 is a diagram of typical train printers.

6.1.3 Terminals

A final form of I/O device is used both for input and output; this is the *terminal*
or *cathode ray tube* (CRT). This device is similar to the combination of a typewriter and a television screen. There is a keyboard on which to type data to be
submitted to the computer. The keyboard has a standard typewriter layout, with

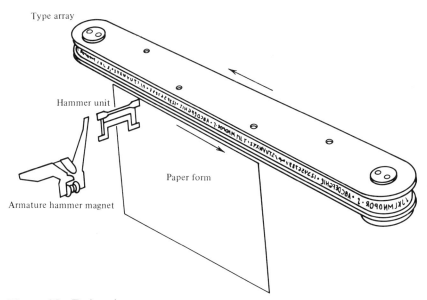

Figure 6.5 Train printer.

perhaps some additional control keys. The screen displays characters, either echoed from keys pressed on the keyboard or from signals generated by the computer. The screen is usually about 6 inches by 9 inches in size. Most screens can display 24 lines of 80 characters each.

Some terminals generate, receive, and display only uppercase letters and digits, while others may use uppercase and lowercase letters; some also generate extra graphical symbols. Most terminals generate the characters on the screen by a dot matrix method, like that for a dot matrix printer, often in a 7-by-9 or 9-by-11 grid. In the *graphics mode* some terminals can also plot individual points on the screen, showing a line as a connected series of closely spaced dots. There are even color CRTs that generate output in a number of colors.

Display terminals have no moving parts in the display portion, so they are both more reliable and faster than mechanical printers. Because they can display approximately 24 lines, they are convenient for programming applications, where it is seldom necessary to refer back to output produced more than 20 lines prior to the present line. These terminals are also especially convenient for program development or data entry, where a printed copy is not needed until the computing session is concluded.

Depending on the features they provide, computer terminals cost between $700 and $3000. These terminals usually communicate with a computer over telephone lines or over direct lines. Over telephone lines, terminals usually communicate at speeds up to 300 bits per second, while terminals wired directly to computers can achieve speeds up to 19,600 bits per second.

6.2 STORAGE DEVICES

The devices described so far have all been I/O devices that communicate information between humans and computers. The section that follows contains information on I/O devices used for long- or short-term storage of information. These devices nearly all use magnetic recording of information on an iron-oxide material. There are some interesting differences in the speed and capacity of these devices, however. The two basic types of magnetic storage devices are sequential and direct or random access devices.

Sequential devices are designed for retrieving the information in exactly the same order in which it was recorded. For example, you may want to use a sequential device for retaining a copy of a program. Computer memory is too small to permit retaining in memory versions of all programs developed, so it is common to back up programs on a storage device in order to be able to retrieve and execute these programs later. A sequential device is appropriate because you will record the program statements in order and read them from the device in the same order.

By contrast, a library may retain a copy of its card catalog on a computer storage device. To find books about xylophones, you would not want to start at the beginning of the device and search serially through entries about aardvarks, castles, foghorns, lampreys, the National Archives, robots, and the planet Venus. You can access the pieces of information on a direct access device in any order, regardless of the order in which they were recorded. This chapter contains descriptions of both sequential and direct access devices.

6.2.1 Sequential Devices

There are two types of sequential devices in general use: cassette and reel-to-reel tape recorders. Both use a ribbon of magnetic recording tape very much like that used for home audio recordings. Cassette recorders are exactly the same recorders used for amateur audio enthusiasts. They are relatively inexpensive (under $50), which makes them especially popular with users of small microcomputer systems. These devices are slow, but their speed is tolerable for small amounts of information or for infrequent accesses. For example, a program stored on tape may take 1 minute to read but may then execute for 30 minutes or more.

Reel-to-reel recorders are used for major computing systems. This type of tape drive is also known as a seven- or nine-track tape drive, in reference to the manner in which data are stored on the device. Data are recorded in seven or nine parallel stripes (which are invisible) running the full length of the tape. There are different recording methods, but all employ a signal that is either high or low; high often indicates 1 while low may indicate 0. If there are nine tracks of such signals, 9 bits of information can be recorded across the width of the tape.

The density at which data can be recorded ranges from 200 to 6250 bits per inch. (This figure is measured as how closely bits are packed along any one track; since a nine-track tape has nine tracks across the width of the tape, there will actually be 9*200 to 9*6250 bits per 1-inch segment of tape.) The most common densities are 800 or 1600 and even 6250 bits per inch (bpi). Figure 6.6 shows how bits are recorded across the surface of a tape.

Characters, words, or bytes of information are normally recorded across the width of a tape, so that 9 bits can be recorded as one character or one unit across the tape. Stray signals may alter the data recorded on a tape, so extra checking information is often recorded to help detect cases where the original data has been disturbed. One checking signal is called *parity*.

There are two types of parity: *odd parity* and *even parity*. With each group of

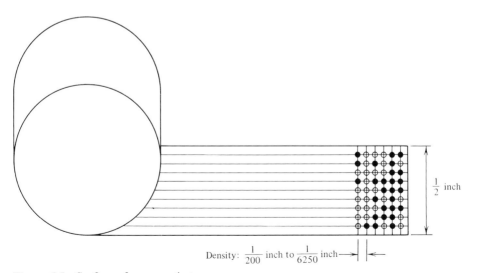

Figure 6.6 Surface of a magnetic tape.

bits, an additional bit of information is recorded to show whether there were an even or odd number of 1 bits in the recorded data. With odd parity, this extra bit is 1 if the number of 1 bits in the original data was even, and the extra bit is 0 if the number of 1 bits in the original data was odd. Another way of looking at this is to look at the original bits plus the parity bit as a unit: in odd parity the parity bit is selected so that there will be an odd number of 1 bits in the unit. (An even number of 1 bits in the original data plus a 1 in the parity bit makes an odd number of 1 bits in the group.) Even parity is defined analogously, with the parity bit making an even number of 1 bits in the unit. A number of binary values and their odd parity bits are shown next.

Binary number	Odd Parity Bit
01100110	1
11111111	1
01000110	0
00000001	0
00000000	1

Parity is used on magnetic tape devices. Each time a group of bits is recorded, the parity bit is computed and recorded. When the data is brought back into memory, a new parity bit is computed for the data bits read. If the new parity bit does not match the one recorded on the tape, it is known that an error occurred during the transmission of this data.

Parity cannot detect all possible errors; for example, it will not detect errors where two bits both change from 0s to 1s; however, the most frequent error is a single-bit error, and parity can detect all of these. Parity is easy to compute, and it does not take excessive space; even using one track out of nine reduces the total capacity of a tape by only 11%. Using one parity track and eight information tracks allows 8-bit quantities of information to be recorded across the width of a tape. Thus a nine-track tape usually contains one 8-bit character or byte of information per horizontal "slice." If memory words are 16 or 32 bits long, they are recorded as two or four successive 8-bit characters on a tape.

Magnetic tape drives achieve very high speeds for transfer of information between the tape and computer memory; transmission rates over 300,000 characters per second are not uncommon. These speeds can be achieved only if the tape is moving fast. A tape cannot instantaneously move to a fast speed; there must be a period of time for acceleration (and for deceleration, when the tape stops). During the acceleration time, data cannot be read, since recording densities of 200 or more bits per inch are possible only when the tape unit is moving at the same speed when playing back (reading) as when recording. This speed synchronization is not possible until the tape is moving at its full running speed. Thus, at any point where the tape unit will need to stop and later start, there is an unrecorded portion of tape called a *tape gap.* A tape gap allows the tape to slow to a halt and then return to full speed.

The amount of data between two gaps is called a *physical record.* A physical record is the smallest amount of information that may be read or written in one read or write operation. Each physical record is surrounded by gaps, so that there is time for the tape mechanism to start and stop.

A tape is divided into individual blocks called *files* or *data sets*. Each file is a related series of physical records. For example, if a tape contains copies of the statements of several programs, each program would be a file, and the individual statements would be separate records in the files. Data for computation can also be retained on a storage device. Thus a file may be either a program or a group of data items. The notion of a file is a logical distinction: programs vary in size, and each file on a storage device may be of a different size. On some devices special symbols are recorded between files to separate one from another; these symbols are called *end-of-file marks,* or simply EOF marks. A picture of a tape with records, gaps, and files is shown in Figure 6.7.

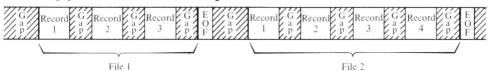

Figure 6.7 Magnetic tape with multiple files.

A gap is from 0.60 to 0.75 inch on a tape, depending on the recording density. On a nine-track tape, assuming a density of 800 bits per inch and a gap of 0.6 inch, if records are 80 8-bit characters each (such as the image of a punched card, with its 80 columns encoded as 80 characters), each record will take 0.1 inch (80 characters * 1/800 inch per character). If each record is 0.1 inch long and each gap is 0.6 inch long, only 1/7 of the tape is used for recorded information; the remaining 86% of the tape surface contains only gaps—effectively useless space. If, however, 20 card images are written as a single physical record, each physical record is 2.0 inches (20 * 80 characters * 1/800 inch per character), and the gaps take up only 0.6/(2.0 + 0.6) part of the tape, or 23%; 77% of the tape is used for data. The process of recording many pieces of information in a single physical record in order to increase the utilization of the tape is called *blocking.*

Each piece of information to the programmer forms one *logical record,* or what the programmer thinks of as one record. However, multiple logical records are combined into one physical record or one *block* to expand the size of a unit recorded. One apparent key to efficient use of a tape surface is to increase the blocking factor, that is, write more logical records per physical record.

There is a flaw to this reasoning, however. Whenever data is read from the tape, one entire physical block is read, and it is placed in memory. Then the desired logical record is found within the physical record, and the data from this logical record is used. Since each I/O operation on the device accesses one physical record, enough space must be reserved in memory to hold one physical record. Thus it would be possible to increase the size of a physical record until it was greater than the size of available main memory. The same is true for output: there must be a space in main memory large enough to assemble different logical records prior to writing them as one physical record. The main memory space for assembling or separating logical records is called a *buffer.* There is thus a tradeoff between increasing physical record size but needing to increase the space in memory allocated to buffers. No magic formula dictates how large to make a physical record; the primary guideline is simply to make it as large as can easily be accommodated.

There are two different kinds of records on magnetic tape devices: fixed-length and variable-length records. In fixed-length records, each record is of the same size. For example, you may be recording images of data cards, or identical output lines from some program. In both cases all logical records will be exactly the same size (number of characters) long. Therefore, if logical records are blocked at a rate of five logical records per physical record and if each logical record is 100 characters long, the physical record will be 500 characters long and the logical records will begin with the first, the one hundred and first, the two hundred and first, the three hundred and first, and the four hundred and first characters. Clearly, if all records are the same size, by simple multiplication it is possible to locate any logical record within a physical record. The records described are shown in Figure 6.8.

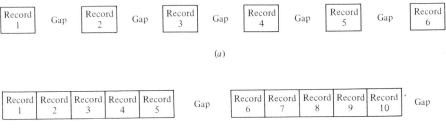

(a)

(b)

Figure 6.8 Multiple logical records per physical record. (a) Individual records. (b) Blocked records.

There are two methods by which records can be made of fixed length. Either the programmer can be required to write records of only the one size, or the programmer can be allowed to write any length records, with the computer padding (extending) or truncating (chopping off) any wrong-length records to make all records the same size. Figure 6.9 shows fixed-length records.

Variable-length records are records that may not all be the same size. For example, reports from sales representatives may be recorded on a storage device. The reports may have a narrative section in which the sales representative writes a description of the nature of the latest interaction with the client. While some sales representatives may respond in just a few words, others may take several sentences or even a few paragraphs. It is wasteful of storage space to extend the short responses to a length that will suffice for the most long-winded sales agent. The solution is a variable-length record, where only as much storage space is used as is needed for a given response.

An I/O device and a program both need to know where a variable-length record ends. This can be done by a special terminator character to mark the end of the record or by a length indicator preceding the record to tell how long the record is. These two approaches are shown in Figure 6.10.

Regardless of which approach is used, it is possible to find the second logical record within a physical record by (1) locating the end-of-record character at the end of the first logical record (if a terminator character is used), or (2) skipping

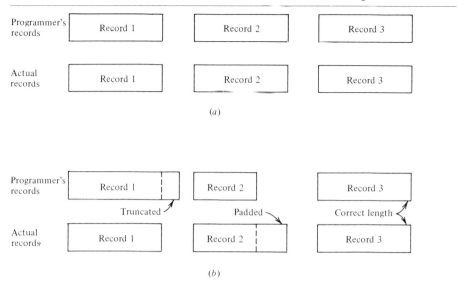

Figure 6.9 Fixed-length records. (*a*) Programmer's records all of the correct size. (*b*) Programmer's records padded and truncated.

over the number of characters indicated in the length field for the first record (if each record is preceded by a count of its number of characters). The third record is found by skipping past the first and then skipping past the second logical record. It should be obvious that the end-of-record terminator must be a special character that cannot be recorded as a symbol within a logical record. Similarly, it should be clear that the count field (which tells the length of each logical record) must be accurate.

Both fixed- and variable-length records can be recorded on magnetic tape. These records are recorded in blocks, which may consist of one or more than one logical record, as shown in Figure 6.11 on the next page.

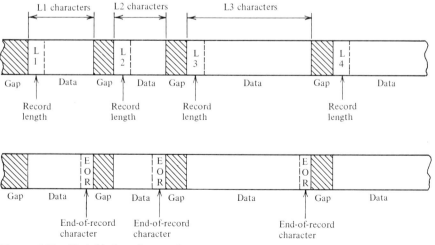

Figure 6.10 Variable-length records.

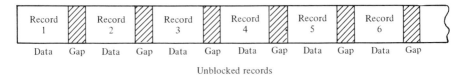

Unblocked records

Blocked records

Figure 6.11   Records on a Magnetic Tape.

Magnetic tape is very convenient for long-term backup or *archival* storage. For example, many businesses need to keep accounting records for long periods of time; furthermore, they must be able to reconstruct data that may be lost or damaged. For this reason, they maintain weekly, monthly, or quarterly logs of transactions, so that if the data for September 1981 become inaccessible, they can begin at August 1981 and reconstruct the September data and then check the reconstruction against the October figures. Seldom is it necessary to go to one of these ancient backups, but they must nevertheless be kept. Such backup versions are frequently kept on magnetic tape, since it is reasonably inexpensive (approximately $15 per reel), and one reel can hold up to 200 million characters of information. Because of the sequential nature of tape, however, its application as a storage medium is limited.

6.2.2 Direct Access Devices

One last kind of storage device is the magnetic disk. This type of device is called a *direct access device,* in contrast to tapes and other devices [which permit only sequential access to their data; i.e., in order to access data item number *n,* it is necessary to access all (*n*-1) preceding data items]. Direct access devices permit access to data in any order; that is, it is possible to read or write record 27, followed by record 104, followed by record 5, without counting through records 28, 29, 30, . . . 102, 103, and then backward from 104 to 5. There are two varieties of disks: *floppy disks* and *hard disks.* Both operate under similar principles; the similarities will be described first.

A disk is a circular platter of material on which magnetic information can be recorded. The disk resembles a phonograph record, although it does not have the actual grooves that a record does. A recording arm is positioned over the surface of the disk; the arm has one or more recording heads that can read or write data on the disk surface. Although the disk does not have grooves, imagine invisible concentric circles on the surface of the disk. Each of these circles is called a *track.* Each track may contain one or more records, depending on the capacity of the track (i.e., the circumference of the disk) and the sizes of the records. Figure 6.12 shows the arrangement of tracks and recording heads on a typical disk.

A disk is mounted in a disk drive and continually revolves at a constant speed,

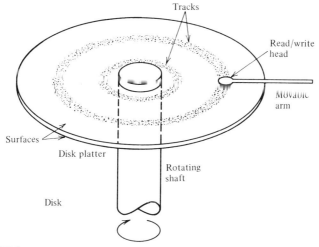

Figure 6.12 Disk.

like a phonograph record. Information is recorded or read as it passes under the read/write head.

On most disk units the read/write head is located on the end of an access arm. The arm can move in or out across the surface of the disk, accessing any track. On other units there is an individual read/write head for each track on the disk.

There are two delays associated with reading or writing information on a disk: seek or access time, and rotational delay. *Seek time* is the time needed to move the read/write head over the proper track. *Rotational delay* is the time needed for a disk platter to rotate until a desired piece of data is directly under a read/write head. For disk drives with one head for each track there is effectively no seek time, since no movement takes place to locate the proper track. On all disks, however, it takes an amount of time for a data item to revolve to the read/write position. Disk units achieve transfer rates of up to 3 million characters per second, while the delays due to access or rotational delay are on the order of a few thousandths of a second.

Some models of disks use multiple platters stacked one above another, with space for an access arm between. In these models the disk platters are an inseparable unit, called a *disk pack*. All read/write heads on these units move in parallel, so that at any given time all heads will be scanning the same relative track on all disk surfaces. There are thus a number of tracks that can be accessed in succession without any head movement. The set of all tracks in the same relative position of a pack is called a *cylinder*. Such a disk pack can hold up to 500 million characters. Both variable- and fixed-length records may be recorded on disks, although some computer systems may permit only one type. A disk pack and its read/write access arms are shown in Figure 6.13.

In some units single disk platters or disk packs are removable from the disk drive, so that a large amount of information can be stored *offline*. (Offline means not directly accessible. Papers filed in a filing cabinet are offline, compared to papers face up on an orderly desk; the papers in the filing cabinet are not immediately accessible, while the data on a desk surface is accessible to the casual

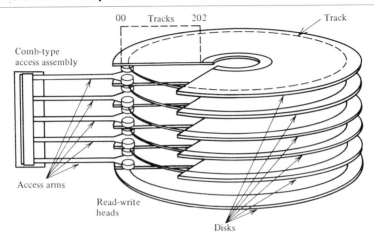

Figure 6.13 Disk pack.

glance.) In other disk units manufacturing and operating tolerances are so critical that it is not possible to allow people to remove and insert the disks in the disk unit. Nonremovable disks usually have a greater density of data than removable disks.

Hard disks, which are the original type of disks, are as just described. They are rigid (as opposed to flexible) and are often encased in a plastic canister to protect the surfaces. They range from 5 to 14 inches in diameter, grouped in packs of 1 to 11 platters. Rotational speeds, capacities, and approximate costs for a number of disk drives are shown in the following table.

Platter size (inches)	5	8	14
Number of platters	1 to 2	1 to 6	1 to 11
Average access time (milliseconds)	170	25 to 70	30 to 70
Average rotational delay (milliseconds)	8.3	8 to 10	12.5
Capacity (million bytes)	6.3	5 to 60	15 to 500
Approximate cost from	$1000 up	$1500 up	$4000 up

Floppy disks are more frequently used with mini- and microcomputers. These disks range from 5 to 8 inches in diameter. They are thin and flexible (hence the name floppy disks). They are kept inside a cardboard jacket to protect the recording surface, although they can be taken out and exposed to the open air with no major damage. Costing roughly $5 each, they are an inexpensive direct access medium for the home computer user.

Holes punched through the disk are used for timing. On some disks positioning information is obtained by (photoelectric or mechanical) sensing of a punch that marks the "beginning of a track."

In contrast with rigid disks, floppy disks have a much lower capacity. For example, a typical 5-inch rigid disk holds 6.3 million characters, while a 5-inch floppy disk may hold as few as 100,000 characters and up to a maximum of 1 million characters. Access time for floppy disks ranges between 0.1 and 1.0 seconds, while access time on a rigid disk is between 0.025 to 0.070 seconds. There are two major advantages of floppy disks over rigid disks for certain applications, however. First, floppy disk drives are generally much less expensive than rigid disk drives, putting them more confortably in the range tolerable by hobbyist computer users. The price of a single floppy disk platter, usually in the $5 to $10 range, is also not prohibitive. Second, floppy disk platters are removable from the drive. Thus, although one platter holds much less information than a similar-sized rigid disk, it is possible to change platters and store large quantities of information on several platters. Thus a user willing to trade speed and high capacity for lower cost and manually changing disk platters in the drive will find floppy disks a useful I/O device.

Direct access storage is convenient for data that must be accessed frequently because the access time for these devices is typically small. Libraries of programs are frequently kept on direct access devices so that a program can be found and readied for execution in a short time.

6.3 I/O CONTROL

The discussion in the last chapter on interrupts was necessary to present the following information on I/O. There are a variety of forms of I/O activity, and more than one form may be used on a given machine for different devices. The access point from a computer to an I/O device is called a *port*. You may think of a port as a collection of circuits to accept I/O commands, transfer data, and synchronize the transfer of the data with the speed of the CPU.

I/O occurs at a speed unrelated to the speed of the CPU. For example, you may request a character of data from a terminal keyboard. The person typing the character operates much more slowly than a CPU. Thus, in the time it takes one person to type a character, 1 million or more instructions could be executed. For this reason it is necessary to identify the desired I/O device, request a piece of data, pause for the data transfer to occur, and check to see that the requested item has been supplied before proceeding.

6.3.1 Nonprogrammable I/O

The simplest form of I/O is called *nonprogrammable, memory-mapped I/O*. This is a type of I/O in which each device is associated with a set of fixed addresses. These addresses are used exactly as main memory addresses are, except that these addresses are not a part of main memory. One address associated with a device is a status location; different bits in this memory location show whether the device is working, or if it has completed its data transfer, for example. Each device also has a location for data. If you want to write a piece of data to such a device, you first test the status location for the device to see if it is free. If it is, you place the data to be written in the data location for the device, and the data placed is transferred to the device. The status becomes busy, and it becomes free again when the device has completed the I/O transfer. Input is handled analogously.

With this form of I/O each device performs only one standard operation for all requests. Devices with both an input and an output capability, such as keyboard terminals, are treated as two separate devices; one the keyboard and the other the display screen. This way, the only operation performed to the keyboard is input, and the only operation performed to the display screen is output.

6.3.2 Programmable I/O

A more involved means of I/O is *programmable I/O.* In this form the device receives 1 or more control words to indicate what operation(s) to perform. In fact, these control words can be thought of as a program for the I/O device to execute. The commands may indicate how many characters of data to transfer, to/from which memory locations to transfer it, what operation to perform (read or write), and what additional "control" operations to perform (e.g., advance the paper in a printer, move the read/write head in a disk, or select the next card in a card reader). The commands are written in a machine language appropriate for the I/O device. The device interprets the commands and transfers the requested data.

Another important notion related to I/O is the notion of a bus. A *bus* may be thought of as a path for data transfer between two devices. The bus must also have a control mechanism in order to limit uses of the bus to one at a time. Data is sent between memory and I/O devices by means of a bus.

Many computers, particularly mini- and microcomputers, are oriented around a single bus. The PDP-11 is the epitome of this structure; each device, as well as memory and the CPU, is connected to one bus, which the manufacturer calls a *UNIBUS.* This form of system organization is shown in Figure 6.14.

With this structure, the CPU competes with I/O devices for the use of memory. The CPU normally has use of memory, since the number of CPU accesses to memory is larger than the number of accesses by I/O devices. However, an I/O device can have priority over the CPU for use of the bus. If the device has only one piece of information to transfer to/from memory, it simply takes control of memory for one memory cycle, transfers the data, and leaves memory to the CPU again. This form of memory access by an I/O device is called *cycle stealing,* since one memory cycle is preempted from the CPU.

However, the device may be a high-speed device, having a number of characters of information to transfer to/from memory. In this case the device can halt the CPU for enough time to transfer all the data. This form of data transfer is called *CPU lockout,* since the CPU is locked out of memory for a period of time.

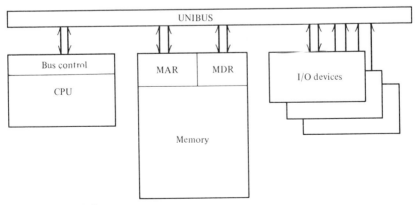

Figure 6.14   Unibus structure.

6.3.3 Channels

Larger computers have channels to perform I/O activity. A *channel* may be thought of as a simple computer to perform the I/O commands. A channel has the ability to sequence through a series of instructions, monitor the status of the I/O device, count the amount of data being transferred, and report status back to the CPU. The channel is the interface between an I/O device and a computer.

A channel may have one or more devices attached and active at one time. One type of channel is called a *multiplexor channel,* which is usually used for slow-speed devices (such as card readers and printers). Such a channel polls each device, taking one character from each ready device at a time. It then transfers the characters to memory. The multiplexor channel sustains I/O operations on a number of different I/O devices at once.

In contrast, the *selector channel* handles a channel program for only one device at a time. It is used primarily for higher-speed devices. Data is transferred in a burst by one of these channels.

A third type of channel is called a *block multiplexor channel,* which is connected with very high-speed devices such as disks. It is able to sustain operations on more than one device at a time, although data transfer occurs on only one device at a time. The other devices may be occupied in some mechanical task, such as positioning the access mechanism.

6.3.4 I/O Interrupts

After an I/O operation has been initiated, the CPU is free to continue other computation. The user can either enter into a loop, testing for I/O completion, or can continue with other computation, occasionally checking back to see if the I/O is finished. A more reasonable model is for the CPU to be left free to handle other computing without having to check the I/O status. With an interrupt mechanism, the I/O device will generate an I/O interruption when the I/O operation is complete.

6.4 SUMMARY

1. I/O devices may be divided into those for human interaction with the computer and those for short- or long-term storage of information. They differ because media for human interaction usually have the data represented in a visible form, as well as perhaps punched holes or some other means for machine sensing. Data is generally packed much less densely on media for humans, and devices that process these media are typically much slower.

2. The most popular media for human interaction are punched cards, printed paper, and CRT terminals. The first two are convenient for use away from the computer site, while the latter is appropriate where a hard copy is not needed, such as during program development or data entry.

3. Records on magnetic media may be stored in blocked or unblocked format, as fixed- or variable-length records. Between two successive (physical) records there is a gap to permit starting or stopping the device or for other functions related to reading or writing the data.
4. Magnetic tape is a sequential storage medium, with an access time longer than that of the disk. The best applications for it are ones where data is being stored for a period of time or as a backup.
5. Magnetic disks are direct or random access devices. Records recorded may be retrieved in any order, including sequentially. Magnetic disks contain one or more platters, with each platter having a number of concentric tracks of recorded data. An access mechanism moves to the proper track, and a read/write head senses the recorded information. Platters vary between 5 and 14 inches in diameter.
6. Rigid magnetic disks are high-density devices of reasonably high capacity and transfer rate; they are also of fairly high cost.
7. Floppy disks have substantially smaller capacity and longer access time than rigid disks, but they are also lower in cost.
8. With nonprogrammable I/O, the user must separately execute each I/O command to be performed. With programmable I/O the user submits a series of commands to a channel, and the channel communicates with the I/O device, passing the commands to the device one at a time. When the device is finished, it generates an I/O interruption to signal completion of I/O activity to the CPU.

6.5 TERMS USED

The following terms have been used in this chapter.

Punched card reader
Printer
Dot matrix printer
Line printer
Drum printer
Train or chain printer
Terminal
Cathode ray tube (CRT)
Storage device
Sequential device
Tape recorder
Cassette tape recorder
Reel-to-reel tape recorder
Seven- or nine-track tape drive
Parity
Tape gap
Physical record
Recording density
Blocking

Logical record
File
Data set
Buffer
Fixed-length record
Variable-length record
Magnetic disk
Direct access device
Floppy disk
Hard (rigid) disk
Track
Read/write head
Access arm
Seek time
Access time
Rotational delay
Disk pack
Cylinder
Offline storage
Removable disk
Port
I/O port
Data transfer synchronization
Bus
Nonprogrammable I/O
Memory-mapped I/O
Programmable I/O
UNIBUS
Cycle stealing
CPU lockout
Channel
Multiplexor channel
Selector channel
Block multiplexor channel
I/O interrupt

6.6 QUESTIONS

1. What I/O devices are available on the computer(s) to which you have access? What are their characteristics (speed and capacity)?

2. A punched card contains 80 columns, and each column has 12 positions where a hole may be punched. How many different characters can be encoded in the 12 punches of any one column? (*Hint:* Think of the 12 punches as binary digits: a 0 represents "no hole" and a 1 represents "hole." This question is then equivalent to asking how many different binary numbers can be represented in 12 bits.)

3. A limiting factor on card reader speed is that each card must move over

some sensing medium, such as lights or electrical contact brushes, for the card reader to sense the values punched on the card. Can you think of a different card reading mechanism that does not require card movement? (If you can, quickly patent your idea, and then talk with a computer peripheral manufacturer about marketing your idea.)

4. In Section 6.1.2 you read about train printers, where the print train contains different numbers of each character to be printed, for example, two Es, one Q, three As, and so forth. For any programming language you may know, such as PL/I, PASCAL, or FORTRAN, list all the symbols that may appear in a program written in that language (these are the symbols that would have to be available to print a source listing of such a program). Assuming there are 256 positions for a character on the print train, what would be a good distribution of characters on the print train: how many As, how many Bs, and the like?

5. Assuming 1600 bits per inch on a nine-track magnetic tape, assuming records are blocked at 3200 characters per block, with a logical record of 80 characters, and assuming a gap of 6/10 inch, how many records can be recorded on a standard 2400-foot magnetic tape?

6. What is the odd parity character associated with each of the following bytes?
    (a) 01110011
    (b) 11111110
    (c) 01010101

7. Show how a 10-byte record containing the characters WONDERFUL ! would be represented as:
    (a) A fixed-length record.
    (b) A variable-length record with a length field.
    (c) A variable-length record with an end-of-record mark.

8. Explain the differences among a *file,* a *physical record* (or *block*), and a *logical record.*

9. Since tracks are concentric circles, the tracks closer to the center of a disk will be "shorter" (have a smaller circumference) than tracks closer to the edge of the disk. In spite of this, most disks record the same quantity of data on the inner tracks as on the outer tracks. Can you think of any reasons for this practice?

10. In what kinds of computing situations is nonprogrammable I/O more appropriate? When is a channel that can execute a program of I/O commands more appropriate?

part 2
Supporting Software

chapter 7

Software Support for Execution

This chapter introduces programming aids necessary to execute a program. There are brief descriptions of supervisory programs, as well as text editors, assemblers, compilers, linkers, and loaders. Assemblers, compilers, linkers, and loaders will be examined fully in Chapters 8, 9, and 10, and the supervisor will be discussed in Chapter 11. This chapter concludes with a short description of the steps involved in producing a program, from its initial preparation to its execution.

7.1 SUPERVISORY PROGRAM

A *supervisor* is a piece of software that controls use of all facilities of a computing system. It may also be called a monitor, an operating system, or an executive. In small systems the user has exclusive use of a machine and all its resources. Thus there is no need to enforce sharing. However, on large machines, there may be many users who want to share the facilities of the computing system; they also need a means for scheduling and distributing the use of the resources among users. The supervisor attempts to distribute resources equitably among requesting users. The supervisor usually includes a number of utility programs, such as programs to assist in entering programs, performing I/O, and using the facilities of the computing system efficiently.

On small machines the supervisor is known as a *monitor* or an *executive system;* on larger machines it is called an *operating system.* The term *monitor* conveys the notion that this support system is in the background, ready to provide services on request, but it enters execution of a user program only on the user's demand. An *operating system* actually controls execution of each user's program, at times intervening in this execution (e.g., to redistribute ownership of computer resources among the users).

The most popular supervisory program for Intel 8080-based machines is *CP/M*. This supervisor provides support to use a terminal as a standard I/O device. CP/M also provides a file structure, so that (with a file medium such as a floppy disk) a user can create a library of programs and data and access them simply by name.

Most operating systems are called *multiprogramming systems*. Multiprogramming is a technique in which there may be a number of programs ready for execution at any one time, and these programs all compete for the computer system's resources: the CPU, memory, and I/O devices. For example, at one time there may be several different programs in different parts of memory, all waiting to use the CPU. Users may voluntarily relinquish use of the CPU when they need to wait for some I/O activity to be performed. The operating system may also suspend execution of one program and allocate the CPU to another user in order to promote more equitable use of resources.

There are three primary operating systems provided for the PDP-11 by the manufacturer; these are *RT-11, RSTS,* and *RSX-11.*[1] These systems differ in the number of users they support and the kinds of services they provide to each user. RT-11, for example, allows either one or two jobs to execute concurrently, one job receiving preference for computer services and the other receiving computer services only when the first is not using these services. This mode of processing is known as *foreground/background processing.* RSTS is a *timesharing system.* A timesharing system has a number of users, frequently interacting with the computer by means of terminals, so that the time one user spends thinking or typing is overlapped with computation for another user. In this way many users can believe that they each are in exclusive dialog with the computing system. RSX is a *general-purpose system* designed to support a number of users with different computing needs. UNIX is another operating system for the PDP-11.[2] This system was created by Bell Laboratories. UNIX is basically a time-sharing system, but it allows a great deal of communication and sharing among users of the system. It provides a flexible file system and a large number of language processors and support programs.

The IBM 360-370 machines run a variety of support systems, such as OS-MVT, OS/VS1, and VM/370. They are designed to support a number of concurrent users. It is possible for each computing facility to tailor the support system to individual needs, deleting unused features, and thereby reducing the size and execution time of the support package.

Remember these points about supervisory programs.

1. Most computer users—even users of small systems—use some form of supervisory program to assist in program preparation and execution. Supervisors are called by names such as *monitors, executives,* or *operating systems.*
2. A monitor or executive is a support system that is available on demand by a program to support use of various components of the computing system.
3. An operating system helps a program to use the devices and facilities of

---

[1] RT-11, RSTS, and RSX-11 are registered trademarks of the Digital Equipment Corporation.
[2] UNIX is a registered trademark of Bell Laboratories, Inc.

a computing system. It also oversees execution of programs and reallocates resources in order to improve the use of all system facilities.

7.2 TEXT EDITORS

The first step in running a program is to produce a copy of the program in some form acceptable to the computer. Sometimes this is done on punched cards using a keypunch. At other times, it is done by direct interface with the computer through a display terminal. A *text editor* accepts data from a terminal, permits corrections and modifications to this data, and arranges for the data to be filed for later access.

You may begin dialog with a computer by invoking a text editor. This is true for time-sharing systems, where you provide input directly to the computer by means of a keyboard terminal. You specify the name of a file you either wish to create or modify. The text editor searches the computer file system, locates a copy of the file (if it exists), and awaits further commands.

For new files, you have no option but to begin to enter the file. For old files, you have the option of adding more data to the file, inserting data in the middle of the file, deleting a part of the file, or changing part of the file. After making the changes you wish, you stop the editor, and the editor saves your newly modified file in the computer file system.

A text editor can be either a line editor, a cursor editor, or a screen editor. To a *line editor,* a file is simply a series of lines, much like the lines on a printed page. You can insert, delete, or replace one or more lines, and you can make changes to a single line at a time. Each line is a separate unit. A *cursor editor* (also called a *context editor*) operates on a file as a series of consecutive characters, not individual lines. The cursor (a position in the file) begins at the first character in the file. There are commands by which the cursor can be moved forward or backward some number of characters. Ends of lines are not important to a cursor editor; a command to replace 10 characters, when the cursor is positioned 5 characters from the end of a line, will replace the last 5 characters, the end-of-line character (which is also a character), and 4 characters from the next line. To a *screen editor,* a file is a series of *pages,* each page being just as much material as will fit onto the screen of the display terminal. The cursor starts at the top left corner of the screen; by commands, the cursor can be moved up, down, right, or left. You can insert or delete characters or full lines at the point where the cursor is positioned. There are also commands to change the screen contents to a previous page or to a later page. A screenful of characters remains on the screen until a new page is called for.

Text editors are part of the group of utility programs provided with a monitor or operating system. It does not matter which editor is used; they all perform the same task. Some people prefer one style of editor to another, however. Text editors are used to prepare files of data as well as source programs.

7.3 ASSEMBLERS

An assembler is a program that accepts a program written in assembler language as its input. It produces as output the machine language equivalent (called the object code) of that program. It also prepares a source listing and other pieces of information. The internal design of assemblers will be studied in Chapter 8.

7.4 COMPILERS

A compiler is a program that operates similarly to an assembler. A compiler accepts a program as input and produces the machine language (object code) equivalent of that program as output. The program input to the compiler, however, is not in assembler language; it is in a higher-level language. Examples of higher-level languages are FORTRAN, PL/I, PASCAL, and COBOL.

A *higher-level language* is usually closer to a natural language (such as English) than assembler language is. Higher-level languages use words such as READ, PERFORM, IF, REPEAT, and STOP for their basic commands. One higher-level-language statement often translates into many machine language instructions. Because each higher-level-language statement can do the work of a number of assembler language statements, a higher-level-language program usually has fewer statements than an assembler program to do the same task. Because it has fewer statements, a higher-level-language program usually corresponds more closely to the actual description of steps in an algorithm. Because they are shorter, higher-level-language programs have fewer places for error, so they can be easier to debug. Figure 7.1 shows the operation of a compiler or an assembler.

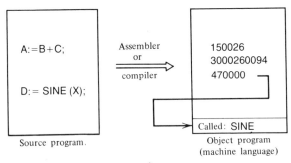

Figure 7.1 Language translator.

7.5 LINKERS

A program may invoke certain other procedures. At the assembler language level, the direct calls are apparent. In a higher-level language, however, the compiler may translate one or more statements into a call to a procedure to perform some particular task. For example, some machines have no hardware instructions to perform floating point arithmetic, but these computations can be simulated by software. When translating a program containing floating point computations, the compiler may invoke a procedure to do the floating point simulation. The user program contains only a simple statement such as

    A := B*3.5

which contains no apparent procedure call. The translated program, however, may involve a call to compute this floating point answer. I/O operations also frequently involve hidden procedure calls.

The support procedures called by a translated program are provided as a part of the operating system with the compiler. However, the compiler does not insert the code for a called procedure into the object code of the original program. Instead, the support procedures reside in a library; when the translated program is made ready for execution, a copy of any needed support procedure is obtained from the library. A program may also explicitly call routines that are part of a common library shared with other users. Prior to executing this program, it is necessary to *link* the program. To link a program is to locate all references to procedures not defined in the program and then include copies of the object code of these procedures with the object code of the program. A program that performs these tasks is called a *linker.* (A linker may also be called a *linkage editor* or a *linking loader.*) Figure 7.2 shows the process of linking.

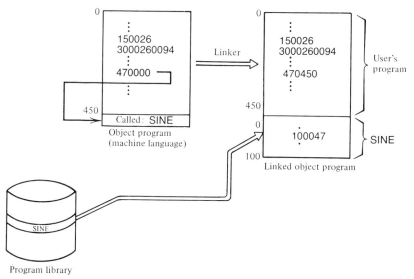

Figure 7.2 Linking.

7.6 LOADING AND RELOCATION

After copies of all called routines have been obtained, the program may be placed in memory. In a single-user machine it may be known that the user program will always start at, for example, address 01C8 . (Parts of the monitor may reside in locations 0 - 01C7 .) An origin statement can be used to tell the assembler where a program will start and, therefore, what location counter value should be associated with the first byte of object code. All address references will then be based on this starting point. Figure 7.3 shows the assembly of a program that has a fixed initial location.

Recall that many users share the resources (including memory) of a multiprogrammed computer. One program may be located in different memory spaces when the program is run at different times. Therefore, as a program is compiled or

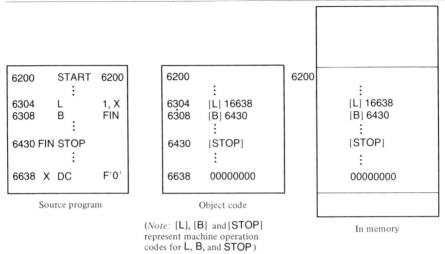

6200	START	6200
	⋮	
6304	L	1, X
6308	B	FIN
	⋮	
6430 FIN STOP		
	⋮	
6638 X DC		F'0'

Source program

6200	
	⋮
6304	[L] 16638
6308	[B] 6430
	⋮
6430	[STOP]
	⋮
6638	00000000

Object code

(*Note:* [L], [B] and [STOP]
represent machine operation
codes for L, B, and STOP)

6200

	⋮
	[L] 16638
	[B] 6430
	⋮
	[STOP]
	⋮
	00000000

In memory

Figure 7.3 Program with a fixed initial location.

assembled, it is not possible to predict where the program will be placed for execution. For this reason programs are translated as if they began at location 0 . (They are said to be *0-origin* programs.) When the program is linked and loaded into memory, address references must be corrected to show the true location where the program resides. This process of changing addresses to reflect the true location of a program is called *relocation;* it is performed by a program called a *loader.* Relocation is shown in Figure 7.4.

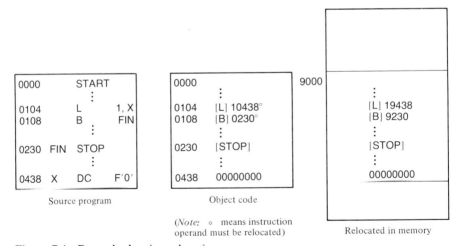

0000	START	
	⋮	
0104	L	1, X
0108	B	FIN
	⋮	
0230 FIN	STOP	
	⋮	
0438 X	DC	F'0'

Source program

0000	
	⋮
0104	[L] 10438°
0108	[B] 0230°
	⋮
0230	[STOP]
	⋮
0438	00000000

Object code

(*Note:* ° means instruction
operand must be relocated)

9000

	⋮
	[L] 19438
	[B] 9230
	⋮
	[STOP]
	⋮
	00000000

Relocated in memory

Figure 7.4 Example showing relocation.

Most machines have hardware that simplifies relocation so that not all addresses need to be changed when the program is placed in memory. One such device is a *base register*. This register contains a base address that is added to memory references in the program. Therefore, the instruction

    L   1 , X

where X is 438 bytes from the origin of the program, is translated as

L   1,0438.

However, when the CPU tries to execute the instruction and computes the oper-
and address, the contents of the base register (6200) is added to the address in
the instruction (0438) to produce the real machine address (6638). The
actual machine address is computed during program execution.

7.7 RUNNING A PROGRAM

The first step in running a program is to prepare the program for input, either on
cards or some other medium or by use of a text editor. This is called the *source*
program. The source program is submitted to a compiler or an assembler, depending on whether it is a higher-level- or an assembler language program. The compiler or assembler translates the program, producing an *object* program and a
listing of the source program. The object program may be placed in a library, in
order to be called by other procedures, or it may be passed directly on for execution.

When the object program is to be executed, it must be linked. A linker
searches libraries for any procedures called but not defined. The object code for
these routines is bound with the object code of the original program. A loader
takes this set of object code and places it in memory, relocating address references
that need to be updated to reflect actual memory locations. Finally, the supervisor
causes the CPU to branch to the first instruction of the program, and execution of
the program begins. Figure 7.5 shows all the steps identified in preparing the
program for execution.

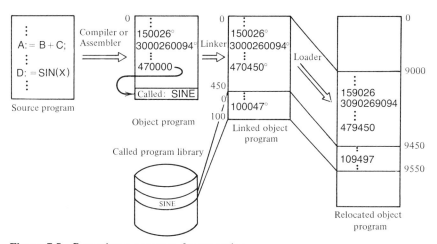

Figure 7.5 Preparing a program for execution.

This completes the overview of software program support facilities. In the
following chapters assemblers, compilers, loaders, and relocation will be examined
in more detail.

7.8 TERMS USED

Since this chapter is an overview of the software systems in use during program execution, many terms have been introduced that will be defined in later chapters. As usual, these terms have been marked with an asterisk (*). You should be familiar with all the terms presented in this chapter.

Supervisor
Computing system resources
Monitor*
Operating system*
Executive*
CP/M
Multiprogramming
RT-11
RSTS
RSX-11
Foreground/background processing*
Timesharing*
Text editor
Line editor
Cursor editor
Context editor
Screen editor
Assembler*
Machine language program
Source listing
Compiler*
Object code
Higher-level language
Support procedure call
Link
Linker*
Linkage editor*
Linking loader*
Library*
Loader*
Relocation*
0-origin program*
Base register*

chapter 8
The Design of Assemblers

The next two chapters contain information on language translators. This chapter describes assemblers, with some additional assembler commands and some information on the internal structure of an assembler. The next chapter contains information on compilers for higher-level languages. These chapters will give you a better understanding of two important pieces of systems support software. Furthermore, understanding the way a compiler works and understanding the ultimate target code for computers will help you to program more easily and more effectively. It will help you to understand error messages and appreciate the limitations placed by certain languages. Finally, assemblers and compilers are examples of programs of complex structure. Studying the algorithms from which compilers and assemblers are built will help you to mature as a programmer.

8.1 BACKGROUND AND DEFINITIONS

You already know that an assembler translates programs written in assembler language into machine language. The assembler language of each machine depends on the machine commands executed by the machine. The machine language of one computer is usually not the same as for any other.

It is possible to have an assembler that runs on one machine, called the *host machine,* and produces code for a different machine, called the *target machine.* For example, you might have an assembler that runs on an IBM 360-370 but produces machine code for an Intel 8080-based machine. This type of assembler is called a *cross assembler.*

The code produced by a cross assembler usually is not intended to be executed by the machine on which the assembler runs. Thus it is not possible to assemble and then execute a program on the same machine. (A program called a *simulator* can allow one machine to execute the machine code of another machine.)

There are several good reasons for using a cross assembler, however. It might be that the host machine is faster, has more memory, has more temporary storage space on I/O devices, or is more readily available. An IBM 360-370 is a larger machine than an Intel 8080, and it is usually multiprogrammed (shared by a number of programs). For this reason it is frequently easier to gain access to or run large programs on an IBM 360-370. An IBM 360-370 might be a good host machine for a cross assembler for an Intel 8080 because the IBM machine might be more readily available to a number of people at one time. The Intel 8080 is then free for debugging those projects, a task for which it is better suited.

The structure of all assemblers is similar. In fact, if an assembler is carefully designed, it is fairly simple to convert it from assembling and generating code for one target machine to assembling and generating code for another machine. Therefore one basic assembler could generate output code for a number of different machines. Given the design for a basic assembler, it is not difficult to produce cross assemblers for a variety of machines. The rest of this chapter discusses assemblers in general—both cross assemblers and those for which the host machine is also the target.

An assembler language consists of three kinds of instructions.

1. *Symbolic Machine Instructions.* These are instructions that translate directly into machine language instructions, such as LOAD, STORE, ADD, and the like. One symbolic machine instruction translates into one machine instruction by a simple translation of the mnemonic op code into a machine language op code and a conversion of the operands from symbolic form to the form required for the machine language command.

2. *Assembler Directives.* In addition to machine instructions, there are commands to direct the assembly process itself. For example, there may be commands to force the source listing of the program to the top of a new page or title a listing. A command to reserve an amount of storage or declare a constant is also a directive to the assembler, since these commands do not translate directly into machine language. Other assembler directives will be described later.

3. *Macroinstructions and Conditional Assembly Statements.* (Not all assemblers accept these commands.) A *macro instruction* (also written *macroinstruction* or *macro,* for short) is a shorthand way of writing a number of machine instructions. If you have a repeated series of instructions that must be coded many places in the program, it is easier to define one macro and invoke it many places. A macro is similar to a subprogram in that it is invoked, does something, and returns to the point of invocation. A macro produces machine instructions and assembler directives. Macroinstructions are replaced by machine instructions and assembler directives, and these are then assembled normally. *Conditional assembly* instructions control the order in which statements are assembled. They may be used both inside of and outside of macro definitions.

8.2 SAMPLE ASSEMBLER LANGUAGE INSTRUCTIONS

In this section you will see some typical assembler language instructions of the three types just described. These examples will be the basis for the rest of the chapter.

You have already seen a number of machine instructions. These include LOAD, STORE, ADD, SUBTRACT, COMPARE, and BRANCH instructions, which were described in Section 4.4.

8.2.1 Assembler Directives

A number of assembler directives were described in Section 4.3. Such directives as the listing controls (PRINT ON and OFF, SPACE, and TITLE), storage declarations (DC and DS or .BYTE and .WORD) and program assembly commands (CSECT, START, and END) were shown in that section. Two other assembler directives that should be discussed at this time are equate and origin.

The equate directive permanently associates a label with a value. This label is recorded in the table of all labels used in the program, so that in the future the label has the same meaning as the constant value. One form of an EQU statement is

label EQU *value*

Other assemblers use a notation such as *label* = *value*. The purpose of this statement is not what it would seem, based on a knowledge of higher-level languages. This statement is *not* used to assign *value* to *label* during execution; instead, it has effect only as the program is being assembled. It simply provides a symbolic name for a constant value. The value may be a numeric constant or a constant expression, or it may be a fixed address within the program. One use of EQU is to provide synonyms for labels in a program or to assign labels to parts of a storage area.

One use for the equate statement is to assign a symbolic name for register numbers. Recall that on the PDP-11 there are eight general registers, although register 7 is the program counter and register 6 is, by convention, the stack pointer. Two equates, such as

```
SP=6    and
PC=7
```

make it easy to remember these associations and make a program more self-documenting. Similarly, the IBM 360-370 has 16 registers to hold intermediate values or use for addresses. If you are implementing a stack and also keeping count of the number of items in the stack, the following equates would be appropriate.

```
STACKPTR EQU  5
COUNT    EQU  8
```

With 16 registers, it can be difficult to remember what result is contained in which register. With mnemonic names the problem is substantially simplified. Not only do you remember which register is used for what, your program shows the reader the reason for operating on a certain register.

Suppose you want to analyze FORTRAN statements. These statements are fixed field, with the statement number in columns 1 to 5, a continuation mark in column 6, the statement body in columns 7 to 72, and a sequence field in columns 73 to 80. You might declare an area of storage to contain 80 characters and then subdivide this area with additional labels to mark the positions of each of these four components. This is shown next.

```
FORTSTMT  DS   80C
STMTNUM   EQU  FORTSTMT      (starts same place as FORTSTMT)
CONTINUE  EQU  FORTSTMT+5    (starts in column 6)
STMTBODY  EQU  FORTSTMT+6    (starts in column 7)
SEQNUM    EQU  FORTSTMT+72   (starts in column 73)
```

Remember that DS 80C declares 80 consecutive storage locations, and the label FORTSTMT is associated with the first of those 80 locations. FORTSTMT is the address of column 1. Thus FORTSTMT + 1 is the second location (column 2), and so FORTSTMT + 5 is actually column 6.

This sequence of EQU statements has several advantages. First, it documents the program by providing more descriptive labels for sections of FORTSTMT; SEQNUM is obviously more meaningful to someone reading this program than FORTSTMT + 72 would be. Second, it adds a measure of bugproofing to the program. It required a bit of explanation to show why column 6 was FORTSTMT + 5, not FORTSTMT + 6; it still seems more natural to use FORTSTMT + 6. When you are coding a program, it is tempting to make such simple slips. Furthermore, in large and complicated data structures, it is not easy to remember the positions of the various components. It is far easier to define all of these by a set of EQUs and then use the labels, instead of actual positions. Finally, the EQUs permit easy change to a program. It is unlikely that the format of FORTRAN statements would change, but in structures that you create, you may need to add a field or change the size or placement of one. It is cumbersome to go through a program, changing all occurrences of FORTSTMT + 72 to FORTSTMT + 75. It would be easier to have the whole program refer to one label, SEQNUM, so that changing the one EQU for SEQNUM would cause values in all statements that refer to SEQNUM to change. Thus wise use of EQUs can contribute to good programming.

While assembling a program, the assembler maintains a counter, called the *location counter,* that shows the position of each statement in the generated object code. The position of each statement is calculated relative to the start of the program. The ORG directive assigns a value to the location counter. Recall that on a multiprogrammed computer it is impossible to predict where a program will reside during execution. On single-user machines, however, it may be possible to predict this. If, for example, the monitor occupies addresses 0 to 07F3, the program will begin at location 07F4. It will be desirable to generate code that uses that fact; then no relocation is necessary. Furthermore, the program listing shows true memory addresses. The ORG statement can assign a value to the location counter. On some machines you would code something like

```
ORG    07F4H
```

(the H shows the constant is hexadecimal), while on others you would say

. =07F4H

or

*=07F4H

Regardless of the form, these statements assign the value 07F4 to the location counter and proceed to assemble the program as if the next location were 07F4. (In the last two forms, . and * refer to the location counter.)

8.2.2 Macro Instructions

A macro instruction is one assembler language statement that may produce a number of machine and assembler language instructions. A macro is a bit like a subprogram in that you define the macro and then call it independently. However, the similarity ends because a macro has its effect during the *assembly* of a program, not during its *execution*. That is, a macro generates regular machine and assembler language statements. By the time program execution begins, only the assembled machine language instructions remain; no trace of the macro is retained.

Suppose, for example, you need to load the larger of two values at a number of different places in the program. This code requires only four statements: a LOAD, a COMPARE, a BRANCH, and another LOAD. It is not worth coding a subprocedure to perform this task. A macro can save you from repetitious coding. A sample of a macro to do this is as follows.

```
           MACRO
&LABEL     LARGE    &VAL1 ,&VAL2
&LABEL     L        1 ,&VAL1          get first value
           C        1 ,&VAL2          see if second is larger
           BNL      *+8               if larger in reg 1, skip next load
           L        1 ,&VAL2          get second value (larger)
           MEND
```

In this example, &LABEL , &VAL1 , and &VAL2 are *symbolic parameters*. When the macro is invoked, they are replaced by a string of characters supplied in the call. Every place in the macro definition where &VAL1 appears, &VAL1 is replaced by the first operand supplied on the call to the macro.

A macro is *called* or *invoked* by coding the name of the macro (the mnemonic on the second line: LARGE) and an appropriate set of operands. For example, this macro might be called by

LARGE   NUM,A

This call will place either the value of NUM or the value of A into register 1 , depending on which is larger. When a macro is called, code is generated that results from substituting the value passed for each of the symbolic parameters. The code generated from the call of the preceding macro would be as follows.

LOOP	LARGE	NUM , A	
+LOOP	L	1 , NUM	get first value
+	C	1 , A	see if second is larger
+	BNL	*+8	if larger in reg 1, skip next load
+	L	1 , A	get second value (larger)

(The + signs along the left side show that this is the code generated from the macro call. In this call, LOOP , NUM , and A replace the symbolic parameters &LABEL , &VAL1 , and &VAL2 . The program is then assembled just as if the programmer had coded the L , C , BNL , and L instructions originally.

A macro can be used in a number of situations. First, as before, a macro is a good choice for a short block of code that must be repeated in a number of places if the code is not large enough to warrant its being made into a separately called subprocedure. Second, if a sequence of instructions is complicated or hard to remember, it is easier to code the instructions once in a macro definition and then invoke the macro at any places needed. For example, if the instructions to set up a series of arguments and call a subprocedure are complex or hard to remember, a macro can reduce the errors from miscoding. Finally, a macro can reduce your coding effort if you can write macro definitions to perform higher-level operations and then use the macros as extensions to the assembler language instructions.

The assembler processes macro calls and later assembles the program. As we study assemblers, you will see the process of generating code from macro calls and translating the resultant code into machine language.

8.3 THE ASSEMBLY PROCESS

Section 4.1 discussed the major activities of an assembler. They are to:

1. Perform numeric conversions and arithmetic.
2. Translate mnemonics to their binary codes.
3. Convert symbolic addresses to machine addresses.

The first task is not complicated and will not be discussed further here.

The second task seems simple. What is needed is a table of all possible mnemonics and the corresponding numeric op codes. There is a complication, however: not all instructions have the same machine language format. For example, on the IBM 360-370 there are five different forms of instructions, and there are also a number of special variations from the standard forms. These different instruction forms must be identified by their mnemonics, since an A (add) instruction has different kinds of operands from those for an AP (add packed decimal) or AH (add halfword) instruction. The table kept by the assembler must contain the op code for each instruction and an indication of the form of the machine code.

Finally, the assembler must determine machine addresses. For example, a program might contain the following statements.

```
LOOP    L    5,COUNT
        . . .
        B    LOOP
```

As the assembler analyzes a program, it keeps a table of all labels seen and the location for the object code associated with each label. When the assembler processes the preceding program, the instruction with label LOOP might be at address 0460 . When processing the branch statement, the assembler consults the table and generates code using 0460 as the operand address in the branch. It would produce the following machine language instruction.

<branch opcode>	0460

However, the branch might also have been a forward branch, as in the following case.

```
        B     BEYOND
        . . .
BEYOND  ST    5,MAX
```

In this case, label BEYOND will not have been seen by the time it is used as an operand (i.e., when the branch instruction is being assembled). The assembler will not know the address associated with BEYOND , since that label is defined on a statement that has not yet been assembled. This problem is called the *forward reference problem* for assemblers. There are two solutions to the forward reference problem: one- and two-pass assemblers.

Two-pass assemblers are the more obvious solution to this problem. A *two-pass assembler* processes each source statement twice. During the first pass, the assembler reads the entire source program, saving a copy of each statement on a storage device. In this pass the assembler looks only at the labels of the instructions and at enough of each operand to determine how much code each statement will produce. This data is enough for the assembler to build a table of all labels and where their assembler code will be located. The assembler keeps a counter, called the *location counter,* that is increased by the number of bytes of object code every instruction will occupy. Each time a label is found, it is entered in a table along with the current location counter value. The table built this way is called the *symbol table.* Pass one of a two-pass assembler is depicted in Figure 8.1.

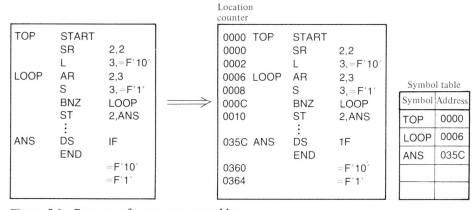

Figure 8.1   Pass one of a two-pass assembler.

During the second pass, a two-pass assembler generates code. This involves transforming each mnemonic op code into the appropriate machine language code and supplying addresses for the operands. Since the symbol table was built during pass one, all symbols defined in the program will already have been associated with a location in the program (the location counter value). This is the address of the symbol within the program. Therefore the operand addresses can be determined just by consulting the symbol table. The program listing is also produced during the second pass. The second pass of the assembly process is shown in Figure 8.2.

The two-pass solution is straightforward because it involves only looking at each statement and determining how much code it will produce. However, it also takes a considerable extra amount of time to process each statement twice; furthermore, building a temporary file of statements for reprocessing in the second pass may not be acceptable because there may not be enough storage device space on which to save the program statements. To overcome these disadvantages, one-pass assemblers exist.

A *one-pass assembler* examines each input statement only once. It builds a table of forward references (references to labels that have not yet been defined) and creates an indirect reference table. For example, if BEYOND is the first forward reference found, it becomes the first entry in the forward reference table. In place of a branch to BEYOND, the assembler creates an indirect branch to the first entry in the forward reference table. As the label BEYOND is defined, the true address of BEYOND is placed in the indirect branch table. When the statement

     B   BEYOND

is executed, the branch extracts the true destination address from the forward reference table, and the branch to BEYOND succeeds.

A one-pass assembler requires more bookkeeping than a two-pass assembler, and the machine code it generates may take slightly longer to execute.

Both one-pass and two-pass assemblers must process certain statements in addition to machine instructions. Assembler directives such as EJECT and SPACE affect the source program listing. The assembler adjusts the location counter to reflect the amount of space reserved by directives that allocate space

0000	TOP	START	
0000		SR	2, 2
0002		L	3, = F'10'
0006	LOOP	AR	2, 3
0008		S	3, = F'1'
000C		BNZ	LOOP
0010		ST	2, ANS
		⋮	
035C	ANS	DS	1F
		END	
0360			= F'10'
0364			= F'1'

[SR]	22
[L]	30360
[AR]	23
[S]	30364
[BNZ]	0006
[ST]	2035C

(a)

1B22	
5830	0360
1A23	
5830	0364
4770	0006
5020	035C

(b)

Figure 8.2 Pass two of a two-pass assembler. (*a*) Machine code before substitution of operation codes. (*b*) Machine code with operation codes for IBM 360-370 computers.

for variables and constants. The origin statement supplies a value to the location counter, and the EQUATE statement establishes a label and a corresponding value to be put into the symbol table. Assembler directives are processed at the same time as machine instructions.

We will conclude this section with a description of the assembly algorithm. *HIPO* is an acronym for *Hierarchy plus Input, Process, and Output.* This is a convenient means for describing a program module. A HIPO description indicates where the program sits in relation to other programs (its hierarchy—which program modules call it and which modules does it call), what input data it uses, what algorithm it uses to transform the data, and what output it generates. A two-pass assembler will be described next, using the HIPO technique.

HIPO Description of a Two-Pass Assembler

HIERARCHY
An assembler is a stand-alone routine, called by the executive system. It calls a number of subprocedures to perform the following tasks, but we will concentrate now only on the assembler, as if it were one large program.

INPUTS
An assembler language source program.

PROCESS

Pass 1

1. Read a single source statement. Write a copy of it in a temporary file of source statements.
2. Determine if the statement has a label. If yes, enter the label and the current location counter value into the symbol table. (Statements such as ORIGIN and EQUATE statements cause a different value to be placed in the symbol table.)
3. Consult a table of legal mnemonics and the form of the statement to determine the length of the machine code into which this statement will translate. Increase the location counter by that amount.
4. Repeat steps 1 to 3 for each statement up to the end of the program.

Pass 2

5. Reposition the file of source statements produced in step 1 to the first statement.
6. Read a source statement.
7. Consult a table of legal instruction mnemonics to determine the opcode for that operation. Determine the addresses of the operands, perhaps by looking them up in the symbol table.
8. Generate the proper machine language code using the opcode and operand addresses determined in step 7. This code may be written on a storage medium, such as a disk or tape, it may be transcribed to a medium such as punched cards, or it may be stored directly in main memory.

9. If desired, produce a line for the program source listing. If there was an error in the statement, generate an appropriate error message for the listing.
10. Repeat steps 6 to 9 until the final source statement has been processed.

OUTPUT

A copy of the machine code for the program, either in memory or on some I/O medium; optionally, a printed listing of the source program and its generated object code.

8.4 LOAD-AND-GO ASSEMBLERS

Most assemblers produce object code on a storage device or on cards. This code is later loaded into memory for execution. The code can be saved, and the same program can be executed many times from just one assembly. (Saving reassembly obviously saves time, but it can be used only on debugged programs that will not require changes from run to run.) Recording the object code on a storage device and then later bringing the code into memory takes time. Relocation is also needed for this object code, and that adds to the time needed. Nevertheless, for programs of substantial size, there can be a savings in time from not having to retranslate the program each time it is used.

An alternative for programs under development is a *load-and-go* assembler. This assembler does not produce object code that can be kept from one run to the next. Instead, it places the object code it produces directly into core and executes it as soon as all statements have been assembled. No time-consuming relocation is needed, since the actual memory address of each statement is known when it is being assembled. Therefore all statements can be relocated as they are assembled. A load-and-go assembler is especially appropriate for a student environment, where a program is frequently changed from one run to the next (while the program is being debugged) and where the programs are small enough that the overhead of relocation is a substantial part of a program's total run time.

8.5 MACRO ASSEMBLERS

Recall that a macro instruction is a shorthand way of writing a number of instructions in one instruction. The assembler then converts the macro instruction into the appropriate series of machine and assembler language instructions. This must be done before assembly, since a macro instruction is a *pseudo instruction,* meaning that it is not a part of the conventional assembler language. In other words, the assembler will not find the mnemonic for a macro instruction in the table of legal assembler language mnemonics; the assembler must convert the macro instruction to its corresponding machine or assembler language statements.

Use of a macro consists of two parts: a *definition* of the macro, and one or more *calls* to the macro. The definition contains a series of model statements: forms of statements that are to be generated. These statements may make use of arguments that are similar to the arguments passed to a subprocedure. Each call to the macro supplies values for the arguments. *Conditional assembly statements* can also be used to control the order in which statements are generated.

For each macro call, the assembler must locate the macro definition, determine the values supplied for the symbolic parameters, and produce the necessary assembler language statements. A macro assembler usually requires at least one additional pass over the source code to locate and expand macro calls. This additional pass is followed by regular program assembly. The process of macro expansion is shown in Figure 8.3.

8.6 SUMMARY

There are a number of important features to remember about assemblers.

1. An assembler is machine specific, since it translates programs written in the assembler language for one particular machine. There are, however, similarities in form among all assemblers. Cross assemblers run on one class of machines but produce code for a different group of machines.

2. There are three classes of instructions processed by an assembler: machine instructions (those that can be performed directly on a machine), assembler directives (instructions that pass information directly to the assembler), and macro instructions (those that are expanded into a number of machine instructions and assembler directives). The assembler expands macros, acts on assembler directives, and translates machine instructions into machine language.

3. As a part of translating a program, the assembler performs numeric conversions and simple arithmetic, translates mnemonics to binary code, and converts symbolic addresses to machine addresses. The first two are direct processes. In order to convert labels to addresses, the assembler builds a table of all labels defined in the program and the address (within the program) of each label. This table is called a symbol table.

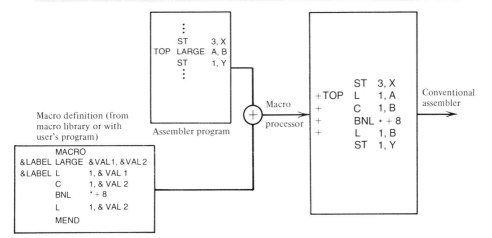

Figure 8.3 Macro expansion.

4. Load-and-go assemblers do not produce object code on an auxiliary storage device; they produce the object code directly in memory in a form that is already relocated.

8.7 TERMS USED

Assembler
Assembler language
Cross assembler
Symbolic machine instruction
Assembler directive
EQU (Equate)
ORG (Origin)
Macro instruction
Conditional assembly statement
Delimiter
Location counter
Symbolic parameter
Forward reference
Two-pass assembler
Symbol table
One-pass assembler
Object code
Load-and-go assembler
Macro assembler
Macro definition
Macro call

8.8 QUESTIONS

1. During which pass of a two-pass assembler would each of the following activities occur?
   (a) Notice that a statement has a label.
   (b) Print a source program listing.
   (c) Process an ORG statement (which assigns a value to the location counter).
   (d) Examine a character string constant to determine how many bytes of memory it will occupy.
   (e) Generate code for the instruction B LABEL (a branch).

2. Some assembler languages permit the equate (EQU) assembler directive to be used like a *named constant;* that is, an equated symbol may be used in most contexts where a constant could be. For example, an equated symbol may be a register number (as in L   R5,X), it may be a repetition factor (as in DC (TABLSIZ)F'0'), or it may be a name for a piece of immediate data (as in MVI   FLAG,ON). In which of these three contexts does the equated symbol need to have been assigned a value *before* the statement in which it is used as a named constant? (*Hint:* Which of these contexts would have an impact on another pass one activity by the assembler that could not be postponed until after the equated symbol had been defined?)

3. In a higher-level language it is perfectly normal to say "X : = X + 1". Why doesn't R5 EQU R5 + 1 have the same effect? What does this latter expression mean?

4. Name three kinds of assembler language instructions that do *not* affect the location counter.

5. Assembler language programs may not have duplicate labels. Clearly, in the expression L   1,X or B   LOOP there must be no ambiguity about where X or LOOP is within the program. The expansion of macro LARGE in this chapter had LOOP   LARGE   NUM , A and + LOOP   L   1,NUM as its first two lines. Why isn't label LOOP considered a duplicate by the assembler?

6. What are some circumstances in which a two-pass assembler might be less appropriate than a one-pass assembler? What are some circumstances in which a two-pass assembler might be more appropriate?

7. Once a program has been assembled, can the symbol table be discarded? Is it needed during execution of a program? Why or why not?

chapter 9

Compilers and Higher-Level Languages

Assembler language programming is fairly popular for a number of reasons. Some machines have no other language in which to program; this is particularly true of microcomputers. (That situation is changing, however, as more translators for higher-level languages are being made available for microcomputers.) Certain functions, those related to the unique hardware of a given machine, are available only to assembly language programmers. In order to make optimum use of a particular machine architecture, it is necessary to program in the assembly language for that machine. As an educational device, working in assembler language is essential to understanding the internal structure of a computer.

However, there is substantially more programming done in higher-level languages than in assembly language. Programming in a higher-level language is usually faster, since a higher-level language program will normally have fewer statements than its assembler language counterpart. There are thus fewer places for error. Higher-level-language forms are closer to the way people think. A major advantage of higher-level-language programs is that they are portable; that is, with appropriate translators, they can be run on a variety of machines having radically different structures. Finally, higher-level languages often permit arranging and structuring the data in a way that is closer to the conceptualization of the problem than is directly possible in assembler language.

This chapter begins with an overview of some of the more popular higher-level languages. It is probable that you know one or more of these; you should also learn to recognize the names and characteristics of the others. Next, some of the elements of languages will be presented. The chapter concludes with a description of the elements of a typical compiler.

9.1 COMMON PROGRAMMING LANGUAGES

This section contains brief descriptions of the more common programming languages. There are a range of language types: some commercial, some scientific, some time-sharing oriented, some designed for large machines, and some for small machines. This is certainly not an exhaustive list; in fact, many fine languages have been intentionally omitted because of space. The motivation here is to give you a feeling for some of the strengths of different languages and an appreciation for situations in which they are most appropriate.

9.1.1 FORTRAN

FORTRAN is among the oldest of the computer languages. The acronym FORTRAN stands for FORmula TRANslator. Designed in the middle 1950s, it has undergone a number of revisions since then. Because of its age, there are many FORTRAN programs in use on a large number of computers.

When originally designed, FORTRAN was intended for scientific computation. For this reason, both real (floating point) and integer computation are supported. Mathematical functions, such as logarithms, exponentials, and the trigonometric functions, are standard features. Conversely, the language has a limited facility for character manipulation or for structuring data in forms other than single variables, vectors, and arrays.

Although you might interpret that FORTRAN is primarily used in numerical computations, this is not exactly true. Because of its long life and because it is supported on almost all machines, FORTRAN is widely used in applications such as plotting and graphing, simulation, and even some commercial uses. Although FORTRAN is not ideal in these applications, good programmers have designed a number of "extensions" to the standard language by means of special-purpose subprocedures to endow FORTRAN with some of the features it lacks.

An internationally standardized FORTRAN exists. This standard is revised from time to time, most recently in 1977; work is already underway to create the next standard version. Standardization helps make programs portable because all compilers then produce equivalent results for the same program. Because of the large body of programs written in FORTRAN, it is certain to be in use for a long time.

9.1.2 PASCAL

PASCAL is a relative newcomer to the language scene. Beginning in the early 1970s, much attention has been paid to *structured programming,* which is a process of writing a program in a clear, concise form that reflects the thought process from which the program was designed. Structured programming is easier if the program structure closely resembles the structure of the algorithm. FORTRAN, for example, lacks certain language features that would make structured programming easier. Restrictions on the conditional (IF) and the repeat (DO) structures make the structuring of a program more difficult in FORTRAN.

The designers of PASCAL learned from the shortcomings of some other languages and presented a language with a flexible set of control structures that were limited enough to be easy to learn. PASCAL has some features that make it easy to arrange data in a natural way. For example, if you were writing a program to record data on a group of college students, you might want to record the class (senior, junior, etc.) of each student. PASCAL lets you define a data type CLASS ; CLASS would then have four possible values, as declared here.

    TYPE CLASS = [FRESH, SOPH, JUN, SEN];

CLASS is a type, analogous to floating point, integer, or character. Variables can be declared to be of type CLASS , as shown

    VAR CL1, CL2: CLASS;

Now the value of CL1 or CL2 is any one of the four values FRESH , SOPH , JUN , SEN . Assignment statements can be written

    CL2 : = SOPH;

and conditional statements can then be formed

    IF CL1 = SEN THEN . . .

Of course, you could achieve the same thing by assigning a numeric code to each of the four values (1 for FRESH , etc.) and using the numeric codes in the program. For classes it is not hard to remember the correspondence of 1 = FRESH , 2 = SOPH , and so forth. However, if the items in the list were colors (RED , BLUE , YELLOW , GREEN) instead of classes, there would be no obvious reason to associate RED with 1 . Thus a program that used constant names, such as RED , would be easier to follow than one that used a numeric code for the colors. This feature of PASCAL makes *readable* programs possible. There are also numerous control structures that can make programming simpler. These structures include REPEAT-UNTIL, WHILE-DO, CASE, IF-THEN-ELSE, and procedure nesting.

A principal advantage of PASCAL has emerged within the past few years: PASCAL is becoming the *de facto* standard higher-level language for microcomputers. There are compilers for the popular microcomputers, and PASCAL programs are being published in technical articles. PASCAL has thus become a medium for microcomputer users to share their programs.

9.1.3 BASIC

Another language popular with microcomputer users is BASIC. This language was originally designed for time-sharing use. BASIC is usually accompanied by an editor that permits the user to enter and modify text, save programs, and then execute the programs. BASIC programs are usually interpreted, not compiled. This means that the program is not translated to machine language, but that each statement is examined as it is executed. A compiled program usually runs faster, since each statement is decoded just once; with an interpreted program, a statement in a loop that runs 100 times is decoded 100 times. On the other hand, with interpreted programs, the entire program is available during execution. If an error occurs during execution, the interpreter can say "*An error occurred during execu-*

tion of line 150 ." Furthermore, with many BASIC interpreters, the programmer can obtain information in the event of an error. For example, since a BASIC interpreter keeps the entire program during execution, the programmer can inquire "At termination, what was the value of variable A?" Some systems even allow the programmer to change the values of some variables and go back into execution of the program.

Another advantage of BASIC is that it has a fairly simple statement syntax (structure). For this reason compilers or interpreters for BASIC programs can be fairly small. Because of its simplicity, BASIC is an easy language to learn. It is an ideal language for mini- and microcomputers with limited memory. Until recently BASIC was a dominant language among microcomputer users for sharing programs; that lead is now being taken by PASCAL.

9.1.4 COBOL

COBOL is an acronym standing for COmmon Business Oriented Language, and that tells the purpose of the language. COBOL is a relatively old language, like FORTRAN; like FORTRAN, it is standardized, and like FORTRAN, it has a tremendously large following.

One interesting feature of COBOL is that a programmer can access many files of data having different forms. Some of these files may be on direct access devices, while others may be on magnetic tape, punched cards, and printers. Another strong feature of COBOL is its attention to output format. There are extensive facilities for converting the values so that they appear in just the form needed. For example, when printing checks, the value 123456 may be desired as $1,234.56, but the value 5 should be printed $****0.05. COBOL provides the means to direct the output form of a value. It also has a mechanism for searching a file for one or more particular records or for sorting a file into order based on a key in each record. These are common business needs.

As noted, there are many COBOL programs in constant use today. Furthermore, the COBOL language is under continual study and revision, so that new features are added to the language as needed. The standard language includes a full language and a subset language. The full language is complicated enough that it is inappropriate for most minicomputers, but the subset language is widely available on small computer systems.

9.1.5 ALGOL

The ALGOL language was designed in the late 1950s as a result of collaboration between the European computing community and a number of U.S. computer manufacturers. The language has never achieved great success in the United States, however.

ALGOL is oriented to the solution of scientific problems. When it was designed, it was based on the experience with FORTRAN, so it had a more flexible set of control structures than FORTRAN did. It introduced the idea of nested procedures (procedures defined within other procedures) and scope of variable declarations (a variable being accessable to all procedures contained within the procedure in which the variable is declared).

9.1.6   PL/I

PL/I appeared in the early 1960s under the influence of IBM, and it is still used virtually only on IBM machines. PL/I statements resemble some elements of FORTRAN, ALGOL, and COBOL. In fact, it was designed to have the numeric capabilities of FORTRAN, the commercial uses of COBOL, the control structures of ALGOL, and the access to all features of the machine, previously available only in assembler language programming. A substantial amount of PL/I programming exists. PL/I compilers tend to be large enough that they are available only on large-scale computers.

This has been a brief introduction to some of the more popular languages for small and large computers. Many important languages have been omitted, but it is impossible to discuss all languages here. The purpose of this section is to introduce you to some of the names of languages and their features.

9.2   LANGUAGE FORMALITIES

As you know, a compiler translates programming language statements into machine language instructions. Just as it is impossible to translate nonsense syllables from English into French, it is also impossible to translate grammatically ill-formed programming language statements into machine language. The compiler needs some means of deciding whether a statement is proper or not.

A *grammar* is a precise description of the form of a language. Most programming languages can be described by grammars that generate only all the legal statements in that language. A compiler applies a grammer to a statement, testing whether the statement can be produced from the grammar. A programming language grammar has a number of *productions* (also called *rules*). The rules contain *nonterminals* (also called *variables*) that represent arbitrary parts of the produced statement; the rules also contain *terminals,* symbols in the language. A production consists of a single nonterminal and a series of terminals and nonterminals. A production rule means that the single nonterminal may be replaced by the series of terminals and nonterminals. There may be more than one production for a given nonterminal. A production is often written with the single variable on the left, an arrow or ::= , and the variables and terminals on the right. For example, here is a set of rules that will produce signed or unsigned integers of any length.

```
<integer> ::= + <unsigned integer>
<integer> ::= - <unsigned integer>
<integer> ::= <unsigned integer>
<unsigned integer> ::= <unsigned integer> <digit>
<unsigned integer> ::= <digit>
<digit> ::= 0
<digit> ::= 1
   . . .
<digit> ::= 9
```

Where two or more productions have the same variable on the left side, the productions may be combined into one by writing all right sides, separated by | symbols; for example, <d i g i t > could be written as

<digit> ::= 0 | 1 | 2 | 3 | 4 | 5 | 6 | 7 | 8 | 9

In a grammar one variable is distinguished and is known as the *start symbol.* In the preceding example, the start symbol is < i n t e ge r > . A statement in the language generated by the grammar is legal if it can be produced starting with the start symbol, and following a finite number of steps, in each step replacing one variable by the right side of a production for that variable. As an example, the integer +42 can be generated by the following sequence of replacements.

<integer> --> + <unsigned integer>
          --> + <unsigned integer> <digit>
          --> + <digit> <digit>
          --> + 4 <digit>
          --> + 4 2

The process of compiling involves checking each statement to verify that it is legal according to the grammar for the programming language.

9.3 COMPONENTS OF COMPILERS

Compilers consist of four major components: lexical analysis, syntax analysis, semantic analysis, and code generation sections. This section contains a brief description of each of these four elements. Each description concludes with a HIPO structure for the element, similar to the HIPO analysis of an assembler in Chapter 8.

9.3.1 Lexical Analysis

A compiler processes certain statement types. Compiling includes checking the form of a statement for its legality. From the standpoint of *form,* the following two statements are the same.

```
1.  IF I=I THEN I:=I;
2.  IF INDEX=LIMIT THEN        { END OF LOOP }
        SUBSCR := MAXVAL;
```

The first form uses only one variable name, and it is all on one line; the second form uses four different variable names, it contains a comment, and the statement is split across two lines. There are countless other variations possible on this statement form.

The *lexical analyzer* processes the input and does two things.

1. It records which specific variables and constants were used in the statement.
2. It reduces the input to a series of *tokens.*

A token is an indicator passed from the lexical analyzer to the rest of the compiler, showing what type of item was found in the input. For example, the lexical analyzer does not pass the characters I and F ; instead, it consults a table of keywords in the language and passes a message that it has found the keyword IF .

After processing the preceding statements, the lexical analyzer will record the names of variables found and in what positions they were found. It then passes the following information to the rest of the compiler.

<IF keyword>
<variable>
<equals sign>
<variable>
<THEN keyword>
<variable>
<assignment sign>
<variable>
<semicolon>

Each item enclosed in < and > brackets is a token; actually, the lexical analyzer would pass a numeric code, with consistent code values throughout the compiler.

The lexical analyzer reduces a source program to a standard form. Most higher-level languages are tolerant of blanks in the source program; that is, an arbitrary number of blanks are permitted between tokens. Good programmers use blanks (indentation) to set off certain segments of code. Although this is meaningful for the programmer, it is unimportant to the compiler. The lexical analyzer deletes blanks (except in a character constant). Similarly, comments are unimportant to the compiler, so the lexical analyzer deletes these. The lexical analyzer also collects constants, converting integer and floating point numbers, character strings, and other constants, and stores them in tables.

The lexical analyzer is called every time the rest of the compiler needs a token. It reads input lines as needed and prints the source listing (if requested). This design has another advantage: the lexical analyzer is the only module of a compiler that needs to see the raw source program; the rest of the compiler works with the regularized tokens identified by the lexical analyzer.

HIPO Description of Lexical Analyzer

HIERARCHY
Called by parser

INPUT
Source program

PROCESS

1.   One at a time read characters of the source program until the end of one token can be identified.

2. If requested, print a line of the source program listing each time a new source input record is read. If error indications are received from the parser, produce these with the source listing.

3. Return the one token located to the parser.

OUTPUT

Source listing, if requested; token to parser.

9.3.2   The Parser

The *parser* attempts to match the tokens found by the lexical analyzer to legal statement forms, trying to determine what kind of statement it is processing. It applies productions one at a time to try to match the input source program. The sequence of productions used by a parser in matching a source input is called the *derivation* of the input. The example to generate $+42$ in Section 9.2 was an example of a derivation.

The two basic forms of parsers are top-down and bottom-up parsers. A *top-down* parser begins with the start symbol for the grammar and tries to derive a statement having the same form as the input statement. The top-down parser replaces one nonterminal with the right side of a production for that nonterminal. It performs replacements as many times as necessary, using any productions.

A *bottom-up* parser starts with the input statement and tries to reduce it (replacing right sides of productions by their corresponding left sides) to the start symbol. The bottom-up parser thus starts with the input and tries to work backward to the start symbol. If you read it backward (bottom to top) the example in the previous section shows how $+42$ could be reduced to the start symbol.

Both top-down and bottom-up parsing can be visualized as building a tree showing the derivation of the input statement. Such a tree is called a *derivation tree*. (This tree is similar to a family tree in that it has one item at the top, and the branches descend from that; the tree widens as it goes down.) A top-down parser begins at the top of the tree and works down; a bottom-up parser begins with the ends of the branches and tries to move up toward the root of the tree. Both top-down and bottom-up parsers will produce the same tree from a given statement. A sample derivation tree is shown in Figure 9.1.

A top-down parser is often able to give better error diagnostics if an input statement is not legal. This is true because the parser has already built a portion of the tree and discovered a branch that will not match the input. At that point, the parser can enumerate the tokens that would be legal as the next input token. For example, a top-down parser might produce the following messages if it encounters two adjacent variables.

UNEXPECTED IDENTIFIER
ARITHMETIC OPERATOR EXPECTED
RELATIONAL OPERATOR EXPECTED
(EXPECTED
; EXPECTED

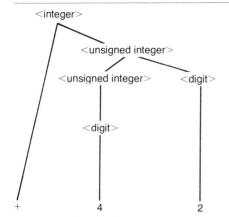

Figure 9.1 Derivation tree.

That is, given what has already been derived, the parser might be able to produce a derivation for ..A + B.. or ..A<B.. or A(B.. or ..A; B.., but ..A B.. does not match the partial derivation tree constructed so far.

There are more parsing techniques known for bottom-up parsers. For simple languages, very fast and small bottom-up parsers can be constructed.

HIPO Description of Parser

HIERARCHY
Top-level routine; calls lexical analyzer, semantic processor, code generator

INPUT
Tokens from lexical analyzer

PROCESS

1. Obtain the next token from lexical analyzer. Place it at bottom of derivation tree being constructed.
2. For a top-down parser, try to find a production that will lead from the last unmatched nonterminal closer to the bottom of the tree. Apply this production, producing a series of nonterminals and connections to existing terminals.

   For a bottom-up parser, try to find a production whose right side is an image of the unmatched terminals and nonterminals at the bottom of the parse tree. If one is found, match the terminals and nonterminals in its right side and enter an unmatched nonterminal corresponding to the left side of the production (i.e., use the production to reduce the tree).

   If all possible productions show the newest terminals can never fit into the tree, pass an error indication to the lexical analyzer (which prints the source listing).
3. If a production was applied, call the semantic processor to interpret the meaning of the production.

4. Repeat steps 2 and 3 until no more productions can be applied.
5. Repeat steps 1 to 4 until the entire source program has been processed. If a complete tree was formed to match all input tokens, the source program has been successfully parsed.
6. When the parse is complete, invoke the code generator to produce an executable version of the internal code generated by the semantic processor.

OUTPUT
None.

9.3.3 Semantic Analysis

Syntax analysis or parsing is the examination of the *form* of a statement. Semantic analysis is the interpretation of the *meaning* of a statement. At the same time the parser is recognizing the form of a statement, the semantic analyzer is recording information to permit the right machine code to be generated.

Semantic analysis usually goes on in parallel with parsing. Each time the parser applies a production (or a reduction, for a bottom-up parser), the semantic analysis routines perform a similar action for code generation later. For example, suppose the parser is recognizing an arithmetic expression and applies the following production.

$<$expression$> ::= <$expression$> + <$term$>$

The semantic analysis routine knows that later a machine language instruction will have to be generated to add the quantities represented by $<$expres-sion$>$ and $<$term$>$.

In many compilers the semantic analysis routine generates a kind of internal code. This is a pseudo machine language code for a hypothetical machine. A later pass converts pseudo machine code to the actual machine code for the machine on which the compiler runs. Just as cross assemblers are useful, there are also situations in which a compiler is needed to run on one machine but to produce code for another machine. With this separation of activities, the first three components of a compiler (lexical analyzer, parser, semantic analyzer) are standard; the code generation routine is all that varies from one machine to another. Then only the code generation routine needs to be rewritten to produce code for a different machine. In this way, one compiler can form the basis for a family of compilers.

Other compilers never produce real machine code; instead, they stop with the intermediate pseudo code. When the program is run, a provided utility program "executes" this internal code. In effect, the utility program simulates the effect of a machine that had the pseudo code as its machine language.

HIPO Description of Semantic Processor

HIERARCHY
Called by parser each time a production is applied

INPUT

Indication of which production was applied; correspondence among actual labels, symbols, and the like, and token codes (e.g., variable I is most recent <v a r i - ab l e> token).

PROCESS

1. Locate the labels and symbols that correspond to the token codes in the production applied.
2. Generate internal pseudo machine language instruction(s) to achieve the effect of production applied. For example, when the production

   <expression> ::= <variable> + <variable>

   is applied, assuming A and B are the actual variables that were matched when this production was applied, the semantic processor might generate code that looks like the following statements.

   LOAD   A
   ADD   B
   STORE temporary location

OUTPUT

Internal pseudo machine language code.

9.3.4 Code Generation

After the semantic analysis routine has produced an internal form telling what operations to perform and on which quantities, the last phase of compilation is code generation. Code generation is reasonably straightforward.

The resulting code can be optimized. Semantic analysis simply produces internal code without attention to the context of the original statements. However, with a little attention, the compiler can produce code that makes better use of the machine facilities. For example, assume the following three statements appear in this order in a program.

```
IF HOURS>40 THEN GROSS := GROSS + .5*(GROSS-40);
WHTAX := .05 * GROSS;
FICA := .12 * GROSS;
```

Since GROSS appears in all three statements, a machine language programmer would try to put GROSS in a register and reference it from the register for all three statements. (Recall that execution of an instruction referencing a register is usually faster than an instruction referencing memory.)

An optimizing compiler attempts to use an efficient sequence of instructions for each computation. Sometimes an optimizing compiler will reorder instructions for more efficient execution. An optimizing compiler may also replace one operation by another if the replacement is shorter or faster. For example, if addition is faster than multiplication, X := 2*A might be replaced by X := A+A. An optimizing compiler may move certain computations out of loops.

Consider the following loop.

```
FOR I := 1 TO 10 DO
   BEGIN
      PI := 3.14159;
      CIRCUM[I] := PI*I
   END
```

Clearly, the value of PI does not change inside the loop; it is therefore inefficient to replace its value each time the loop executes. An optimizing compiler would move the code for the PI := 3.14159 statement outside the loop. Although this is clumsy programming, there are instances in which the code generator, not the programmer, puts constant computations inside a loop. The optimizing compiler moves the invariant computation outside the loop to reduce execution time. There are a number of facets of code optimization; this section has only introduced the general notion.

Another feature handled during code generation is checking. Some compilers (especially student-oriented ones) will check the legality of some statements before their execution. For example, in the statement

```
RAD := XVAL;
```

XVAL must have a value before it can be assigned to RAD. If XVAL has never received a value, this statement assigns an unpredictable value to RAD. The programmer might make a mistake as the program is being entered and write XAVL in place of XVAL. In that case, even if XVAL had a value, there would not necessarily be a value for XAVL. Some compilers generate code to check that each variable has been assigned some value, either from input (READ), assignment (:=) or data initialization (FORTRAN DATA or PL/I INIT statements). Some compilers also verify that a subscript expression is within the declared limits for that subscript.

One final task performed during code generation is assignment of locations for variables and constants (although this may be done earlier by some compilers.) Each time the programmer declares a variable

```
VAR I,J: INTEGER;
```

or uses a constant

```
I := 20;
```

the lexical analyzer notes this in a table of labels and constants, called the *symbol table*. (The same type of table was produced by an assembler.) During code generation, the proper number of words of storage must be set aside for variables and constants. Furthermore, the correct values must be placed in the constant locations. (The value 20 would have to be placed in a location for the preceding example.) These things are done during code generation.

HIPO Description of Code Generator

HIERARCHY
Called by parser when derivation tree completed

INPUT
Internal pseudo machine language code from semantic processor

PROCESS

1. Allocate storage for variables and constants used in the program just parsed. Place the proper binary values in the locations assigned to constants.
2. Convert internal pseudo machine language code to real executable machine code, performing optimization or inserting checking code, if desired.
3. Produce a version of the generated code either in main memory or on some external storage medium such as disk, tape, or punched cards.

OUTPUT
Executable machine language program.

9.4   SUMMARY

1. Some programming languages are large and complex; others are small and simple. Some are oriented toward business applications, while others are more appropriate for scientific uses or for special applications. Compilers for these languages run on different machines.
2. A grammar is a formal description of a programming language. Grammars consist of production rules; these rules are applied in succession to generate legal statements of the language.
3. The four major components of a compiler are lexical analysis, parsing, semantic processing, and code generation.
4. The lexical analyzer takes the input program and breaks it into standardized objects called tokens. It also records all variables and constants.
5. The parser examines the tokens and attempts to match the input statements to legal forms in the language. Top-down parsers try to produce the input statement, while bottom-up parsers try to reduce the input to the start symbol of the grammar.
6. The semantic analysis routine interprets the meaning of each statement, creating an internal form from which machine code can be generated.
7. The code generation routine takes the internal representation of the program and produces executable machine code that does what the program intends. It is responsible for any code optimization as well as allocation of storage for constants and variables. Some compilers do not generate code; instead, they stop with intermediate code and supply a utility program to simulate the effect of executing that intermediate code.

9.5   TERMS USED

Commercial programming language
Scientific programming language

FORTRAN
PASCAL
Structured programming
BASIC
Interpreted program
COBOL
ALGOL
PL/I
Grammar
Production
Rule
Variable
Nonterminal
Terminal
Start symbol
Derivation
Lexical analyzer
Token
Parser
Top-down parser
Bottom-up parser
Production of grammatical forms
Reduction of input program
Derivation tree
Semantic analysis
Intermediate code
Code generation
Interpretation
Code optimization
Storage allocation

9.6 QUESTIONS

1. Which of the languages listed in Section 9.1 would be most appropriate for each of the following tasks?
   (a) Writing a program to print paychecks for all employees of the state of Tennessee.
   (b) Writing a program to convert metric to U.S. weights and measures for a demonstration program on a microcomputer.
   (c) Solving a system of simultaneous equations in 50 variables.
   (d) Writing a program to form paragraphs and pages from input text to sell to microcomputer users.
2. Using the grammar of Section 9.2, show how each of the following strings is produced by the grammar.
   (a) -426
   (b) 500

3. Is the grammar in Section 9.2 unique? That is, can you find another different grammar that generates exactly the same strings?

4. With the grammar of Section 9.2, is a derivation unique? That is, for each string generated by the grammar, is there only one sequence of productions that will generate that string?

5. In FORTRAN an identifier (variable) begins with a letter and consists of up to 6 letters or digits. For example, I, MEAN, XBAR1, and A1B2C3 are acceptable identifiers, but 1WAY and @123 are not. Write a grammar that generates exactly the legal FORTRAN identifiers.

6. *(More challenging.)* Write a grammar that generates all the legal arithmetic expressions formed using variables and the binary arithmetic operators + , − , * , and / . The terminals of this grammar may be <variable>, + , − , * , and / .

7. What are the similarities between pass one of a two-pass assembler and the lexical analyzer of a compiler? What are the differences?

8. Number the productions of the grammar in Section 9.2 from 1 to 15. Then write the series of numbers of productions in order applied during the top-down parse of the string +48. Do the same for a bottom-up parse.

9. If you translated the statement A : = B + C * D by hand, you would probably generate code similar to

    ```
    LOAD    C
    MULT    D
    ADD     B
    STORE   A
    ```

    However, for the statement A : = B + C + D , you would probably generate

    ```
    LOAD    B
    ADD     C
    ADD     D
    STORE   A
    ```

    Can you explain your algorithm for deciding when to load B immediately and when to defer using it until after having computed something else? (*Note:* This is the basic problem of code generation. Although there may be many streams of code that will produce a desired effect, compilers want to select a series of instructions that will match the code of good assembler language programmers coding the same thing.)

10. What is the motivation for generating an internal code form of a translated program and then converting that internal form to executable machine code?

11. Question 7 of Chapter 8 asked if the symbol table of an assembler needed to be kept during execution. Does the symbol table of a compiler have to be kept? Why or why not?

chapter **10**

Loaders and Relocation

This chapter contains information on what happens to a program after it has been assembled or compiled. *Loading* a program means placing it in memory and readying it for execution. On some small computers loading is done as part of the translation process. On other machines the object code produced by an assembler or compiler is written on an I/O device. It must then be loaded into memory for execution to occur.

10.1   RELOCATION

Relocation was introduced in Section 7.5. In this section you will see when relocation is needed and exactly how it is done.

Most compiled or assembled programs are 0-origin. That is, object code is produced for them as if the programs were to be placed in memory location 0. Consider the following program fragment.

```
LOOP   some instruction
       B . . LOOP
```

The statement labeled LOOP is located somewhere within the program; assume it is 320 bytes from the start of the program. The branch instruction B LOOP will be assembled as if it were a branch to location 320 in memory. Figure 10.1 shows the translation of this branch.

When the program is executed, it may, however, not be placed in location 0. Suppose, for example, the program is loaded beginning at location 10000. Then the branch statement should reference location 10320. The value 10000 is a *relocation factor* for this execution of the program. It is added to all addresses within the program to convert them from 0-origin addresses to real memory

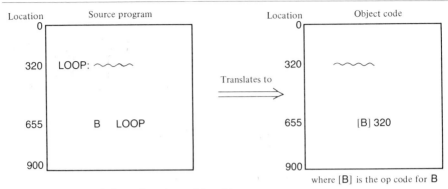

Figure 10.1   Translation of a relocatable address.

addresses. An address that must be relocated in order to execute the program is called a *relocatable address.*

Some addresses, however, are not relocatable addresses. Consider, for example, memory mapped I/O, as described in Section 6.3.1. This is a form of I/O in which one or more unique addresses are associated with each device; although these are not the addresses of actual memory locations, they seem just like words of memory. To write to an I/O device, you store a value in the memory address associated with the device; to read from a device, you fetch (e.g., by a LOAD) the value at the assigned address. These addresses are fixed; for example, the printer might be associated with address 74730. Any program accessing the printer will use address 74730. If a program is located at address 10000, the relocation factor 10000 should *not* be added to address 74730. We say that address 74730 is an *absolute address,* since it should not have a relocation factor added to it prior to its use.

The assembler or compiler must produce a list of the relocatable addresses so that they can be adjusted before the program is executed. There are a number of ways this can be done.

10.1.1   No Relocation

On some machines it may be possible to predict exactly where a program will be placed for execution; this can be known during assembly. For example, on a single-user microcomputer, the monitor always occupies the same addresses; the remaining memory is available to the user. The first word directly after the monitor could then be the start of the user program. This start address does not change.

Suppose, for example, the monitor occupies addresses 0 to 137. The program could then begin at address 138. The assembler could be directed to produce a program with an origin of 138, so all internal addresses would be correct. The code generated could be placed directly in memory beginning at address 138 and executed without change. Such a program is called a *fixed-origin program.* Figure 10.2 shows a user program translated to use origin 138.

10.1.2   Program Counter-Relative Addresses

A simple means of relocation is to have relocatable addresses be assembled relative to the program counter. That is, each address reference in the program is

Location	Object code		Statement		
0138		TOP	START	X'138'
0138	1B22		SR	2,2
013A	5830 0498		L	3,= F'10'
013E	1A23	LOOP	AR	2,3
0140	5B30 049C		S	3,= F'1'
0144	4770 013E		BNZ	LOOP
0148	5020 0494		ST	2,ANS
⋮			⋮	
0494		ANS	DS	1F
0498			END	
0498				= F'10'
049C				= F'1'

Memory

0	
	⋮
0138	1B22
	5830 0498
	1A23
	5B30 049C
	4770 013E
	5020 0494
	⋮

Figure 10.2   User program translated with origin 138.

composed of two parts: the value in the program counter at the time the instruction is executed, and a positive or negative value to be added to the program counter. The program in Figure 10.2 would then look like this.

    320   LOOP   some instruction

                   . . .

    360   B   LOOP   effectively   B   − 41

When the branch is executed, the program counter will contain 361 (the address just after the branch instruction). Since 361 + (−41) = 320, this code produces the correct relative address.

Now consider how the program is correctly relocated. When this program is executed, the operating system places the value 10000 in the program counter in order to select the first instruction of the program. When the branch instruction is executed, the program counter will contain 10361; 10361 + (−41) = 10320, the correct relocated value. If the program is placed instead in location 5000, all addresses in the program are correctly relocated when the program counter is loaded with the initial value of 5000 prior to execution. Absolute addresses do not have the program counter value added to them. Figure 10.3 shows how this type of relocation works in practice. A variation of this form is used in the PDP-11.

This method is simple and effective. Addresses can be calculated quickly during execution, since the program counter is always available to address decoding circuitry. This method is limited, however, because addresses outside the pro-

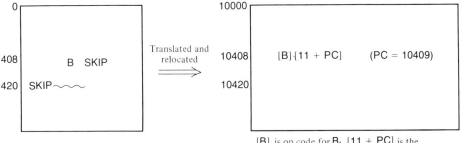

[B] is op code for B; [11 + PC] is the encoding of " 11 instructions beyond the current address in the program counter "

Figure 10.3   Code relative to the program counter.

gram must be handled differently. These address references can arise if a program is assembled in separate parts or is combined with shared (library) subprocedures.

10.1.3 Base Registers

Instead of having the program counter implicitly included in all relocatable address references, some machines use separate registers, called *base registers*. A base register contains a real address (often the address of the start, or base, of the program—hence the name base register). The value in the base register is added to each relocatable address formed during execution. On some machines the programmer manages base registers; on others the base registers are out of the normal control of the user. A base register contains a fixed address, usually at the top of the program. Unlike the program counter, it does not change as each instruction is executed.

One base register gives effectively the same characteristics for relocation as code that is relative to the program counter. In fact, the instruction

    B   LOOP

effectively becomes

    B   320+(contents of base register)

which resembles an instruction that is relative to the program counter.

With base registers, it is also possible to address some operands without having the base register added to the address; absolute addresses should not be relocated, so the contents of a base register should not be added to an absolute address. Absolute address references operate with no base register.

With more than one base register it is possible to have a number of separate program segments, each with its own base register. Each instruction indicates which base register is to be used for relocation and what displacement is to be added to that base register.

Multiple base registers permit sharing of code between two programs, and they permit pieces of a program to be assembled or compiled independently; each of these has its own base register during execution. A two-part program with two base registers is shown in Figure 10.4. Base registers are also efficient for calculat-

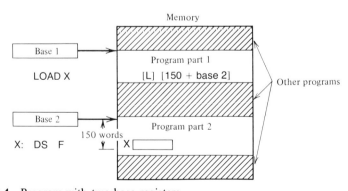

Figure 10.4 Program with two base registers.

ing actual addresses, since the base register is readily accessible to the CPU. The IBM 360-370 uses a form of base register for relocation.

However, there can be disadvantages to using base registers. If the user is responsible for maintaining the values in the base registers, putting the wrong value in a base register is an extra source of error. If the base register is one of the general-purpose registers, the programmer has effectively lost a register that could otherwise be used for computation.

10.1.4 Translated Addresses

A more complicated but much more flexible relocation mechanism is to translate all addresses. This relocation scheme is known as *paging, virtual memory,* or *dynamic address translation.* Each program address consists of two parts: a *page* number and a *line* number. As an example, assume that the line number is the rightmost 2 (decimal) digits of the address, and the page number is the rest. Address 320 is then line 20 of page 3. Each page is 100 (decimal) lines or addresses or words in size. The program is artificially divided into a number of pages, each 100 words long.

Real memory is divided into 100-word units, called *page frames.* A page of a program could be placed in any available page frame without regard for where any of the rest of the program was. Also needed is a *translation* or *page table.* This is a table of page numbers and the addresses of the page frames containing those pages. For example, the preceding program might use the table in Figure 10.5.

Page table				Memory	Address
Page number	Frame address			Other pages	14200
. . .	. . . . .			Page 2	
2	14200			Other pages	
3	96800				
. . .	. . . . .				
				Page 3	96800
				Other pages	

Figure 10.5 Address translation.

During execution, each address reference is broken into the page number and the line number. The page number is looked up in the page table, and the line number is added to the frame address from the page table. For example, address 320 would translate into 96820, since 320 is page 3, line 20, as shown in Figure 10.6. From the page table, page 3 has frame address 96800. The frame address plus the line number is 96800 + 20 = 96820.

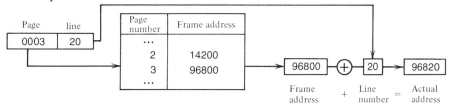

Figure 10.6 Address calculation with Translated addresses.

Translation of addresses is potentially a slow technique, since each address must be broken into the page and line numbers, and the page number must be found in the page table. Computers using translation often have additional hardware to improve the efficiency of the translation. Address translation permits efficient use of computer memory, since programs can be split into separate pages and placed in any available page frames; it is not necessary to have one block of contiguous memory as large as the program. (In fact, not all pages of a program need to be in memory for the program to execute.) Some IBM 370 computers use a form of address translation as well as multiple base registers.

Whatever relocation method is used, a program must be relocated before it can be executed. (No relocation is needed, of course, if the program has been translated with an origin of exactly the address where it will be loaded. This is possible on single-user computers, such as many of the microcomputers.) Relocation permits a program to be broken into parts, with each part assembled separately. If a program is composed of separately assembled or compiled pieces, some of those pieces could be placed in a library so that other users could share them. Loading and library fetches will be studied in the next section.

10.2 PROGRAM LINKING

One of the major advantages of computers is that they permit different programmers to work on one project, sharing the work load. Higher-level languages are built around the concept of the subprocedure (subprogram or subroutine), with each subprocedure considered a separate unit. A program consists of a number of different subprocedures, each written perhaps at a different time and by a different programmer. The higher-level languages have established conventions on how arguments are to be passed and how control is to be transferred. At the programmer level, then, there is little complication in calling a procedure. However, there is some additional work that must be handled by software in order to connect two independent program units. Binding two or more procedures together is known as *linking*.

Linking includes several steps.

1. Determine which procedures have been defined in the user program. Most higher-level languages allow the user to define one or more procedures in a program. These procedures and their positions within the supplied object code must be recorded.
2. Determine which procedures have been called in the user program. The list from step 2 minus the list from step 1 gives a list of routines called but not defined.
3. Locate a usable copy of any procedures called but not defined. (Notice that these procedures may call others, so it is necessary to increase the lists in steps 1 and 2 for each procedure definition.)
4. Collect all procedure definitions, noting the relative location of each procedure. Report on any procedure definitions still missing.

5. Place the entire program unit in memory, relocating it as necessary. Set the value of the program counter to the start of the program unit (i.e., branch to the start) and begin execution of the unit.

In the rest of this section we will see how linking is handled by a number of different operating systems.

10.2.1   No Relocation/Linking

Section 10.1.1 showed that on some single-user computers relocation may not be necessary. The translators are informed exactly where their output (the translated program) will reside, and they produce code that uses exactly those addresses. No relocation of the program is necessary. In such a system it is also possible to use subprocedures written at different times.

For example, assume you are writing a program and you wish to use a special-purpose subprocedure called SHOW for graphics displays. The author of SHOW might have decided to write it so that it would use addresses 27350 and above. You have only the object code of a translated version of SHOW. In your program you might use an equate statement to indicate that SHOW was associated with address 27350. The statement

    CALL   SHOW

is assembled as if it were

    CALL   27350.

You would then load both your program and SHOW into memory, being sure SHOW was placed at 27350. During execution, the call would transfer to location 27350, the entry point for SHOW, and after it finished, SHOW would return to your program. This process can be used with any number of routines; as your program is translated, you only have to supply the addresses of other routines that will be loaded with yours. A possible layout of memory is shown in Figure 10.7.

This mechanism is simple, but it has one serious flaw. Suppose you wanted to use both SHOW and a routine to compute the trigonometric sine. Also suppose

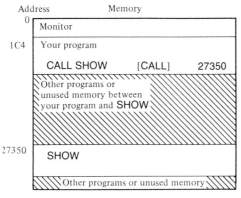

Figure 10.7   Multiple procedures in fixed memory locations.

that the author of the sine routine placed that code at 27350. One memory location cannot contain code for both SHOW and SINE. Furthermore, both routines are bound to those addresses, since they have been translated assuming the procedures would be located there. The use of SHOW and SINE in the same program is impossible.

A possible solution is to have two copies of SHOW, one that runs at address 27350 and another that runs in some other address, say 13660. However, address 13660 might overlap an address used by a routine to compute standard deviations. The assumption is that the three routines, SHOW, SINE, and STDEV would not be needed together. Of course, the three might be needed together, and then you would be right back where you started.

This problem is not one of those that "might occur but in practice really doesn't." As more and larger programs are written for a particular machine, the chances are stronger that one program will overlap another. This is a serious flaw with avoiding relocation, and this problem was the primary motivating factor behind libraries and utility programs to manage a program library.

10.2.2 Program Libraries

In order to save time retranslating programs that are in final form, the object code of a subprocedure can be saved in a library. A *library* is a collection of object code and a table of pointers. The table of pointers (called a *directory* or *table of contents*) tells what procedures are contained in the library and where they are located. The library can be kept on any convenient storage medium (cassette tape, reel-to-reel tape, or direct access device); it is even possible, although cumbersome, to keep a library on punched cards or paper tape. (In the latter case the directory would be apt to be written on paper for human use; for the other media, the directory would be machine readable.)

Each program in the library is translated with a 0-origin. Each indicates what procedures it calls; it also contains any other notes needed for relocation. Since each routine has a 0-origin, with proper relocation, it can be placed in any memory locations. Thus, a program and all of its called subprocedures could be located in any free memory space. There is no difficulty with one routine being mutually exclusive with another because of overlap of address space.

A utility program called a *linker* takes a procedure and searches a library to locate copies of any procedures called but not defined in the first procedure. The linker binds the object code for all of these routines together to form one object program ready for relocation. The linker changes addresses in branches or calls between the linked procedures so that each correctly references the others. When the program is to be run, the entire collection of routines is relocated as a unit, just as if it were a large program. An example of changing addresses in calls is shown in Figure 10.8.

The use of subprocedures permits programs to be written in more than one language. Each subprocedure can be written in whatever language is most convenient or most appropriate, and these separate language modules can be combined at execution time.

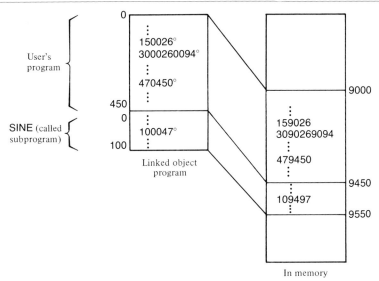

Figure 10.8 Relocating called procedures.

10.3 LOADING

Loading is the final process prior to a program's execution. A *loader* is a program that brings a fixed origin or relocatable program into memory, modifies relocatable addresses as necessary, and begins execution of the program. A program that has a fixed origin will not need relocation before it is executed. The program counter can be set to the first address of the program (this address is called its *entry point*), and the CPU continues to execute the instructions of the program one by one.

If, however, the program is relocatable, certain addresses must be changed to reflect the actual memory addresses at which the program will execute. When the program was translated, the compiler or assembler created a list of any addresses that needed relocating. The loader adds the relocation factor to these addresses. It then sets the program counter and begins execution of the program. Relocation of a program is shown in Figure 10.9.

The loader also performs any "cleanup" necessary after the program has executed. This cleanup might include releasing resources no longer needed by the program or attempting to find another program to load and execute. Effectively, then, the loader "calls" the program as if the program were a subprocedure. In this way execution of the loader is suspended during execution of the program. The program completes by returning to the loader, which performs any necessary cleanup functions.

10.4 SUMMARY

1. Relocation is the process of taking a translated program, assigning it to a set of memory locations, and revising addresses within the program to reflect the memory addresses assigned to the program.

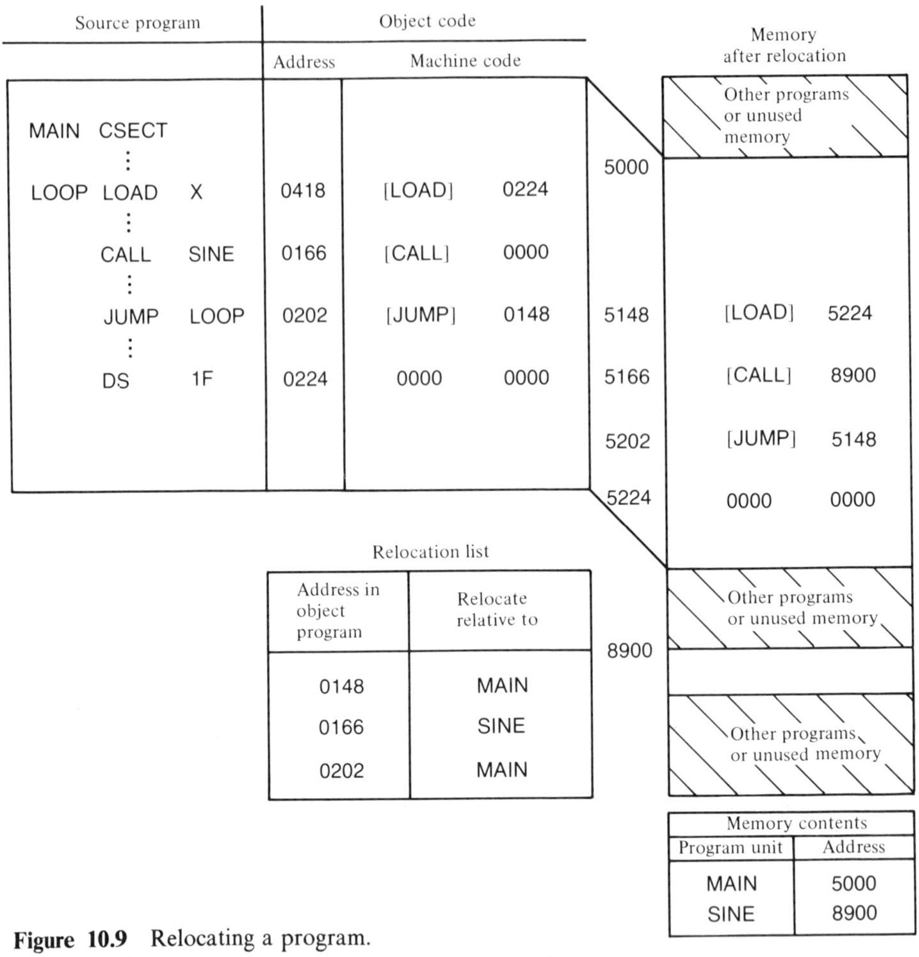

Source program		Object code			Memory after relocation

Figure 10.9 Relocating a program.

2. Programs may be relocated by use of the program counter or a base register. In both cases an operand is translated into a displacement to be added to the value of the program counter or the base register during execution. The program counter or base register plus the displacement form a real address. Only one register, the program counter or the base register, must be changed in order to relocate addresses that were translated relative to it. This mechanism is fast to use.

3. Addresses can be translated during execution in a paging or virtual memory mode. In this method a table in memory is used to convert each address in a program to a real address. Each address is translated from virtual to real every time it is used. In this way a program is seen as a number of disjoint pieces (called pages) that do not have to be located consecutively in memory.

4. Linking is combining a program with all of the subprocedures it calls. Linking may involve searching libraries to find the called procedures.

5. After a program has been linked, it is ready to be loaded (relocated)

and executed. The loader effectively calls a program. The program stops by returning to the loader, which disposes of the program and attempts to relocate the next program.

10.5 TERMS USED

Relocation
0-origin program
Fixed-origin program
Relocation factor
Relocatable address
Absolute address
Program counter-relative address
Base register
Displacement
Translated address
Paging
Virtual memory
Dynamic memory management
Line number
Page number
Page frame
Page table
Linking
Program library
Directory
Linker
Loaded program

10.6 QUESTIONS

1. Not all labels of a program are relocatable. For each of the following labels, tell whether it is relocatable or not.

   (a) LOOP   LOAD   X
   (b) L1   EQU   *   (reference to location counter)
   (c) LOOP   B   TOP
   (d) R5   EQU   5
   (e) CARD   EQU   CARDFORM + 20
   (f) X   DC   F ' − 1 0 0 '

2. Can a program call itself? That is, is there anything in the linking or loading process that would prevent this?

3. If the program counter is being used for relocation (i.e., addresses are computed as the contents of the program counter plus or minus some displacement), absolute addresses must be differentiated so that the location counter will not be added to them. This can be done either by special instructions, "absolute instructions," whose operands would *never* have the location counter added, or by a single bit in the instruction operand part to tell

whether the operand is absolute or relative to the program counter. What are the advantages and disadvantages of each representation?

4. Assuming instructions are all 2 bytes long, what will be the displacement added to the location counter to reference:
   (a) The current instruction (e.g., LOOP B LOOP)?
   (b) The instruction after the current instruction?
   (c) The instruction before the current instruction?

5. Can program counter-relative addressing be used to call a library routine that is not assembled or compiled with the current program? Why or why not?

6. If three successive statements all refer to the same operand (e.g., LOAD X, MULT X, STORE X) will the displacements generated to fetch the operand in these three statements be the same if program counter-relative addressing is used? Will the displacements be the same if a base register is used?

7. Using the page translation table in Section 10.1.4, to what address would 203 translate? To what address would 359 translate?

8. Differentiate between "linking" and "loading."

9. What information does a compiler or assembler transmit to assist in linking the translated program? What information does a compiler or assembler transmit to assist in loading a translated program?

10. What is the advantage of having all page frames the same size?

11. What can be done if a program is 40,000 words long and there are two free blocks of memory, each 25,000 words long, but these blocks of memory are not adjacent, assuming
   (a) a single base register is used for relocation?
   (b) page translation is used for relocation?

chapter 11

Monitors and Operating Systems

Throughout this book the terms *monitor* and *operating system* have been used, and they have been defined as support programs that help the user make full use of the facilities of the computer. Depending on the size of the computer, the operating system may provide few or many services. A monitor or an operating system provides three kinds of services.

1. *User Services.* Provide programs that the user needs to call in order to use the machine. This category includes programs such as assemblers, compilers, linkers, and loaders. Certain subprocedure libraries, search and sort programs, and utility programs to copy collections of data are also parts of the operating system directly called by the user.

2. *Support Programs.* Provide programs that support the users' programs in execution, although this support structure may be invisible to the user. For example, the programs that handle interrupts are important to completing execution of a user program, even though the user never calls these directly. Also in this group are device drivers, which handle the interface between a user program and an actual I/O device, and programs that do accounting, to record who used the computer and which computer facilities were used.

3. *Resource Allocators.* Provide programs that permit and even enforce sharing of computer resources among a number of users. This item includes programs that schedule jobs for execution, those that allocate temporary and permanent space on I/O devices, and those that distribute use of the CPU among ready programs.

These are the three major components of an operating system. However, any one operating system may not contain items from all three categories, and some systems may not provide all of the services described under one category.

Section 11.1 contains a short introduction to terms that will be needed throughout the rest of the chapter. Then operating systems for each of the three sample machines—Intel 8080, PDP-11, and IBM 360-370 computers—will be described.

11.1 BACKGROUND DEFINITIONS

A *uniprogramming* system has only one program able to use the resources of a computer at one time; most microcomputers are uniprogrammed. That is, one user powers up the machine, enters or modifies a program, executes it, collects any results, and eventually leaves the computer for someone else to use.

A *multiprogrammed* computer is shared among a number of users. Since there is (generally) only one CPU, only one program can actually be in execution at one instant. However, running a substantial program on a multiprogrammed machine may entail a number of activities: reading data from a magnetic tape, printing result values on a printer, and executing instructions with the CPU. These activities are *asynchronous,* which means that they occur at different rates. On large computers they are handled by independent modules, so that more than one of them can go on in parallel.

Consider, however, a program that has the following kinds of statements:

```
READ (A,B,C);
D := A+B*C;
WRITELN (D);
```

These three statements must be kept in sequence; the assignment to D cannot occur before the READ of A, B, and C is done, and the WRITELN cannot take place until D has a value. The input, output, and computing activities must be synchronized so that none of these activities begins until necessary data are available. Higher-level languages automatically provide synchronization and, in assembler language, it is possible to test the status of an I/O operation before doing a computation requiring that the I/O be done.

I/O activities are substantially slower than the CPU, often by a factor of 1000 or more; that is, in the time it takes to read one data item, it may be possible to perform 1000 CPU instructions. Figure 11.1 shows a time line for a program that reads and computes using the values read. Two graphs are shown: one for CPU activity and one for I/O activity.

As you can see, the CPU is inactive much of the time. In multiprogramming it is desirable to spread the use of all resources of the computer—including the CPU—among all users. During the time that the program in Figure 11.1 is not using the CPU, the CPU could be transferred to another user. For example, the job in Figure 11.2 requires no input data; it computes for a relatively long period of time and then prints a piece of information.

Figure 11.1   Progress of I/O and CPU on a simple program.

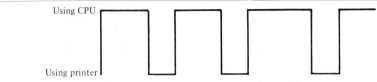

Figure 11.2 Use of CPU and printer by a CPU dominant job.

During the time the first job is using the CPU, the second can use the printer; while the first is occupied with input, the second can use the CPU. This is known as *CPU-I/O overlap*. Notice how this overlap occurs if the two graphs are superimposed, as shown in Figure 11.3.

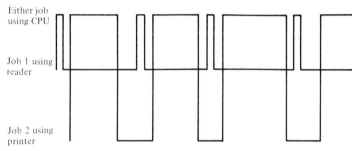

Figure 11.3 Time graphs for both jobs.

This same type of process can occur with more than two jobs. Of course, sometimes the demands of jobs will not mesh as perfectly as they did in Figure 11.3 so some jobs will have to wait for a resource they want. However, multiprogramming can be used to improve the utilization of *all* computing resources. The operating system is the facility from which users request and are granted use of computing resources. The term *degree of multiprogramming* refers to the maximum number of tasks that may be in execution at one time. It would seem that a high degree of multiprogramming is a way to keep many resources fully used. However, this may not be so, since too many tasks competing for a small number of resources means inefficient usage as tasks hold some resources while they have to wait for others.

Small to medium computing facilities may use *foreground-background processing*. In this mode two tasks are selected; one has high importance but limited need for CPU service; the other has lower priority. The first task is the foreground task, and the second is the background task. The foreground task receives CPU service whenever it requests it, even if the background task must be interrupted to provide this. The background task is available, however, to take up the "slack" in the CPU usage.

Designing or managing a large multiprogramming system can be complex, since it is difficult to allocate resources to keep as many resources in use as possible. In a foreground-background system the only major decision is which task is the foreground one and which the background. A foreground-background system is frequently used with experiments, where bursts of data will be presented at times throughout the running of the experiment but, between these bursts, the CPU is not needed. The experiment task becomes the foreground task, and various noncritical analyses of data can fill in the background.

One class of operating system is a *batch* system. In a batch system, users present their programs and all necessary data and can walk away from the system until the job has been processed. A user's job is processed without the user's involvement during the execution of the job.

In contrast to batch processing, *interactive processing* permits the user to interact with a program during its execution. Generally, the user submits such a program through a video display terminal and can supply data during the execution of the program. This variety of processing is called *timesharing* because the time of the computer is shared among a number of users. Since human response and typing time is substantially slower than CPU speed, the CPU can be shared among a number of human users in the same way that it was shared previously between two programs using I/O devices.

Another form of operating system is a *real-time* system. In a real-time system the computer receives signals from outside the system. These signals will occur at a specified rate, and the system must respond to these signals as they occur. Examples of this sort of system are online transaction systems, such as airline reservation systems, and systems that receive data from experiments, such as space satellites or nuclear reactions. These systems transmit data to the computer for processing; the results obtained by the computer are needed, for example, to correct the flight path of the satellite or to operate control rods to control the nuclear reaction.

The remaining sections of this chapter contain descriptions of popular operating systems for each of the three sample computing systems.

11.2 CP/M FOR THE INTEL 8080

CP/M is a popular operating system for 8080-based microcomputers. It is a product of the Digital Research Corporation of Pacific Grove, California. CP/M is a (floppy) disk-based system; this means that major portions of the operating system are maintained on disk, and the operating system establishes a line of communication between disk and user programs. CP/M also creates communication with a console (usually a video display terminal).

An important feature of CP/M is its file-managing facility. Recall from Section 6.2.1 that a *file* is a collection of related data items. Many operating systems provide a way to save files for a period of time and to be able to retrieve them later. These files may be source programs, object programs, data, or any other kind of binary records. A user of CP/M has commands to create, delete, modify, and print or read files of text or programs. CP/M maintains a *directory* for each user; this is a listing of all files owned by a user.

To assist a user in preparing files, CP/M provides a *text editor,* a program by which a user can create a file or make modifications to an existing file. When modifying an existing file, the editor fills an internal buffer with the file, makes modifications to the file in the buffer and, when the user has finished making modifications, rewrites the file on a disk. Another feature of CP/M is a command interpreter to accept and perform commands submitted by the user.

CP/M provides several utility programs for moving and copying data from one place to another. A BASIC translator and an assembler are also standard parts of CP/M. Other languages and utility programs are also available.

All of the facilities described for CP/M are of the first category listed at the beginning of this chapter: user service programs. They provide services to the user on demand. Additionally, there are some hidden support routines that handle interrupts and interface between a processing program and various I/O devices. Support programs were the second category listed at the beginning of the chapter. However, there are no programs of type three—resource allocators—because these were designed for sharing of computer resources. Generally, 8080-based systems are for a single user at a time, so it is unnecessary to have software for sharing with only one user.

11.3 OPERATING SYSTEMS FOR PDP-11S

There are a range of operating systems for the PDP-11. RT-11 is a simple system, designed for either the foreground-background mode or processing a single job at a time. RSTS is a flexible time-sharing system, and RSX is a more general-purpose multiprogramming system. All of these are supplied by the Digital Equipment Corporation, the manufacturers of the PDP-11. Additionally, Bell Telephone Laboratories, through Western Electric, distribute UNIX, a powerful timesharing system.

11.3.1 RT-11

RT-11 is designed for support of one or two concurrent jobs. When running one job, that job has full access to the computer resources; two jobs run in the foreground-background mode, so that one job has inherent priority over the other. RT-11 handles up to two jobs in the foreground-background mode. This system runs on small to medium PDP-11 computers.

The system supports a variety of peripheral devices, especially laboratory devices and graphics equipment. For this reason RT-11 is especially popular in scientific laboratories, where devices controlling experiments are used. The PDP-11 in foreground mode can be executing a program that processes data as it comes in and then, perhaps, activates mechanical devices to control the process of the experiment. In the background mode it can perform statistical computation on the data received. In this way the important task (controlling the experiment) takes precedence over the task that is not time dependent (doing statistical calculations).

RT-11 supports a type of BASIC interpreter called multiuser BASIC. This interpreter can support four or eight BASIC users at once. The BASIC interpreter is only one job to RT-11; it shares the resources it receives among a number of users. In this way this interpreter gives the effect of four or eight people sharing a computer that ordinarily permits only two-user sharing.

11.3.2 UNIX

UNIX is a timesharing system that runs on medium to large PDP-11 computers. Standard features are an editor, several language translators, and various utility programs. The necessary routines to support users—interrupt handlers and device drivers—and resource allocation programs are available.

One important feature of UNIX is its file structure. Every system user (i.e., everybody who is allowed access to the system, whether currently running a program or not) is represented by a directory in the file system. The file system is organized like a tree. Figure 11.4 shows three users, CEH, CPP, and MXS.

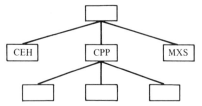

Figure 11.4   UNIX file system showing three users.

Each user can create additional directories, which become subtrees under that user. Suppose, for example, that CPP is working on three projects: BOOK, COMPARE, and LIST. User CPP could set up each of these as a separate directory. When working on any one of these, CPP might want to create a temporary file and, to make it easy to remember, might want to call this file TEMP. The file TEMP under directory BOOK would have the name CPP/BOOK/TEMP.[1] Each slash character (/) indicates which path to take from the current directory. In this way, CPP/BOOK/TEMP is a completely separate file from CPP/LIST/TEMP. Every directory contains pointers to other files, which can be directories, data files, or both. Figure 11.5 shows these directories and several subfiles.

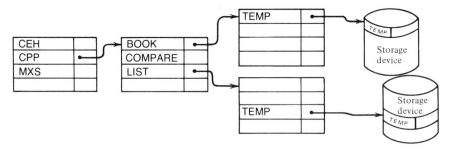

Figure 11.5   User directory with subdirectories.

A user can be positioned at any directory, and references are assumed to start at that directory. Thus, if the user was currently positioned at directory CPP, TEMP would be accessed as LIST/TEMP; if the user was currently positioned at directory LIST, file TEMP would be known simply as TEMP. The chdir command permits a user to move to a higher or lower directory in the file structure.

When a file is created, the owner specifies certain access rights: who may use the file and how. For example, it is possible to set up a file so that any other user can execute the file (meaning it is a translated program) or read the file (see what it contains), but only the file owner can change the file. A user accesses a file belonging to another user simply by specifying the file name. For example, if you

---

[1] This is not quite the correct path name for TEMP because it ignores where CPP may be located in the file structure tree; that is, it does not specify how to find CPP starting from the top of the tree. We will ignore the path from the root to CPP or any other user in this and following examples.

want to print the file PASCOM, which is a file directly under user CEH, you issue the monitor command

pr CEH/PASCOM

The command p r executes a program (also named p r), which prints a file, supplying page headings and page numbers.

To a UNIX user, everything is a file: every program, device, and data file is effectively the same kind of file. Therefore, in order to display file LETTER on the video display terminal that is known to UNIX as TTY8, you execute a command similar to

cat LETTER > TTY8

which copies the file LETTER into the file TTY8, which is the file for the terminal.

A number of user programs are available under UNIX, including ones for formatting manuscripts, writing compilers, and manipulating data files. Two languages available under UNIX are RATFOR (RATional FORtran), a FORTRAN-like language with many extensions, and C, a higher-level language especially well suited for writing systems programs. Compilers for other languages are available.

11.4   IBM 360-370

There are a number of operating systems for IBM 360-370 computers, ranging from simple systems for smaller installations to extremely powerful systems for large installations. Two systems that will be described briefly here are OS-MVT and VM/370.

11.4.1   OS-MVT

OS-MVT is designed for moderately large IBM 360-370 installations. This system is primarily oriented toward batch processing. It runs up to 15 jobs at one time, although any (or all) of the jobs can create independent subjobs a potentially endless number of times. The system can handle large commercial applications, so it has several very powerful data management features. There are four standard file organizations supported for users; one of these, direct organization, lets a user create any different organization for specialized applications.

The system command language removes all selection of actual I/O devices or media from the program itself. This makes it possible to test a program using, for example, card input, and then run the program in production getting input from a magnetic tape. A command language called JCL (Job Control Language) is the means for actual device selection, which is done as a job executes.

Many languages are supported under OS-MVT, including FORTRAN, COBOL, PL/I, and assembler language. Private software vendors distribute compilers for other languages such as PASCAL.

11.4.2   VM/370

VM/370 runs only on the IBM 370 and similar computers. It is an operating system that runs other operating systems. That is, the tasks running directly under VM are different operating systems, and these "suboperating systems" run the actual user jobs. An operating system is simply a program so, at least in theory, an operating system should be able to execute another operating system just as it executes other user programs. Figure 11.6 shows VM/370 running other operating systems.

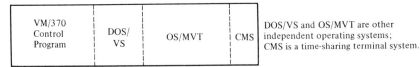

Figure 11.6 VM/370 running other operating systems.

As defined, an operating system allocates the resources of a computing system to the requesting users. VM/370 allocates the resources of an IBM 370-like machine to one or more other operating systems, which in turn allocate resources to users. VM/370 presents each user operating system with some of the resources of the real computer, but each suboperating system believes it has use of an entire machine. Effectively, then, each system under VM/370 has control of a pseudo machine, where the pseudo machine is a machine having just the resources allotted by VM/370. (This pseudo machine is also called a *virtual machine.*) Figure 11.7 shows VM/370 supporting virtual machines.

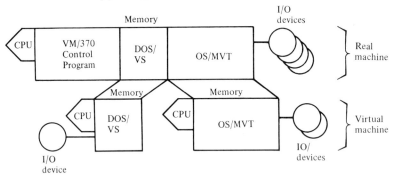

Figure 11.7 VM/370 running virtual machines.

Of course, this two-level allocation of resources introduces an amount of overhead. There are important benefits to using VM/370, however. An operating system is a collection of programs; like other programs, operating systems must be tested, corrected, and extended. Ordinarily, when an operating system is being tested or changed, normal user tasks cannot be run, since they might interfere with the features being tested or the changed system might not be correct and would therefore incorrectly process user programs. Most computing installations have a reserved time for operating systems development; during this time normal user jobs are not run. Under VM/370, it is possible to run two operating systems, one a "stable" operating system that will run the user jobs, and the other a "test" operating system that is under development. In this way it is not necessary to prohibit normal users during operating system modifications.

Another justification for running two operating systems under VM/370 would be if a firm wanted to convert from one operating system to another (e.g., an installation moving to a more powerful system or upgrading to a new computer). Some user programs would have to be modified in order to run under the new system. Changing from one system to the other overnight would prevent executing any programs that need to be changed. Still, these programs would have to be converted at some time. Running two operating systems concurrently would allow unconverted programs to be run under the old system, and the converted ones could be tested and run with the new system. These programs could be converted gradually, as shown in Figure 11.8.

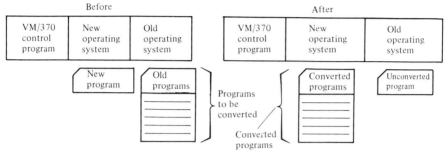

Figure 11.8   Converting programs from one system to another.

VM/370 features are mainly those of the third category for operating systems: providing and enforcing sharing of resources to the users.

11.5   SUMMARY

This chapter has contained descriptions of the features of a number of monitors or operating systems. These systems have ranged from single-user support systems to an operating system that runs other operating systems. The systems have been arranged more or less in increasing order of complexity and number of user services. Each step added items of the first two categories (user services and support) as well as the third category (resource sharing) of operating systems functions.

The probable uses and users of an operating system dictate what amount of these three kinds of facilities should be provided. A single user has little need for a comprehensive resource allocation and sharing system, and machines with large amounts of memory can offer more language translators that will occupy large amounts of space. Since the primary function of an operating system is to provide user services, you should thoroughly investigate the operating system you are using to determine which of its features you can use.

11.6   TERMS USED

Operating system
Monitor
User services
Support programs
Resource allocator
Uniprogramming
Multiprogramming
Asynchronous activities
CPU-I/O overlap
Foreground-background processing

Batch processing
Timesharing or interactive processing
Real-time system
CP/M
File system
Directory
Text editor
Command interpreter
Utility program
RT-11
UNIX
Tree-structured file system
OS-MVT
VM/370
Virtual operating system

11.7 QUESTIONS

1. Are relocation facilities useful to a user of a uniprogramming system? Why or why not?
2. The most obvious resources of a computing system are its I/O devices. What other resources are there in a computing system?
3. Section 11.1 describes overlap of CPU activity for one job with I/O activity for another job. A selfish user might say "It is not helping my program to have someone else using the CPU while I perform I/O activity. Why should I use a computing system that permits this overlap?" Explain why the user's reasoning is faulty.
4. Can a program overlap its own I/O activity with CPU usage? Explain your answer.
5. How can a single user actively use both the foreground and the background of a foreground background system? (*Hint:* Consider compiling a program in the background; what other activities could go on in the foreground?)
6. Using a UNIX file structure tree, show how one user could have two files of the same name (e.g., TEMP) located at different nodes in the tree. Can two identically named files descend from the same immediate predecessor?
7. In batch processing, can you interact with a program during its execution? Can you in time-sharing processing? Can you in real-time processing?

Index

223